Planning and Designing the Office Environment

Planning and Designing the Office Environment

Second Edition

Edited by

David A. Harris,
Byron W. Engen, and
William E. Fitch

VAN NOSTRAND REINHOLD
New York

"Office Landscaping" or "Bureaulandschaft" is . . . a synonym for creative innovation through systematic cooperation of many disciplines.

Dr. R. E. Planas

Copyright © 1991 by Van Nostrand Reinhold

Library of Congress Catalog Number 90-32212
ISBN 0-442-31931-2

Printed in the United States of America

Van Nostrand Reinhold
115 Fifth Avenue
New York, New York 10003

Chapman and Hall
2-6 Boundary Row
London SE1 8HN, England

Thomas Nelson Australia
102 Dodds Street
South Melbourne 3205
Victoria, Australia

Nelson Canada
1120 Birchmount Road
Scarborough, Ontario M1K 5G4, Canada

16 15 14 13 12 11 10 9 8 7 6 5 4 3 2 1

Library of Congress Cataloging-in-Publication Data

Harris, David A., 1934-
    Planning and designing the office environment / David A.
Harris, Byron Engen, William Fitch—2nd ed.
        p.   cm.
    Rev. ed. of: Planning and designing the office environment /
David A. Harris and others. 1981.
    Includes bibliographical references.
    ISBN 0-442-31931-2
    1. Office layout. I. Engen, Byron. II. Title. III. Title:
Planning and designing the office environment.
    HF5547.2.P58   1991
    725'.23—dc20   90-32212
                                                        CIP

Contents

6   POWER AND SIGNAL DISTRIBUTION / 209
David A. Harris

7   SYSTEMS PROCUREMENT / 247
David A. Harris

Acknowledgments

The preparation and updating of this book is an effort to further the basic understanding of the "systems" approach to designing interior office space, specifically that space which is of the open office or landscape type.

A group of professionals in architecture/engineering created this book. Each contributing author is an expert in his field and is dedicated to the systems concept and to the creation of the optimum environment for today's business needs.

This was, then, an interdisciplinary effort. And though the chapters may stand alone, the authors spent many hours developing the integration of their disciplines. They diligently identified the techniques for thorough subcomponent and technology interfaces that were a major concern to each of them.

Many contributed extensively to the original project. Special thanks must go to the past and present members of the Technical Communication Services department of Owens-Corning Fiberglas: to Jean Del Gaudio for supervising the editing and preparation of the text; to Craig Fisher for directing the illustration and design; to Julianne Frost, Patricia Donaldson, Jeff Basting, Chris Berry, Patricia Miller, Irene Kolakowski, and Gayle Harp who spent untold hours planning, illustrating, and keylining; to Mary Jo Ceglio who directed the typesetting; and to Ronald Kirschner, Robson Sweney, and Arnold Knipp for their guidance in this project.

Several persons have contributed suggestions and technical assistance that have been reflected in the original draft of this book. They include Richard Thielmann, Dr. Robert Rudolph, John Doyle, Mary Jo Wiese, James Stillwell, Stewart Byrne, Bruce Williams, and John Halldane. Technical coordinators for the book were Byron W. Engen, David A. Harris, and William E. Fitch.

Finally, we must thank C. E. Peck and D. E. Morgenroth, who were instrumental in making this book possible. This updated edition was prepared by David A. Harris. Byron W. Engen edited the Lighting and HVAC chapters. William E. Fitch edited the fire-safety chapter.

Introduction

Planning and Designing the Office Environment has been compiled for organization management, facility planners, financial investors, and the professionals directly involved in office planning and design. Those professionals include architects, engineers, interior designers, and office planners. These are the people responsible for decision making about office planning and design, and who may need general information concerning

- Specific methods and purposes of the team planning process
- Kinds of decisions to be made
- Bases for these decisions
- Technological demands and possibilities involved in design solutions

We believe this book will increase the reader's knowledge and understanding of these areas, and reinforce and amplify the idea that creativity and innovation are possible in office planning and design solutions.

The purposes of this book are to describe office planning as a process, to discuss in detail some of the more important disciplines and technologies involved, and to describe the process of developing design solutions. Special attention is given to the integration of disciplines and their technologies. Although we do propose an approach to office planning, we do not attempt to define a design methodology. Our aim is to present the major issues and considerations involved in solution development.

In order to understand these issues and considerations, it is beneficial to possess a moderate understanding of office history. Offices began as small groups of persons gathered in one location to perform various tasks. A three-person office was typical: the owner of the business, a secretary, and a bookkeeper. This arrangement is still common today and works well for small businesses. As industrialization spread, the office reflected the rapid growth of businesses, which increased enormously in terms of staff and administration.

One of the first large office plans was the bullpen, in which staff workplaces were arranged in rigid grids of desks and aisles in open areas. Executives occupied much of the prime perimeter space in enclosed, windowed offices.

The single-office plan maintained the same segregation of executives in closed, windowed offices, but placed staff members in several-person enclosed spaces instead of a bullpen arrangement. Various manifestations and combinations of the bullpen and single-office layouts were widely used until about twenty-five years ago, when the executive core plan developed. In this layout, staff members remained in a bullpen arrangement, but were moved to the perimeter of the office. The executives were located in the center of the space and were still provided with enclosed, individual offices.

A recent change in office design and layout has been the open office, sometimes called an open-plan office. Initially, free-standing screens were utilized. These soon gave way to work stations or systems furniture. A popular open-plan design concept called "Bureaulandschaft," or "office landscape," was developed by the Quickborner team. In all cases, the open office utilized part high space dividers. Today the open office is combined with closed offices. This mix of closed and open offices has added a new dimension to design and performance issues.

The fundamental distinction between the closed office and the open office is a simple, but meaningful one: partitioning. In the closed office, partitions between workplaces are interior walls that extend from floor to ceiling. In the open office, partitions, generally in the form of visual/acoustical screens, do not extend to the ceiling. The screens are rarely above five feet tall and may or may not be flush with the floor.

In recent years, office planning and design have changed a great deal. New technological developments and products have come into being to meet the needs of office users and have often simultaneously had to answer more general needs for energy conservation and lower life-cycle costs. Further, in the fields of lighting, acoustics, and fire safety, more realistic and accurate techniques are now being used to define user requirements.

More often than not, the technologies of various disciplines such as heating, ventilating, and air conditioning (HVAC), acoustics, and lighting have developed separately. In some cases, products integrate pieces of the technologies of these disciplines. This is true of several currently available floor systems, ceiling systems, and furniture systems that include task/ambient lighting and power and signal hookups. In other cases, user requirements demand the design of additional or new integrated systems and solutions.

However, office design is not merely an arrangement of products—it is itself a product. Solutions for almost any office planning and design project are many and varied. Final solutions are selected from among alternate solutions, all of which meet the organization's and the user's needs.

Those solutions are based on life-cycle costs, aesthetics, and any functional advantages one alternative may have over another. The end product is a whole whose parts, like the office itself, are mutually dependent and interactive.

This book gives an overview of the planning requirements and the integration of these technical disciplines. Because of the mutually dependent and interactive aspects, the closest teamwork among designers and/or specialists from different disciplines is essential. Such teamwork and integration require a great deal of planning.

Planning defines the frame of reference and the sets of requirements for design and for the technology that design employs. It ensures that these sets of requirements are accurate and comprehensive and that they are based on information which has been systematically gathered and analyzed. Planning is also used to ensure both the integration of the disciplines involved in the planning and design process and the integration of the solutions themselves in terms of the technology and the overall environment.

This is particularly true of the open office. Because it is essentially undivided, the open office demands holistic solutions. Its planning and design must be approached in a way that reflects this demand and creates a fertile environment for the development of innovative solutions. Certain combinations of user requirements can set up a situation in which open-office technologies must be interlocked to a much greater degree than in any other circumstance of office design. The use of sophisticated technology is required if the space is to be successful. We do not wish to imply by this statement that technology is an answer unto itself. Rather, it is the tool designers must use to generate workable solutions.

The first chapter of the book describes office planning as a process, one that begins at the project's inception and continues beyond implementation. This chapter discusses the structure and strategies of the proposed planning approach, as well as the objectives and rationales for its procedures.

Chapters dealing with acoustics, lighting, HVAC, fire safety, the systems procurement process, and finally power and signal distribution follow. In this second edition, all chapters have been updated to reflect current practice. The chapter on power and signal distribution is new. These chapters cover planning, technical, and design considerations regarding their subjects. In every chapter, the need for integration of disciplines and technologies is emphasized and explained. Essentially, the five technical chapters are details or enlargements not of phases of the planning process, but of some of the disciplines the planning comprises.

A number of other fields are included in most planning projects, but we have chosen five to discuss in this book for specific reasons. Lighting, acoustics,

HVAC, fire safety, and the new chapter on power and signal distribution are frequently the most critical technological systems involved in office planning and design projects and can be complex in terms of integration. Further, these are the disciplines whose technologies often must be highly integrated because they are so mutually interdependent.

The fire safety chapter is included because codes represent both constraints and requirements which affect all project disciplines and which must be accounted for in any project. Most current codes do not address open offices, so this chapter discusses the possibilities of adopting a systems approach to fire safety. This approach entails planning for the elements of the systems from the time the decision is made to use an open-plan layout.

Significant changes have occurred in acoustics, lighting, and HVAC since publication of the first edition. These chapters have been extensively revised to reflect new innovative solutions. In the case of acoustics, the industry has adopted new standards for testing, and the mix of open and closed offices has had a profound effect on planning principles.

The book concludes with an explanatory chapter on systems procurement and a whole new chapter covering power and signal distribution. While the procurement process has not changed, the addition of power and signal is indicative of the massive changes that have occurred in how we do business and communicate in today's office. With the rapid change in our power needs, the use of personal computers and new methods of communicating in our business world, the chapter on power and signal is long overdue and will be obsolete almost as it is written. For this reason, we chose a new format that may be helpful in managing this ever-changing technology.

In general, the emphasis in *Planning and Designing the Office Environment* is on open-office planning and design. Revisions in this second edition reflect the trend toward a mix of the open and closed office. The principles of planning do not change with the mix of open and closed offices. What does change, in some cases rather dramatically, are the system performance attributes and test procedures. For example, it is imperative that the closed office partitions be demountable and have a highly sound-absorbent facing if they are to be readily usable in an open-plan environment. Significant changes in ceiling, lighting, and HVAC systems performance have also occurred.

It is not our intention to advocate one layout, open or closed, over another for all circumstances. The appropriateness of a layout is entirely dependent upon the needs of the organization and its users. This idea is central to the planning approach we present.

Chapter 1

PLANNING

Alvin E. Palmer and M. Susan Lewis

Updated by David A. Harris

Today's office is a complex and variable environment. It is constantly in a state of flux, growing in one area, cutting back in another, reallocating and redefining tasks and procedures. The organization must foresee its own change and must develop logical, comprehensive solutions to the needs such change produces. Office planning is a means of defining these needs specifically and of generating their solutions.

The approach presented in this chapter represents a logical progression of steps which, in generalized form, are as follows:

- Define the organization's[1] goals.
- Carefully examine the existing situation.
- Establish detailed sets of user requirements.
- Develop, evaluate, and implement solutions that fulfill these requirements.

This approach is based on techniques designed to ensure that final project solutions are not arrived at by guesswork, but are the results of fully informed decisions backed, in turn, by objective, systematically gathered data.

Often, organizations implement solutions and, shortly thereafter, realize the solutions are inadequate. One reason for this is that the problems and needs to which the solutions speak have not been defined clearly or completely. The planning, for example, may have established that lighting needs in a particular project are uniform throughout the space, but, after move-in, users quickly discover that the uniform lighting provided is not appropriate for all tasks.

Another common cause of inadequate solutions is that the solutions are based on subjective or inaccurate information. An illustration is a project in which the organization chart has been used as the basis for juxtaposing users in the layout, thereby reflecting only the users' formal work flow and communication patterns, and overlooking and hindering their actual ones.

A third reason for unsatisfactory solutions is that they have been preconceived either by the organization or the planning team. An instance of this, and one that happens frequently, would be to say from the beginning that all top management personnel must have closed offices and must be grouped in one area. The result is that these individuals are removed from the users with whom they need close contact.

Finally, if the planning has determined user requirements accurately, solutions will still fail if they are not designed to meet *all* these requirements. The first example, with lighting levels, can be reversed to illustrate this point. Say that specific lighting needs have been established for each user and that these needs vary between users. Nevertheless, because of the difficulty of providing the appropriate lighting for each user and simultaneously maintaining the overall rearrangement flexibility needed by the organization, a uniform lighting system is adopted, with some supplemental task lighting for a few users. The fault here may lie with the organization which, being unconvinced that individual lighting needs are legitimate and believing them to be expensive to fulfill in any case, more or less vetoes their resolution. Or it may lie with the designers who are simply unwilling or for some reason unable to develop solutions that meet the established requirements. Mistakes and failures like these can end in costly wastes of time, energy, and money. They can be avoided through comprehensive, accurate planning and design.

The organization should be viewed as a whole. Its elements—that is, its products, procedures, people relationships, and environment and equipment—are interdependent and should be planned for as parts of a whole and not separately as though they were unrelated. The office users are employed by the organization to produce something: marketing communications, marketing research, personnel services, or what have you. If generating a particular product is one of the organization's goals, then a set of its procedures, people relationships, and environment and equipment are all directed specifically toward achieving this goal.

Two different products, such as marketing communications and personnel services, require two different sets of procedures, people relationships, and environment and equipment. The product, then, or any substantive alteration to it, directly influences the forms and purposes of the other three elements of the organization. Likewise, the other three elements influence and depend upon

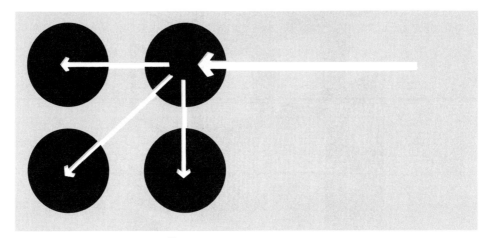

Figure 1-1. Organization effect

each other, and changes in one usually warrant changes in the others.

Traditionally, office planning has addressed environment and equipment, with some attention to people relationships and little to products and procedures. A pleasant environment, however, will not increase user efficiency and productivity if there are unresolved communication or paper-flow problems. By the same token, if procedures are streamlined and users are rearranged to improve communications, but some users are without proper furniture and equipment, or are subjected to too much noise or glare, then obviously not all of the existing problems have been remedied. This is piecemeal planning, and it overlooks the crucial point that the organization is indeed a whole whose parts are dependent upon one another and must function together (Figure 1-1).

The value of comprehensive office planning is underscored by a look at the dollars spent over the life of a building. If the costs of equipment, construction of the building, maintenance, and replacement are added together, their sum will still be only one-tenth of the dollars spent on user salaries and benefits (Figure 1-2). This ratio clearly points up the importance of planning and design—the importance, that is, of identifying and fulfilling user needs in all areas in order to improve efficiency and productivity. Users carry out tasks that are interrelated but often diverse; the office must be planned and designed to support and sustain these tasks both in their interaction and in their diversity.

To support and sustain user tasks, any office requires a certain amount of technology. Planning is the link between this technology and the design of a successful office environment. It establishes the sets of requirements that possible solutions must fulfill. It should also encourage the integration of these solutions in terms of initial and life-cycle costs, and energy usage. Office planning has not adequately emphasized or facilitated such integration.

Figure 1-2. People cost vs. building cost. User salaries and benefits equal roughly ten times the total cost of construction and maintenance over the life of the building.

The need for a planning and design process that is comprehensive and integrated not only in its approach, but also in its solutions, is illustrated by the three matrices shown here (Figures 1-3, 1-4, 1-5). These matrices are not meant as definitive lists of all of the disciplines, office tasks, and office elements/needs involved in a project; instead, they are intended to indicate in broad terms some of the areas in which integration is required if user needs are to be met and a truly task-supportive environment is to be created.

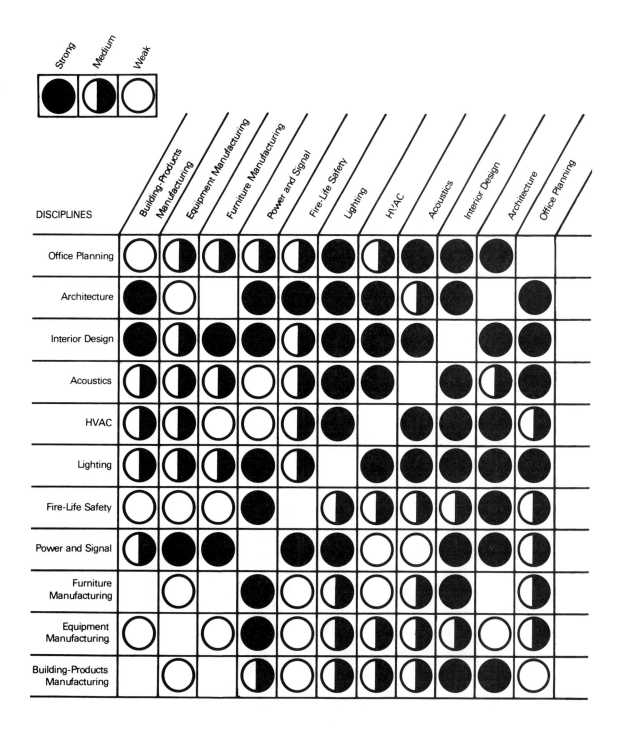

Figure 1-3. Matrix of interaction

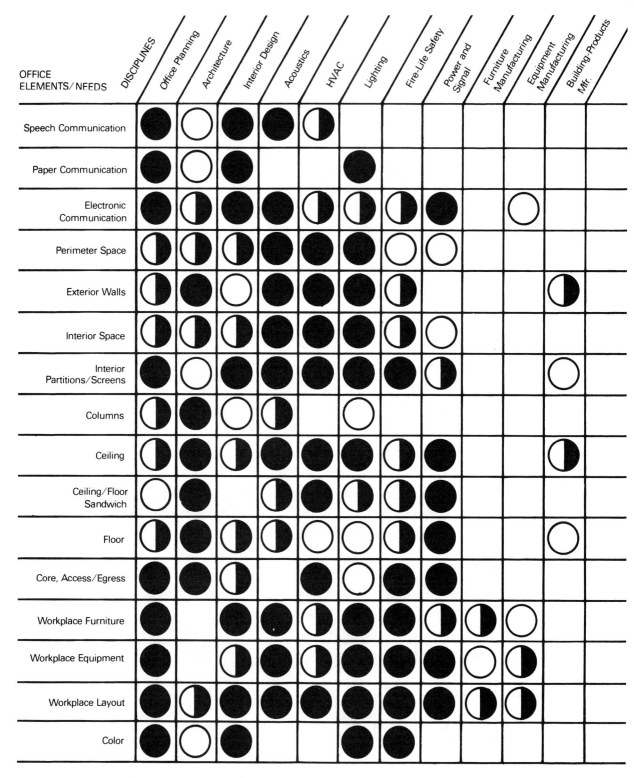

Figure 1-4. Matrix of needs versus disciplines

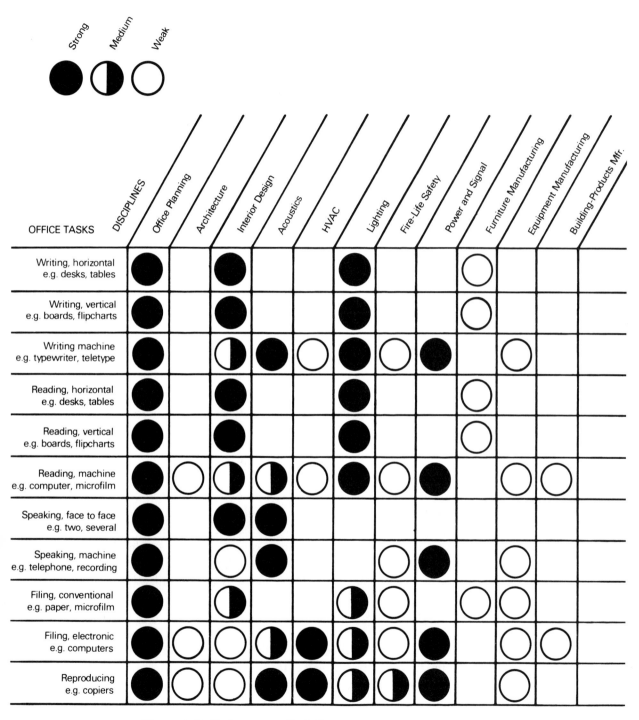

Figure 1-5. Tasks versus disciplines

Planning
Design
Implementation
Follow-Up

Figure 1-6. Cyclical planning

Office planning should also be ongoing. Clearly, it would be counter-productive in the long run to undertake an in-depth planning and design project, implement its solutions, then neglect further planning efforts until changes within the organization have made it necessary to begin a new and again comprehensive project. Consequently, after solutions have been implemented, planning should continue, but on a much smaller scale. Follow-up planning is a matter of maintaining achieved levels of communication, efficiency, and productivity by identifying and resolving new problems as they arise (Figure 1-6).

Like the aspects of the office they analyze, the planning steps described in this chapter are interdependent. The results of one step influence another, just as work flow within the office influences communication, and communication influences work flow. Ultimately, these results combine to define the specific requirements of the organization and its users, and to provide the direction for project solutions. In reading this chapter, you should be aware that many of the planning steps we must describe sequentially here occur concurrently in an actual project. Their concurrence is structured to minimize both time and costs.

In describing this office-planning approach, we attempt to explain the purposes and principles behind planning and the function of each step within the process as a whole.[2] We do not intend this chapter as a set of instructions for carrying out an office-planning project. Nor do we recommend that any organization which has not had experience in office planning and design undertake a project without the aid of an office planner and the other professionals required by the particular project.

PLANNING AND DESIGN TEAM

An essential ingredient in accomplishing comprehensive planning and design is an interdisciplinary planning team which includes consultants or representatives of all the disciplines necessary to the project. The interdisciplinary nature of this team helps to ensure that the planning does not overlook or exclude any element of the organization and that the solutions developed for the project are integrated. In addition, this planning team is participatory; users from all levels of the organization are planning team members. User participation throughout the project is vital, both in terms of problem identification and definition and in terms of testing the suitability of solutions.

Because no office-planning approach can actually guarantee the best possible solutions to an organization's needs, but can only provide the framework for developing such solutions, the planning team takes on extreme importance. The individuals who comprise the team are responsible for interpreting as well as gathering information, and they must ultimately generate innovative solutions which will fullfill *all* user requirements.

The makeup of the planning team depends upon the size of the organization, the time allotted for the project, and the project's scope—renovation of an existing facility or construction of a new one. *There is no set formula for team membership,* nor should there be. The membership must remain flexible and must be tailored to the project.

The planning team is composed of four groups: the core group, specialists, the user group, and the review and decision committee (Figure 1-7). The core group is responsible for the great majority of planning tasks, and consists of a full-time office-planning consultant(s) and in-house personnel. This group is established at the beginning of the project and is usually made up of three to five people, including the office-planning consultant(s); members of the organization who are totally familiar with the organization and have immediate access to all its employees; and users who will later conduct long-term or follow-up planning. In addition to carrying out many of the planning steps, the consultant is responsible for coordinating all phases of the project from its inception through its implementation. The office planner must ensure the project's continuity, and the accurate, complete definition and resolution of the organization's needs.

Part-time consultants and/or in-house professionals, each expert in a particular discipline, make up the specialists. These team members are involved in the project on an as-needed basis, in accordance with the tasks at hand. Specialists such as architects, interior designers, acousticians, lighting consultants, structural engineers, HVAC consultants, fire-safety experts, industrial psychologists, mechanical/electrical engineers, furniture and equipment representatives, and construction contractors are often included. Although their

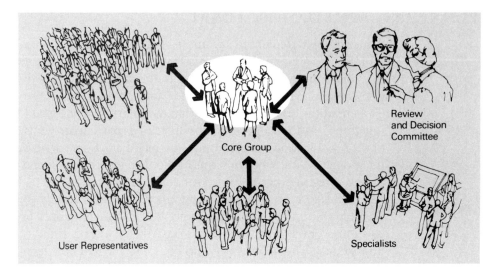

Figure 1-7. The planning team

involvement in the project is not continuous, the specialists are a very important group. They not only help define user requirements, but also design the systems and solutions that fulfill these requirements.

Users are the members of the planned-for organization. The user group may include all the users, or, if this is impossible because of numbers, their representatives. Its purpose is to ensure the users' participation in the planning and design and, through this, their acceptance of and enthusiasm for the solutions. The user group provides information, and positive and negative feedback to the core group. A representative to the user group is usually selected by each of the work groups defined by the communication analysis, described later in this chapter. Each representative to the user group should be able to articulate the needs of his or her work group accurately, and should be generally available to participate in the planning process.

Though the user group may not be formed until the communication analysis has been completed, user participation begins at the outset of the project. Through meetings with all the users, the office planner explains the planning process and its strategies, underscoring the point that solutions will be developed logically in accordance with the users' needs.

The review and decision committee should be made up of management personnel from as high a level in the organization as possible. Its responsibility is to review and maintain familiarity with the planning as it progresses, and to render and/or endorse decisions as necessary. In order to assure the availability of committee members, a schedule of meetings should be established as early as possible in the project.

A planning team structured in this manner is able to operate with maximum efficiency because of its clear-cut definitions of tasks and responsibilities. Redundant activities and project delays are minimized. In combination, these advantages reduce overall project time and therefore project costs. Further, because the user group and the review and decision committee are integral parts of the planning team, planning tasks, findings, and conclusions are thoroughly understood by everyone in the organization. The planning becomes a participatory process, with suggestions, criticisms, and decisions made on an ongoing basis. This avoids any end-of-project misunderstandings or dissatisfactions and ensures that the project maintains proper direction.

Although part of the office planner's responsibility is to coordinate the planning process, the planning team itself has no designated leader. At any given time, team leadership is in the hands of that team member whose expertise lies in the area of primary concern. In other words, if the users' lighting requirements are being finalized, the lighting specialist is the team leader; if the possibilities for building configuration are the subject, the architect becomes the leader. Essentially, the planning team's job is to define the users' environmental requirements in detail and eventually to develop solutions to these requirements. The team therefore creates a loose framework for design. It does not attempt to dictate solutions or to govern design through a design methodology, but provides an environment in which solutions that are both workable and creative can be generated.

PROJECT DEFINITION

One of the first steps in any planning and design project should be to define the project itself. This entails identifying the goals or needs the project is to fulfill, establishing the priority of these goals, and delineating the strategies by which the goals are to be reached.

Clearly, the organization has initiated the project for some purpose and has identified some needs and/or problems that need to be addressed. For example, the organization may want to improve the office environment both for the sake of the users and to enhance public image; it may also want to improve user communication and work-flow patterns. These general goals/needs are the reasons for the project's existence. They should be identified and defined as carefully as possible through discussions between the core group and the organization's top management.

So that the team does not overlook other problems and needs, however, the core group should undertake a problem detection analysis. This analysis serves to enlarge upon and further define the organization's stated needs, and to detect related but previously unidentified problems. The problem detection analysis may be conducted by interviewing a large sampling of users from all levels and job classifications of the organization. Depending upon the number of users involved in the project and the variety of tasks they perform, it may be desirable to interview all users; however, a sampling is generally sufficient to identify any user problems.

In interviewing the users, the core group should gather information on all aspects of the office: efficiency, productivity, communication, work flow, promotion, furniture and equipment, acoustics, lighting, and so forth. If the results of the project are to be comprehensive, then the problem detection must be comprehensive. The organization's goals, needs, and problems must be defined clearly and accurately before they can be answered.

After needs, problems, and goals have been defined, they should be reviewed by the review and decisions committee and placed in order of priority. Generally, they are interrelated and will fall into groups; the relative importance of each group can then be determined. The main reason for putting priorities on goals and problems is timing. For instance, if one of the organization's goals is to begin construction of a new office facility on a certain date, the planning and design of that facility must be scheduled as priority items. Determining priorities early on is an important factor in minimizing the possibilities of later project delays or confusion over scheduling.

Developing strategies, the means by which the goals can be achieved, involves decisions by the review and decision committee and the core group as

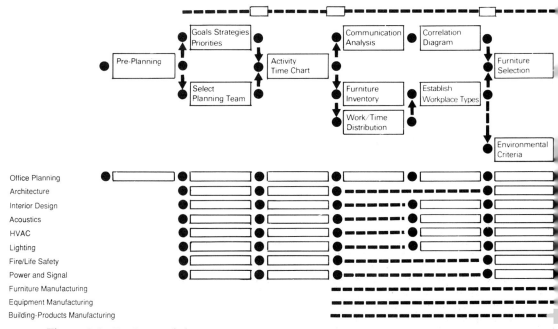

Figure 1-8. Review and decision committee meetings

to which specific planning steps are to be undertaken and which disciplines/ specialists the project requires. For instance, decisions should be made as to whether a filing system analysis ought to be run, or whether a status symbol analysis is necessary. In addition, attention should be given to the scheduling of the planning steps and to scheduling each specialist's participation.

Goals, priorities, and strategies must be jointly determined by the core group and the review and decision committee. Open and continuing communication between these two groups is vital. Discussion and information-gathering sessions with users are also very important and should include as many users as possible from every level of the organization. The core group should make sure that the users are informed of and understand planning activities throughout the planning process.

SCHEDULE

A carefully drawn schedule (Figure 1-8) serves to define and organize the project further, both for the planning team and for the organization. It establishes, for example, an end date for the project and shows how the project is to be accomplished in the time allotted for it. The schedule also indicates when each planning activity begins and ends, how the content of each activity feeds into or depends upon the information and conclusions of another, when each

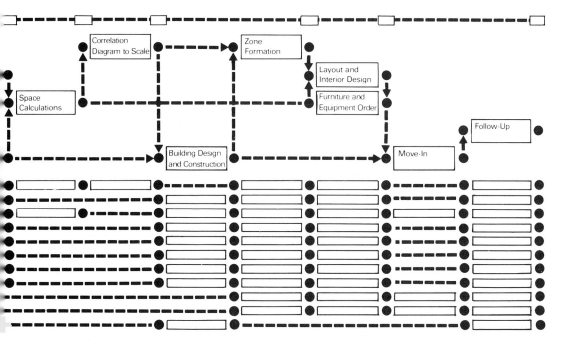

specialist should be brought in, how that specialist relates to the project, and who is responsible for carrying out each planning step—the core group, a particular specialist, etc. In addition, by establishing the time required for the project, the schedule facilitates estimating and budgeting planning costs.

Because of all the information the schedule contains and because it outlines the project from start to finish, it should be shown graphically in the form of an activity time chart. This form makes the schedule, and with it the planning and design process as a whole, easily understandable and accessible to management and users, as well as to the various groups within the planning team. A specialist who is involved early in the project and then halfway through can determine quickly how the project has progressed and how his or her role relates to and affects other planning steps. The activity time chart (Figure 1-8) indicates, in simplified form, how the various planning steps discussed in this book might overlap or run concurrently.

COMMUNICATION ANALYSIS

The importance of the communication analysis to the success of the project cannot be overstated. The purpose of the office itself is to provide an environment that facilitates communication. The purpose of the communication analysis is, quite simply, to track communication patterns. Ultimately, when this information is used as the basis for the layout of the new office space, it ensures that the layout maximizes work flow and communication efficiency (Figure 1-9).

The communication analysis consists of three parts: a communication tally, a matrix of interactions, and matrices of interaction intensity. Its purpose is to measure the communication—that is, the functional relationships between individuals. However, to record the fact that user A relates to users C, F, and G is not enough. It is also necessary to quantify and qualify these relationships; this is the aim of the communication tally. Mistaken information regarding the quantity and/or quality of communication may lead to an inefficient layout, which will surely diminish other, positive effects of the planning and design effort.

The communication tally measures each user's communications over a specified period of time, generally about two weeks. Because the tally actually quantifies and categorizes communications, it is a crucial step in the communication analysis and cannot be approximated through the use of questionnaires or even lengthy interviews without greatly increasing the chances of acting on mistaken, subjective information.

During the course of the tally, users record communications in four categories: personal visit or conference interaction, paper interaction, electronic communications, and telephone interaction. Each user simply logs all

Individual	Code	Phone Calls Received	Total	Papers Received	Total	Visits or Conferences Received	Total	Electronic Communications	Total
L. Vasquez	001								
B. O'Brien	002								
M. Corrigan	003								
J. Aquilino	004								
M. Keano	005								
S. Gabbey	006								
S. Brisman	007								
S. Westbok	008								
T. Willi...									

Name _____
Title/Code _____

Outside Contacts

Contact	Code	Contacts Received			Contacts Made			
		Phone Calls	Papers	Visits Conf.	Phone Calls	Papers	Visits Conf.	...
Sales Office	501							
Warehouse	502							
Other	...							
...								
...								

Figure 1-9. Sample communication tally sheet

communications received, whether these originate inside or outside the organization, and all communications transmitted to outside the organization. Each interaction is recorded under its proper category (personal visit or conference, paper, electronic, telephone) and beside the name(s) of person(s) involved in the interaction. For each user to log transmitted as well as received communica-

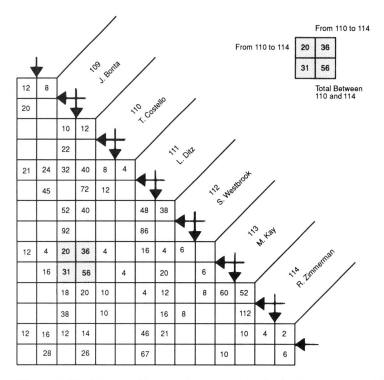

Figure 1-10. Matrix of interactions: combined telephone, paper, visits, or conferences and electronic communications

tions would needlessly double the number of data to be analyzed. Paper interactions are recorded alike, regardless of the number of pages included in a single interaction—a one-page memorandum or a twenty-page report.

At the end of the tally period, communications in each category can be totaled for each user. The totals from each category can then be transferred to a matrix of interactions (Figure 1-10) which shows the totals of communications from one user to another and vice versa, and also shows the total of these two figures.[3] The value of the tally and the resulting matrix of interactions is that they provide an objective foundation for developing layout schemes that will enhance work flow within the organization. The advantage of this factual, quantified approach over interviews or questionnaires is made clear by the surprise many users express when they review their own completed tallies.

At this point, the matrix of interactions can be simplified into a matrix of interaction intensity. Here, the totals of communication interactions between individuals are described graphically with symbols representing weak, medium, and strong interaction totals or intensity. If the least number of communications is 0 and the greatest is, say, 120, then 1 to 40 may be classified as weak, 41 to 80 as medium, and 81 to 120 as strong. The reason for developing this matrix is that it is much simpler for the planning team and the users to review and use.

In analyzing and testing the matrix of interaction intensity (Figure 1-11), it may become apparent that, although the communications between two given users are relatively few, they are critical and should be allotted a greater intensity than their number would seem to merit. For judgments such as this, the planning team must depend on its overall working knowledge of the organization and the frequent review of its measurements and conclusions by the users themselves. Alterations in the results of the communication analysis, though, should be made only if absolutely necessary.

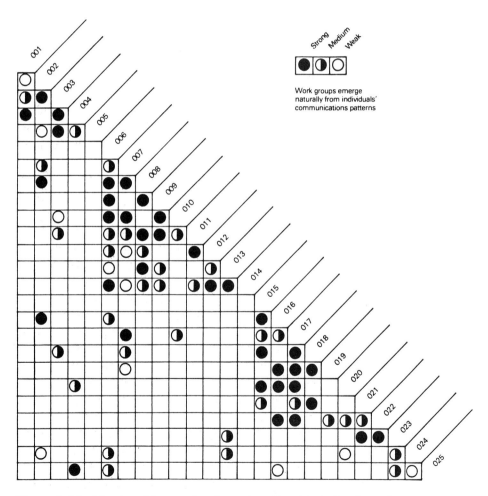

Work groups emerge
naturally from individuals'
communications patterns

Figure 1-11. Matrix of interaction intensity: Graphic indication of communication intensity between individuals

As the information gathered in the communication analysis is reviewed, obvious work groups will begin to emerge. A second matrix, showing the interaction intensities between these work groups, may be drawn up (Figure 1-12). This matrix of work group interaction intensity is merely a simplification of the matrix indicating individuals' interaction intensities, and forms the basis of the next planning step—the correlation diagram. Also, it is from the work groups defined here that representatives to the planning team's user group may be chosen.

At first glance, it would seem that, insofar as it is used to define work groups, the communication analysis is a make-work procedure because such groups could be drawn much more easily from the organization chart. The organization chart, though, useful as it may be for some purposes, is *not* a planning tool. It illustrates the formal structure of the organization, the vertical lines of report and command, which, in terms of work flow and communica-

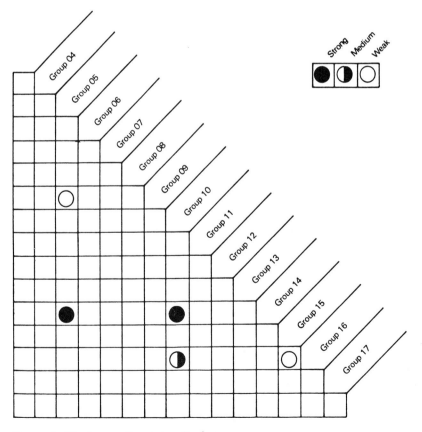

Figure 1-12. Interaction intensity between groups

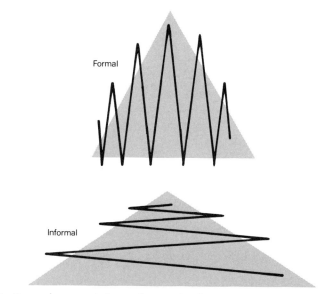

Figure 1-13. Formal versus informal organization structure

tion, are unrealistically rigid. In fact, the organization operates much more informally and horizontally than the organization chart suggests (Figure 1-13), with each individual's capabilities, needs, objectives, and interests affecting his or her communication and work relationships. Within any organization, for example, it is common to find individuals who fall into the middle levels of the organization chart, but who actually have direct access to persons in the top levels. It is equally common for employees to be positioned in one column of the chart, but to carry on their primary work relationships with individuals in another, ostensibly unrelated column.

It is exactly these less formal, more flexible work flow lines, the actual operating lines of the organization, which the communication analysis tracks. When communication analysis work groups are compared with those implied by the organization chart, the actual work groups usually prove to be considerably larger and the number of levels from top to bottom is typically fewer, often by 50 percent.

CORRELATION DIAGRAM

Using the information gathered in the communication analysis, it becomes possible to represent graphically the *ideal* spatial relationships between work groups. This graphic representation is the correlation diagram. It is derived directly from the matrix of work group interaction intensity, and juxtaposes work groups in accordance with the intensity of their interactions—strong,

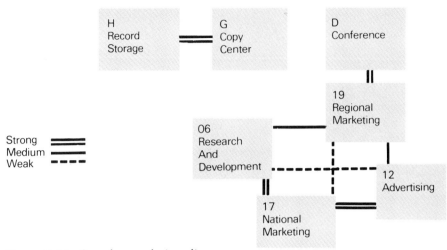

Figure 1-14. Sample correlation diagram

medium, weak, or no interaction. It does not indicate these work groups to scale, but is concerned only with their relative positions.

Developing the correlation diagram may seem simple enough because the planning team has already collected and evaluated the necessary data, but its purpose is to set forth that arrangement of work groups which best supports all user interactions, and this can be a difficult task. If each group is represented by a rectangle, as can be seen in the accompanying illustration (Figure 1-14), then the lines of intensity connecting the rectangles must be as short as possible; in other words, the groups must be as proximate as possible. Obviously, the stronger the interaction between work groups, the shorter their connecting lines should be. After the correlation diagram has been completed to show the ideal relationships between work groups, a correlation diagram indicating individual users should be developed for each work group.

The correlation diagrams are the first steps toward developing a logical arrangement for the organization, and will be referred to again and again throughout the planning and design process. Consequently, they should be reviewed carefully by the users and the review and decision committee.

SUPPLEMENTARY PLANNING STEPS

Depending on the particular goals the organization has established and the problems the planning team has defined and is attempting to resolve, it may be advantageous to conduct a document flow study (Figure 1-15), a filing system analysis, and/or a status symbol analysis. The document flow study may be electronic, paper, or both, depending on the degree to which computers and electronic mail are utilized.

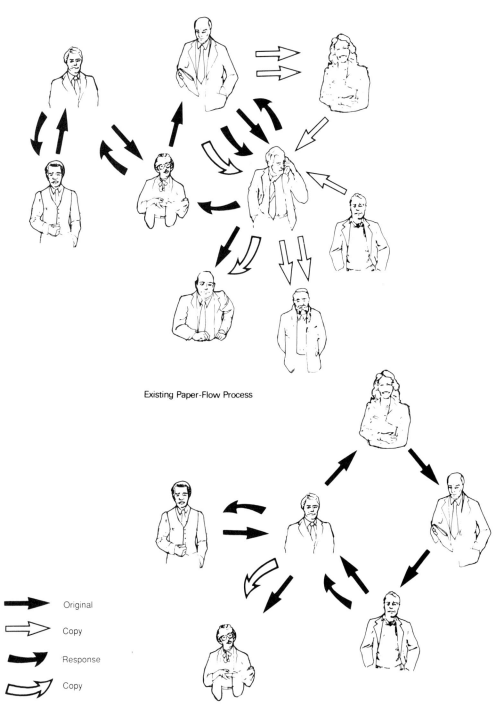

Existing Paper-Flow Process

Revised Paper-Flow Process

Original
Copy
Response
Copy

Figure 1-15. Document flow study

21

Document-Flow Study

Generally, a document-flow study is only required if information-processing difficulties have surfaced, if there are obvious duplications of effort due to inefficient document flow, or if the communication analysis has indicated an abnormally high number of paper interactions. The document-flow study itself is an uncomplicated but time-consuming matter of selecting a typical document-flow network, recording even the smallest processing step as the document moves through the organization, and then streamlining the network as much as possible. In one actual project, the processing steps in a particular document-flow network were reduced from seventy-three to three without alteration in the desired results.

Filing System Analysis

A filing system analysis is much more frequently required than a paper-flow study because of the tendency of most users to surround themselves with paper. The ultimate purpose of this analysis is to design a filing system which ensures that each user maintains in the workplace no more paper than he or she actually uses (Figure 1-16). The principle is a simple one: office space is too expensive to double as a storage area for inactive files. Further, paper is fuel for fire and, for safety reasons, should not be stored unnecessarily within the office.

Files may be divided into three categories: active, semiactive, and inactive. Only active files require storage at the workplace. Semiactive files may be centralized in group areas for easy access when needed. Inactive files, which cannot be discarded but are seldom looked at, may be placed in an archive in

Figure 1-16. Active files. Generally, a user cannot work with more than two feet of files at his or her workplace.

the basement of the facility or in another relatively inexpensive location as long as retrieval capabilities are adequate. Electronic filing should also be considered as a solution to storage problems.

Analyzing the organization's filing system, and designing a new one which functions efficiently and minimizes filing loads within the office, is a complex series of tasks and warrants the expertise of a filing system specialist.

Status Symbol Analysis

Changes within the organization, such as a move into a new facility or the renovation of an existing one, offer an ideal opportunity to evaluate and redistribute status symbols. If there is a likelihood that the new office space will be open plan, a status symbol analysis should definitely be conducted. In any layout type, status symbols in the form of furniture may inhibit workplace flexibility. In the open plan, where flexibility is a prime consideration, such status symbols generally impair rearrangement efficiency, raising workplace rearrangement costs. For example, if an oversized desk is a particular user's status symbol, then each time that user must change workplaces, the desk's contents cannot simply be moved to the existing desk in the new workplace. The oversized desk itself must be moved, as must the desk in the new workplace. If the move is to be made to another floor of the building, the difficulties and costs are compounded.

In addition, when a move into open offices is intended, organization personnel may become concerned that their present status symbols will be eliminated and will not be replaced. Consequently, it is especially helpful to establish guidelines for status in the open plan and to make these clear to all users.

In a status symbol analysis, existing status symbols are inventoried, the users assign a value to each, and these values are averaged. For instance, on a scale of one to ten, an oversized desk might receive a value of four, while a private reception area might rate an eight. The quantity and value of each user's status symbols are then charted on graphs which combine to delineate status distribution within the organization (Figure 1-17). Usually, this distribution will be extremely uneven, with people holding the same job ranks charting out far apart on the graphs.

Following the evaluation of present status symbol distribution, the planning team's task is to develop a workable and continuing system for status distribution in the new space. Again, the fewer items of furniture that are attached to status, the better. If, for example, all personnel of a certain rank are given workplaces with conference tables, but numbers of these personnel do not actually need private conference tables, clearly money is being spent un- necessarily on furniture and space. As long as status symbols are clearly defined

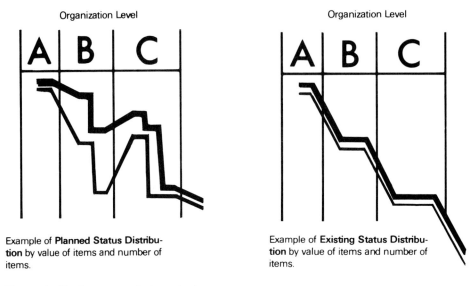

Example of **Planned Status Distribution** by value of items and number of items.

Example of **Existing Status Distribution** by value of items and number of items.

Figure 1-17. Status symbol analysis

and understood by all users, the symbols need not take such a conventional form. It is not so much a question of *what* they are, as *that* they are. Telephone color, ashtray size, nameplate type or location—all can denote status without impairing flexibility and without resulting in wasted space and dollars.

WORKPLACE TYPES

Before the correlation diagrams can be enlarged upon to include work groups to scale, the planning team must gather specific information concerning each user's furniture and equipment requirements. Two steps in this process are an inventory of existing furniture and equipment, and the development of a work/time distribution matrix.

Whether the project involves renovating a facility or constructing a new one, some of the existing furniture and/or equipment may usually be reused. The inventory simply gives the organization and the planning team a list of the items available for reuse. Further, in combination with the work/time distribution matrix, it aids in determining the misuse or disuse of furniture and equipment.

The work/time distribution matrix indicates the kinds of functions the user performs at the workplace, such as typing, filing, writing, conferencing, and telephoning, and the percentage of time spent on each function. This information may be gathered by means of a questionnaire.

When the furniture and equipment inventory and the work/time distribution matrix are examined together, it may become apparent that a number of employees do not use certain items of furniture and equipment presently in their workplaces, while other employees need furniture and/or equipment they do not have. In addition, often some pieces of equipment are used only a small percentage of the time by each member of a group of users and therefore can be shared satisfactorily, reducing equipment duplication.

The work/time distribution matrix should also be used to establish each user's lighting and acoustical privacy requirements. Because these requirements figure so strongly later in the design of the office space, they must be accurate. The core group should carefully review lighting and acoustical requirements with the users to ensure their accuracy, and should revise them as necessary.

On the basis of the work/time distribution matrix, and in light of findings and solutions related to document flow, filing, and status, it is now possible to define workplace types. Generally, as the furniture and equipment needs of each user are determined, it becomes clear that some users' needs are essentially the same. Wherever this is the case, a workplace type may be established and a list of the furniture and equipment required for that workplace type may be compiled. For example, a given workplace type might include the following: a standard desk, a desk chair, a side chair, and two feet of file storage (Figures 1-18 and 1-19). Workplace types should be developed for *all* users.

Furniture and equipment should also be itemized for group workplaces[4] such as shared conference, reception, or semiactive file storage areas, and for special areas. Special areas are those that relate to the organization as a whole

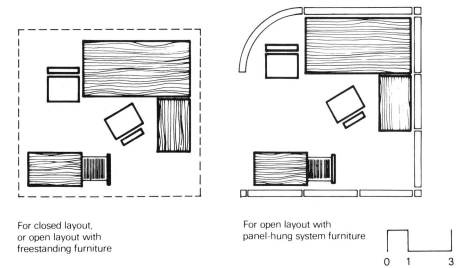

For closed layout,
or open layout with
freestanding furniture

For open layout with
panel-hung system furniture

0   1   3

Figure 1-18. Closed- and open-plan layouts 1

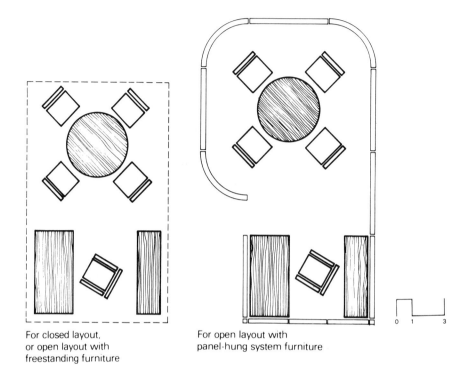

For closed layout,
or open layout with
freestanding furniture

For open layout with
panel-hung system furniture

Figure 1-19. Closed- and open-plan layouts 2

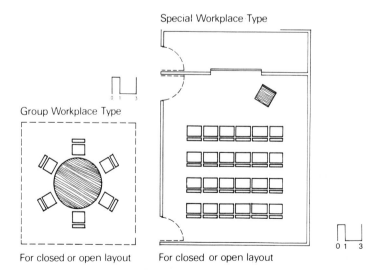

Special Workplace Type

Group Workplace Type

For closed or open layout

For closed or open layout

Figure 1-20. Group workplace layouts

rather than to any particular user or group of users, but that are still parts of the office proper (Figure 1-20). Special areas include libraries, very large conference areas, audiovisual rooms, and lounges, but do not include mechanical equipment rooms or the main building lobby.

Developing workplace types does *not* entail developing workplace square footages. Further, the furniture and equipment requirements of *all* office spaces must be itemized; otherwise, when total space needs are calculated, they will be incorrect.

At this point, the planning team has gathered enough information and has determined the organization's needs sufficiently to decide whether a closed- or open-plan layout is appropriate. In actuality, although the planning team has avoided working toward a specific layout type, this decision will probably have become obvious by this time. Nonetheless, to double-check the validity of the chosen alternative and/or to resolve possible disagreement, the team may formulate a decision matrix. If open and closed layouts are the vertical categories, the horizontal categories should list the aspects of these layouts to be evaluated in terms of the organization's needs. The horizontal categories might include communication facilitation, workplace flexibility, layout flexibility, acoustical privacy, visual privacy, and any generalized costs that can be estimated at this time. If these evaluations are indicated by numbers on a scale of 1 to 10, it is necessary only to compute their totals to arrive at a layout decision.

It is worth pointing out here that the organization may be best suited by a combination of open and closed offices because of varying user needs. There is no reason such a combination cannot be workable. Again, layout is totally dependent upon user and organization needs.

ENVIRONMENTAL REQUIREMENTS

Once the planning team has decided between an open and a closed plan, the core group and specialists should establish environmental requirements for the space within the context of this decision. These requirements should address all aspects of the office space with the exceptions of user juxtaposition and furniture and equipment needs, which have already been established by the correlation diagram and workplace types, respectively.

This planning step is a crucial one because it describes what *must* be accomplished if the space is to be successful. It provides the planning team's specialists with the goals for their designs. These requirements are not design guidelines, but design *necessities*. If they are not met, then the design process will have failed. Neither available technologies nor costs are considered; user needs are the sole focus.

In the case of an open layout, some of these requirements might be as follows:

- All workplaces must be easily rearrangeable to accommodate the formation of new work groups, and the relocation and addition of users.
- All work groups must be identifiable as groups.
- All type A and B workplaces must have confidential speech privacy.
- All type C, D, and E workplaces must have at least normal speech privacy.
- All type F, G, H, and I workplaces require only minimal speech privacy.
- Acoustical systems must be able to accommodate user rearrangement and different densities of users over time.
- All workplaces must be provided with lighting for conventional reading and writing tasks.
- All type B workplaces must have lighting controllable for use of audiovisual equipment.
- All type F, G, and H workplaces must be provided with lighting for machine communication tasks.
- Lighting throughout the space must be able to accommodate the rearrangement and addition of users.
- All storage areas in each workplace must be within the user's reach when he or she is seated at the desk.
- All work surfaces must be nonreflective.
- The fire safety system must be able to accommodate different densities and locations of users over time.
- Type F, G, and H work stations must be provided with furniture that will support the computing system selected for that job function.
- Power and signal must be rearrangeable to accommodate users in different locations and in different densities over time.
- HVAC must be able to accommodate users in different locations and in different densities over time.

Note that these are *requirements* and do not include solutions. The requirements for lighting, for instance, do not address whether the lighting should be direct or indirect, but only what it must provide for in terms of user tasks. Likewise, acoustical requirements do not state that there must be a background masking system; a background masking system is a solution, not a requirement. These requirements state only what is needed, not the means by which these needs may be met.

When the environmental requirements have been defined and listed, they should be presented to the users and the review and decision committee for approval. The users should be involved in this review for two reasons: first, to double-check the accuracy of all requirements and second, to ensure that users understand the requirements and the logic behind them.

FURNITURE SELECTION

Following the development of environmental requirements, the core group and the interior designer should evaluate and select furniture for the new office space. This should be done by laying out a sampling of workplaces using different types or lines of furniture. The sampling should include workplace types for all levels of the organization so that the functional and aesthetic advantages and disadvantages of different furniture types or lines may be evaluated in the context of the project.

If the project calls for an open-plan office, three sets of layouts should be developed. These are necessary because there are three general types of furniture for open offices, and each type has its own layout constraints and freedoms. The three types are freestanding, semi-freestanding, and interlocking or panel-hung systems furniture. Of course, if one of these types is clearly inappropriate or unacceptable to the organization and its users, it is not necessary to develop all three layouts.

When the furniture types have been compared and a decision has been made regarding which type or types are appropriate, the team should proceed with additional layouts in order to select a line or lines of furniture for the open office. The team is not necessarily limited to one line of furniture or to one general type of furniture, but can make choices according to user needs. For instance, one work group may be best served by a particular line of freestanding furniture made by manufacturer R, and another by a line of interlocking furniture made by manufacturer S.

In the case of a closed-plan office, the planning team may proceed directly to selecting a line or lines of furniture because, in the main, closed-plan furniture does not break down into types affecting layout (Figure 1-21).

Whether the new office space is to be open or closed, it may be that no furniture entirely meets the organization's functional and/or aesthetic requirements. In this case, the core group and the interior designer should design modifications to be made to an existing line, or design an entirely new line of furniture to meet the project's needs.

Here is a discussion of the three open-plan furniture types and some of their major advantages and disadvantages.

Freestanding furniture is usually associated with, but is not limited to, a free-form layout (Figure 1-22). It is defined as that furniture in which each item is structurally independent of all others and has only one function. A writing table is only for writing and similar tasks; it has no file drawers attached. Interlocking or panel-hung furniture is designed so that most items are structurally dependent. For example, a partition may have a writing surface, file drawers, and bookshelves attached to it, or will at least accept the attachment of such items. In semi-freestanding furniture, many pieces remain structurally

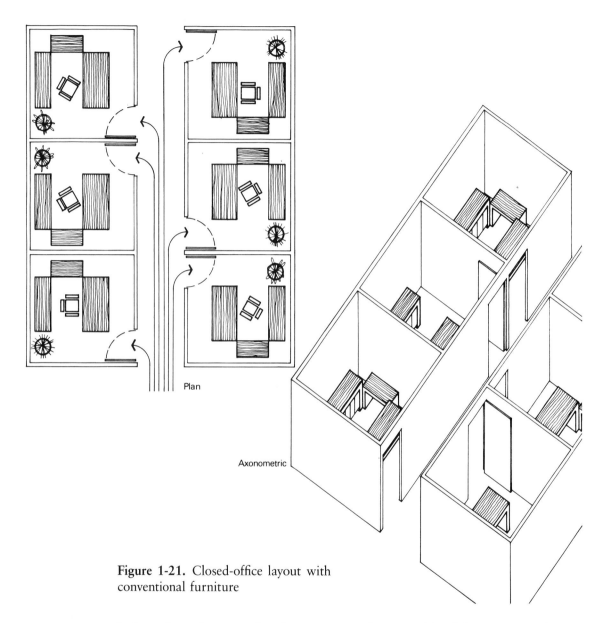

Plan

Axonometric

Figure 1-21. Closed-office layout with conventional furniture

independent of one another, but some may have combined functions, such as a desk with the file drawers attached, or a bookcase, the back of which is an acoustical panel (Figure 1-23).

Panel-hung systems are designed to be laid out in a geometric pattern (Figure 1-24). Although different lines use different patterns, such as rectangles, pentagons, hexagons, octagons, all conform to one pattern. Each line allows more or less freedom to deviate from its pattern. This geometrical

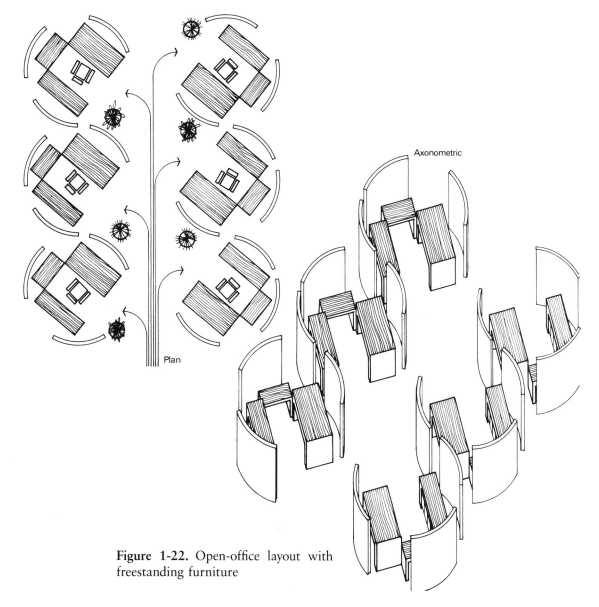

Axonometric

Plan

Figure 1-22. Open-office layout with freestanding furniture

rigidity is both an advantage and a disadvantage. One advantage is that it makes panel-hung systems simpler to lay out than other furniture types. There are fewer choices to be made regarding workplace shape, exact juxtaposition to other workplaces, and even workplace size, because the size must grow or shrink incrementally.

Other advantages are that the pieces of the panel-hung systems are generally interchangeable, and adding pieces to an existing workplace is a

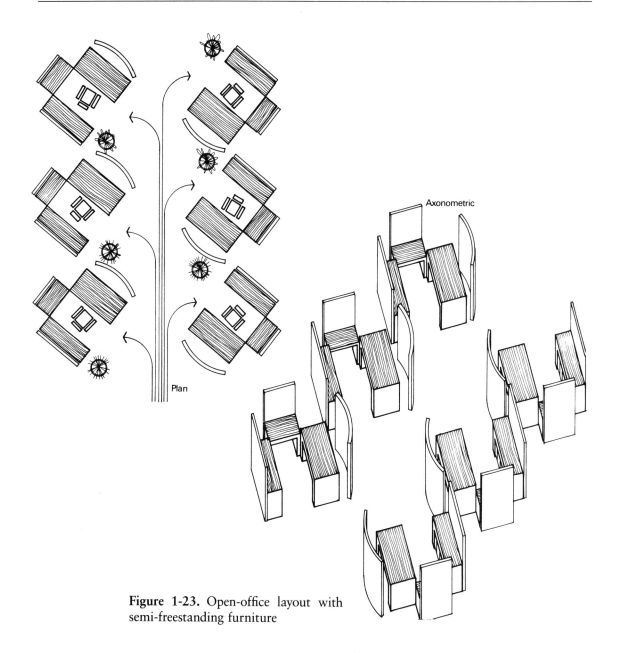

Axonometric

Plan

Figure 1-23. Open-office layout with semi-freestanding furniture

simple matter of attaching the desired items to existing partitions. In other words, a writing surface attached to one partition in one workplace will fit a partition in any other workplace. Further, if a user requires an extra bookshelf, one can be brought from the storeroom or ordered, and added to the user's existing partition. In the same circumstance, freestanding or semi-freestanding systems may require the acquisition of a new bookcase.

However, the geometrical pattern that makes the panel-hung layout easier in some ways may also make the result quite rigid in appearance. Workplaces designed with any single line of systems furniture do tend to look more or less alike. There are variations in size, color, and orientation, but not in the fundamental shape or overall character of the workplaces. Because of this, panel-hung systems seem most suitable for large groups of users who perform basically the same tasks.

As a type, freestanding furniture is the least rigid of the three in terms of layout. There are essentially no layout rules regarding either the patterns formed by workplaces or workplace sizes. Consequently, freestanding furniture may take slightly more time to lay out, but it is more conducive to variation in workplace shape, size, and character.

There is an ongoing debate over freestanding furniture and panel-hung systems concerning which is the more flexible from layout and rearrangement

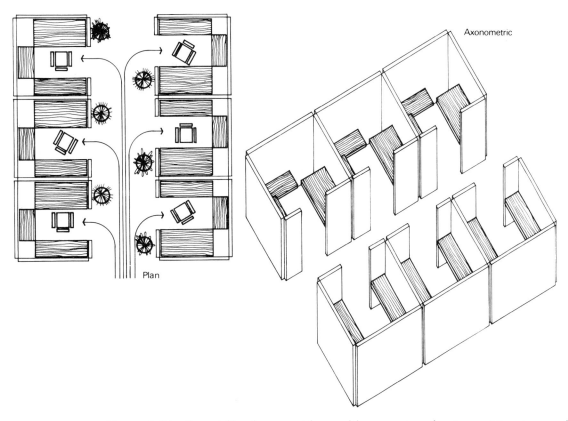

Figure 1-24. Open-office layout with panel-hung system furniture. Most items of furniture are structurally dependent.

points of view. On one side, some office designers and users believe that freestanding is more flexible because it is less rigid as far as layout, because it can accommodate a larger range of workplace types, and because the furniture itself is easily moved or rearranged. Others maintain that panel-hung systems can accommodate any workplace type, and that they are less limiting in terms of layout because each workplace can be designed with less square footage, and therefore user density can be increased. In general, systems workplaces do require fewer square feet than *comparable* freestanding workplaces; depending upon project circumstances, this may or may not be viewed as a great advantage.

The relative costs of rearranging freestanding furniture and panel-hung systems are also hotly debated. It seems that in some situations, such as moving numbers of workplaces from one location to another, panel-hung systems may be less expensive than freestanding furniture. In other cases, adding one or two workplaces to an existing group, for example, it appears that freestanding is less costly. One consideration less open to controversy is that moving freestanding furniture requires no special skills or knowledge, whereas dismantling and reassembling a panel-hung system does call for familiarity with the mechanics of that system.

As one might expect, semi-freestanding furniture shares some advantages with the other two furniture types. As far as layout freedom and workplace size, it has roughly the same characteristics as freestanding, yet it shares an advantage with systems in that it possibly requires less square footage per workplace than freestanding. However, semi-freestanding furniture is somewhat more difficult to move than either of the other types because its components, such as desks with file drawers, are heavier unless they can be dismantled easily. At the same time, it does not preclude the possibility of using at least some of the organization's existing furniture, and this clearly means a savings in initial costs.

Planning for a mix of closed- and open-plan offices requires an additional set of considerations. A key element of planning is the degree of flexibility allowed by the space dividers. In the open-plan office, flexibility is a given. In the traditional closed-plan office, full-height space dividers are fixed and become part of the building. This limitation, however, has given way to a whole array of "demountable" or "movable wall" systems. The optimum solution for a closed-office full-height space divider requires a system that will be compatible with and interchangeable with an open-plan office. In other words, the space divider should be easily reconfigured to be compatible with the open-plan space divider system. In addition, system performance must be compatible with the acoustical, lighting, fire safety, power and signal distribution, and HVAC systems for the project. The result may be that a special ceiling system and high-performance sound-absorbent facing on the demountable partitions will be required. If hang-on component furniture is the norm for the rest of the office, the full-height space divider that will accommodate the same furniture may be desired.

Caution: Mixing closed- and open-plan offices with the intent to move back and forth over the life span of the building will require careful consideration of all the building subsystems. Clearly lighting, acoustical, and HVAC systems designed specifically for the open-plan office will not function properly when closed offices are installed. Likewise, systems designed exclusively for the closed office will not function properly when the full-height partitions are removed. It is imperative that the concept of mixing closed and open offices be part of the original planning process. With appropriate performance criteria established for both concepts at the onset, it is feasible to select and design environmental components that will function efficiently in either layout.

SPACE CALCULATION

The furniture and equipment requirements for each workplace type, in combination with the selection of line(s) of furniture, allow the specialists and the core group to determine workplace square footages.

The square footage for any given workplace equals the area required for the items of furniture and equipment, plus the square footage needed for circulation within the workplace, plus a factor for major circulation within the office space. This formula may also be used to derive group and special workplace square footages, and holds true for any layout type. Because the factor for major circulation differs with layout type, and interior circulation needs depend upon the line of furniture selected, all space calculations should be computed with the help of an interior designer and/or architect, and a furniture representative.

The planning team should also calculate both the square footage required for each work group, and the total square footage necessary to fulfill the organization's office space needs (Figure 1-25). Each work group's existing square-footage requirement is simply the sum of that group's individual and group workplace square footages. The organization's existing square-footage needs for office space equal the sum of all work group square footages, plus the square footages for all special workplaces or areas. In order to reflect any expansion projected for the near future, square footages for projected workplaces should be added to appropriate work group calculations and to the calculations for the whole office.

As square footages are being calculated, each workplace type, including individual, group, and special workplaces, should be graphically laid out *to scale* with all items of furniture and equipment shown in a logical, functional arrangement.

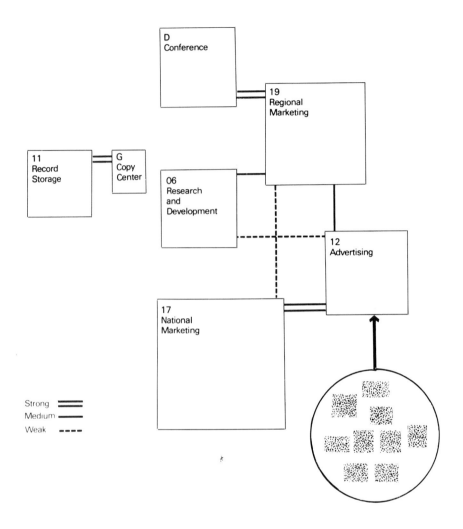

Figure 1-25. Correlation diagram to scale. Work-group square footage equals individual workplace plus group workplace plus estimated future workplace square footages.

The original correlation diagram represented graphically, but not to scale, the ideal spatial relationships between work groups. Now that the square footage of each work group is known, it may be applied to the original correlation diagram to develop a correlation diagram *to scale*. In addition, special workplace square footages should be included in this new correlation diagram so that all of the organization's major office elements are indicated. Individual workplaces should not be incorporated until the final layout is made, later in the project.

BUILDING AND ENVIRONMENTAL SYSTEMS DESIGN

In combination, the space calculations and the established environmental requirements have brought the project to a point at which the building itself—if a new one is to be constructed—and its environmental systems, such as lighting, HVAC, acoustics, and fire safety, may be designed.

Environmental systems design is the primary subject of the remainder of this book and will be discussed in the following chapters. However, several general points are worth making in this chapter.

The Building Parameters

The first is in regard to the building, its space configuration, and its shell. In designing the configuration of the space, the planning team specialists most directly involved, such as the architect and interior designer, should remain in close contact with the core group. This is to make sure that numerous space configurations are examined and the most logical adopted. In a multistory building, for example, it is of the utmost importance that the ideal work group interaction relationships, set forth by the to-scale correlation diagram, be compromised as little as possible by the division of groups among floors.

In terms of cost, the planning team should consider space configuration in regard to both construction and life-cycle costs. For instance, a configuration that minimizes exterior wall area will probably be less expensive to construct than, say, a very elongated configuration. But life-cycle costs for lighting and HVAC may be reduced with the elongated shape because of access to natural light and solar heat. At the same time, such a shape may pose difficult acoustical problems because of the increased square footage of sound-reflective wall surface. In deciding upon final space configuration, then, the core group and specialists must remain aware of the effects of the configuration on user needs, layout, energy consumption, fire safety, and the overall environmental conditions of the space (Figure 1-26).

The building shell is, of course, inseparable from space configuration. It is defined as the building's fixed elements, such as floors, ceilings, exterior walls, columns, and the building core, which includes elevators, stairs, toilets, mechanical chases, and so on. In office design, the essential point is to locate columns and the building core where they will least interrupt or conflict with layout. In the case of a closed-office layout, it may be desirable to locate the building core in the center of the space in order to preserve window exposure for the offices. In an open layout, however, the core is usually better located away from the center so it does not interrupt circulation patterns or user interaction and work flow.

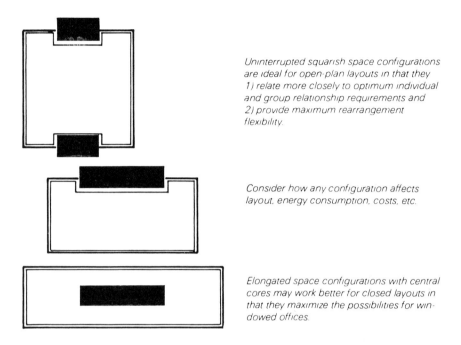

Uninterrupted squarish space configurations are ideal for open-plan layouts in that they 1) relate more closely to optimum individual and group relationship requirements and 2) provide maximum rearrangement flexibility.

Consider how any configuration affects layout, energy consumption, costs, etc.

Elongated space configurations with central cores may work better for closed layouts in that they maximize the possibilities for windowed offices.

Figure 1-26. Space configuration

Systems Integration

The second point is that all design solutions should reflect at least the degree of systems integration that is necessitated by the environmental requirements and the overall conditions of the project. Systems should be integrated in order to avoid negatively influencing the users—for example, HVAC noise should not create acoustical problems. They should also be integrated to minimize life-cycle costs, energy consumption, and construction costs and time. This integration demands close teamwork among the specialists, and between the specialists and the core group.

Environmental Constraints

The third point is simply that, taken together, the design solutions must meet *all* of the environmental requirements established earlier in the project. Otherwise, the solutions cannot be considered workable. If there are several workable design solutions for any given area, these may be considered as alternatives and weighed against each other in terms of life-cycle costs, aesthetics, energy usage, and so forth.

Once the most appropriate solutions have been chosen from among the alternatives, the specialists and core group, still working as a close-knit team, can begin to select and specify products that fulfill the required functions within and meet the intentions of these solutions. If possible, more than one product should be specified in all cases so that bids may be received from manufacturers and initial costs minimized. In all cases, though, the products must fulfill their proper functions within the contexts of the solutions.

If no product exists which fulfills a given solution's functional and/or aesthetic requirements, the specialists must modify an existing product or design a new one. As with existing products, the modified or new product should be tendered to several companies for bids on manufacturing costs.

FINAL LAYOUT

When the facility plan is sufficiently complete, the next planning step, called zone formation, may take place. This step is essentially the application of the to-scale correlation diagram to the plan of the new or renovated facility. Work groups and special areas should be laid out exactly to scale on the new floor plans, and if the facility is multistoried, decisions regarding the division of work groups among floors should be finalized. Depending upon the layout type chosen for the project, the *shape*—not the square footage—of each work group's area or of a special workplace will have to be adjusted to provide optimum major circulation patterns. This is perhaps best explained by the accompanying drawing (Figure 1-27).

In most cases, special areas such as audiovisual rooms and reproduction rooms should not occupy prime space; they are probably better located near the core than along windowed exterior walls. In addition, any extraordinary environmental needs these special areas may have should be accommodated. For example, if an audiovisual room has the dual function of conference room and a window is desired, then there should be some means of controlling natural light within the room.

The zone formation layout should be presented to the review and decision committee and the user group of the planning team. Once these groups have reviewed and approved the zone formation, individual and group workplaces may be added to it. This is accomplished one work group at a time. The arrangement of users within the work group is based on and must diverge minimally from the original correlation diagram developed for each group. All workplaces are shown to scale, though specific items of furniture and equipment should not yet be indicated.

Just as it was necessary to consider major circulation patterns in zone formation, in arranging workplaces within each work group it is necessary to decide both how major circulation will enter the given work group's area and

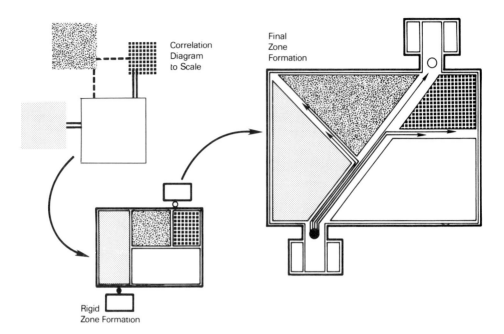

Figure 1-27. Zone formation

how in-group, or minor, circulation may be routed. Three points are worth noting in this regard: (1) access to one user's workplace should never interfere with another's workplace; (2) no workplace should be entered from the rear, i.e., the user should face toward, not away from, the workplace entry; and (3) both minor and major circulation routes should be as short as possible.

The appropriate furniture and equipment may be added to the work group layouts by referring to the to-scale layouts of workplace types compiled earlier in the planning. During this final phase of developing a layout for the organization's office space—though perhaps at this point it goes without saying—it is critical for specialists and core group to be aware of how the layout affects acoustics, fire safety, HVAC, and lighting, and vice versa. For instance, if tall acoustical screens are to be placed in a certain area, they may block air circulation or lighting. Further, the layout should ensure the creation of a subjective space for each work group. That is, each group's space should carry a certain identity that allows its members to relate strongly to the group as a whole. Subjective space may be reinforced through the use of color and graphics, for example, as well as through the layout itself. In general, any large space in which there is little variety in terms of layout, color, graphics, and furniture and furnishings will become boring and may also seem confusing to users and visitors. Monotony is to be avoided.

If a closed-plan layout is being designed, special attention should be paid to avoiding shotgun corridors. They are often dull and usually appear uninviting or even intimidating to users and visitors. Further, the layout should be such that windows are exposed to as many users as possible.

The three open-office layout types also warrant a few special considerations. As with a closed office layout, shotgun corridors are undesirable, not only for the reasons mentioned above, but also because major circulation should conform more to the best configurations for work groups than the other way around.

Major circulation in the open office should be as needed to serve the work groups, rather than following a predetermined grid. All workplaces within one group's space should be oriented differently from those of adjacent groups; this is primarily to reinforce the users' sense of subjective space. Tall furniture, such as screens and bookcases, should not be of uniform height throughout the office; this is to avoid monotony and to eliminate the possibility of creating a single, unbroken plane as large as the office space. On the average, two visual/acoustical screens per workplace are sufficient for visual privacy, but this average may fluctuate up or down as far as acoustical privacy is concerned. Clearly, the number required depends upon the degree of acoustical privacy desired. And finally, plants work well as corridor definers and as *visual* screens. If there is an average for plant use within the open office, it is about one large plant per workplace.

COLOR AND GRAPHICS

Although color and graphics are really design issues, there are a few general points we would like to make about their use in the office.

Color

Color affects people physiologically. For example, reds, in quantity, cause increased heart and perspiration rate, while blues have the reverse effect. Greens and grays are neutral. This is certainly not to imply that any colors are taboo in the office environment, but to say that a balanced color scheme is necessary. A mix of colors also provides variety and is a good means of defining subjective space, in closed and in open offices.

Colors for open-office spaces should be selected with particular care because they affect everyone within the organization. Special attention should be given to color schemes for work groups and to balancing these schemes within and between groups (Figure 1-28).

In addition, and especially in the open office, color can be a powerful shaper of the character, mood, image, and even of the apparent logic or illogic of the space. It can cause the office to seem dull or lively, depressing or cheerful,

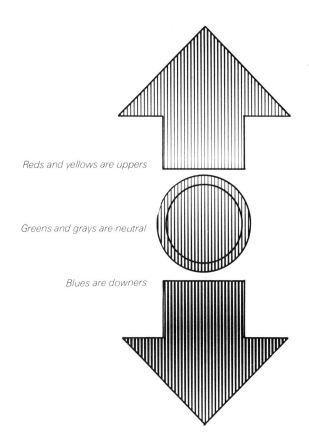

Reds and yellows are uppers

Greens and grays are neutral

Blues are downers

Figure 1-28. The psychological effects of color.

chaotic or orderly, and can, to a certain extent, influence user perception of the size and shape of the space.

Another important consideration is how lighting affects color, and vice versa. The kinds of light sources used in the office space have a direct bearing on our color perception, and excessive color contrasts in the workplace may decrease visual comfort appreciably. Further, the colors chosen for the work environment may alter lighting requirements substantially by their ability to reflect or absorb light, thus affecting initial construction costs, maintenance costs, and energy consumption, not to mention user comfort and productivity. Clearly, then, the planning and design team's lighting specialist must work closely with the core group and the interior design specialist in color selection and placement.

It is worth noting also that color may become a useful element in the organization's fire safety program by denoting emergency exit routes. Graphics too may function well for this purpose.

Graphics

Graphics within the office, whether it is open or closed, should not be approached merely as decoration, though all graphics should, of course, be attractive (Figure 1-29). In general, graphics should serve one or more of the following purposes: to inform, to identify, or to direct. In this way, they become functioning parts of the office. For example, graphics might identify areas and activities of the organization's various work groups, or direct visitors and users to a particular location. Graphics can also be coordinated with color so that the graphics directing visitors to area X, say, are always green, while those directing people to area Y are always red, and so forth. Additionally, graphics work well as status identifiers: a block of blue, for instance, can be used to identify all department heads.

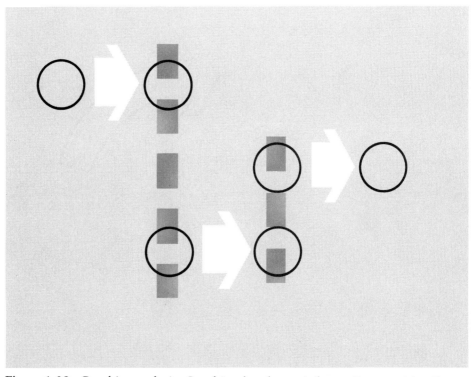

Figure 1-29. Graphics analysis. Graphics that do not inform, direct, or identify are only decorations.

MOVE-IN AND FOLLOW-UP

When the organization's new or renovated office space is ready for occupancy, the move should be conducted as a planning task to ensure a smooth transition for all users and to minimize the disruption of regular office activities. The core group of the planning team should conduct a detailed pre-move-in check to avoid any last-minute delays, because of, say, improper arrangement of a few workplaces, or malfunctioning of certain pieces of equipment.

After the move has been accomplished and all users are settled in their workplaces, follow-up planning should be undertaken. This is essentially a matter of evaluating the success of implemented solutions and of making necessary adjustments (Figure 1-30). The first step in follow-up is a physical and environmental evaluation. This evaluation is primarily a job for certain of the planning team's specialists because it involves measuring whether the lighting, HVAC, power and signal, and other components are performing as planned, and whether the space is acoustically balanced. Measuring, evaluating, and adjusting the acoustical qualities of the whole office and of each workplace are most important if the layout is an open plan. It may be necessary

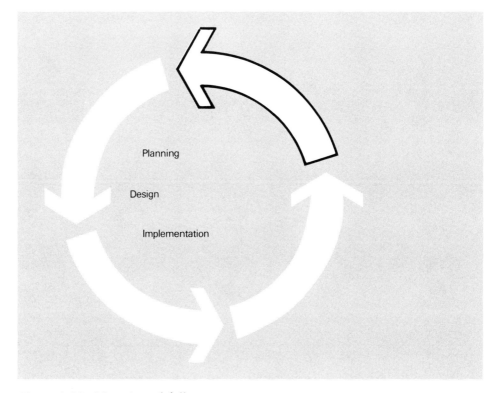

Planning

Design

Implementation

Figure 1-30. Move-in and follow-up

to add or subtract acoustical screens and tune the background masking system, if one has been installed, to the appropriate level. In addition, the layout of open-plan areas should be reviewed and adjustments made if some workplaces are too tight or too open.

Besides their obvious use in determining whether the acoustical controls for each workplace fulfill desired performance levels, the measurements taken by the acoustical specialist also serve to allay any doubts users might have as to the real speech privacy afforded by open-office workplaces. These doubts are understandable. For example, in a closed-office space, the user may feel that he or she has acoustical privacy simply because of the floor-to-ceiling partitioning, when in fact the space is not acoustically private and the user's conversations may be overheard in adjacent offices. But in an open workplace designed for confidential privacy, the user may need to be convinced that his or her speech cannot be understood beyond the visual/acoustical screens. In-place acoustical measurements, then, serve to prove to the users that their workplaces do actually afford them the speech privacy they need.

About a month after move-in has been completed, an employee attitude survey should be conducted by means of a questionnaire. The questionnaire should gather user opinions on *all* aspects of the new office environment, including the following: workplace size and location, work group location, ease of communication of all types, access to information, furniture and equipment, circulation, office temperature, lighting, acoustical privacy, acoustics of the office in general, color, graphics, status symbols, filing systems, special areas. The user should be allowed a range of choices for each question. The point of the survey is to discover what each user's likes and dislikes are regarding the new space, and to identify and solve any problems which might have surfaced.

The results of this survey and of the physical and environmental evaluation should be summarized in written and graphic form for review by the organization's management and users.

Approximately six months after move-in, a second employee attitude survey should be conducted and its results summarized in a second report. In this way, the users' initial and postadjustment responses to the new space may be compared, and further adjustments may be made if needed.

Although these follow-up evaluations mark the end of the formal project, planning for the organization should continue, though not on the same scale. This ongoing planning should be the responsibility of the in-house members of the planning team's core group, who by now will have become familiar with the methodology and approach presented here. Their task is to ensure that the continuing change within the organization is reflected and accommodated by the physical environment of the office. The office space cannot be allowed to become static any more than the organization itself can afford to become static.

SUMMARY

Office planning is a logical progression in which the following must be accomplished: (1) definition of the organization's goals; (2) examination of the existing situation; (3) establishment of use needs; (4) development, evaluation, and implementation of solutions that fulfill user requirements. The organization should be viewed as a whole whose parts are dependent upon one another and must function together. Examples of the elements are the office products, procedures, people relationships, equipment, and the environment. The environment is all inclusive and interdependent. Key items that shape the environment are acoustics, lighting, thermal comfort, safety, power, signal, furniture, and aesthetics.

Planning is the link between technology and the design of a successful office environment. An interdisciplinary planning team includes user representatives and consultants or representatives of all the disciplines necessary to the project. Information gathering is vital and should include as many users as possible from every level of the organization. The more extensive and comprehensive the information gathering process, the more effective the solution will be.

Establishing environmental requirements is a crucial planning step because it describes what must be accomplished if the space is to be successful. Selection of the space layout, including the identification of closed office, open office areas, square foot allocation, and furniture systems should be made solely to satisfy the total user needs.

Follow-up planning, or on-going facilities management, using the same planning principles as those implemented in the planning process, is essential to the success of the project.

Notes

1. For purposes of convenience, *organization* is used to refer to the planned-for group. In an actual project, this group might be an entire company or institution, or a part thereof.
2. Those readers desiring more detailed information on this planning approach are referred to Palmer and Lewis, *Planning the Office Landscape,* New York: McGraw-Hill, 1977.
3. Using a computer for these totals may be helpful, especially in large projects.
4. Group workplaces may serve an entire work group, or a smaller unit of, say, five users within a larger work group.

Chapter 2

ACOUSTICS

David A. Harris

In many ways, a well-designed office is one that goes unnoticed by the users; it does not distract them or draw their attention. This is perhaps true of acoustics more than lighting or HVAC because the acoustical system has few adjustments or controls. It does not turn on or off, nor can the user readily adjust or reposition it daily for different activities. It is simply there, and either it is successful or it is unsuccessful. Undoubtedly, initial design efforts must consider acoustics, since retrofit solutions are notoriously expensive.

The planning team, in generating acoustical solutions, must consider the *whole* space and account for the effects of all other systems. Acoustics becomes a controlling element in the open office. Careful tradeoffs with HVAC, lighting, and other system element designs are usually required to meet user needs for speech privacy. Therefore, before a specialist can begin designing the acoustical system, the first stages of office planning must be completed by the team.

Planners must already have analyzed their organization in its totality— its purposes, its products and/or services, and especially the communication patterns between individual employees and departments. With this foundation, they can effectively answer questions about office layout and speech privacy requirements that are fundamental to an acoustical design:

- Is the closed- or open-office plan preferred?
- Should the office have the capability of being converted to either plan?
- Where should departments and individuals be placed in relationship to each other?
- What will be the location of departments like word processing and computer centers that require special acoustical treatment?

The goal of the acoustical system is to create an environment where employees and clients feel comfortable and can perform their activities efficiently. Such an environment will be aesthetically pleasing if it is free from annoying or unwanted noise. And it will enhance productivity by allowing office occupants to talk comfortably without distracting others or being distracted by those in adjacent areas. In the language of acousticians, the acoustical system should provide "speech privacy" adequate to the needs of the employees and clients of the particular organization. The system analysis generally includes these items:

- Are there individuals or departments who must be accessible to many others?
- What are the privacy needs of individuals and departments?
- Are there some areas where strict confidentiality is required?
- Are there some where the acoustical system is required only to provide freedom from distracting sound?

The critical decision about layout is whether to use a closed or open plan. Both have advantages. Achieving speech privacy and a pleasant acoustical environment in a closed office is less difficult than in an open office. However, the open office can much more readily be changed to match changes in an organization. The planning team therefore needs to understand the acoustical requirements, problems, and solutions that relate to both plans. In particular, it needs to consider these elements:

- Ceilings
- Office partitions in closed offices or screens in open offices
- Other vertical surfaces like walls, windows, and columns
- Floors
- Background sound masking system
- Placement and positioning of occupants

SPEECH PRIVACY

The ideal office acoustical environment will permit occupants to talk easily with a visitor or on a telephone without distracting or being distracted by those nearby. The three principal elements that shape this environment are the noise sources (voices and office machines), the transmission elements (ceilings, walls, floors, etc.), and the noise receivers (the people occupying the office area). It is the responsibility of the acoustician to design transmission elements and background masking systems that will control unwanted sound to the degree required by office occupants (Figure 2-1).

Speech privacy criteria should be established early in the planning process. For example, executive and sensitive areas may require confidential

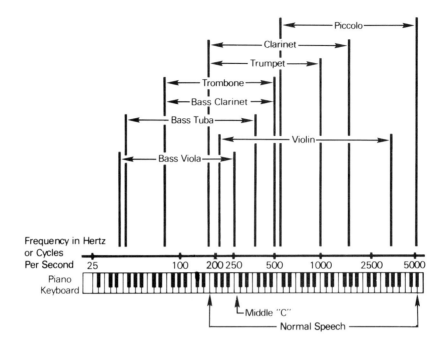

Figure 2-1. Sound frequency. Frequency ranges of several musical instruments shown on a frequency scale which uses the piano keyboard for comparison.

privacy. The effect of confidential privacy is that the sense of a conversation cannot be understood by persons in an adjoining office or work station (only in rare instances is greater acoustical privacy required in an office). Minimum privacy, or the ability to avoid distractions from an adjoining office or work station, is usually necessary for most office workers. Certain work groups or teams require no privacy due to their need for constant interaction.

Note that these privacy requirements are associated with speech communication. While an environment that satisfies speech criteria may be adequate for most office machines, noisy equipment should be analyzed separately and moved to another area if necessary. Fortunately, most modern office machines are designed to be quiet.

Speech sounds for a typical male conversation at 3 feet are approximately 60 to 65 decibels (dB)[1] with a dynamic range of 200 to 5000 hertz (Hz).[2] The middle frequencies from 500 to 4000 Hz are the most important for communication. For total intelligibility, speech sound should exceed the level of background noise by a full 30 dB. (Acousticians refer to this difference in sound levels as the signal-to-noise ratio.) Hence, small changes in the sound source, the sound transmission qualities of sound barriers, the sound-absorbing qualities of reflecting surfaces, or the level of background sound can assure speech

	Decibels	Threshold of Feeling
	120	
Deafening	110	Thunder, Artillery, Nearby Riveter, Elevated Train, Boiler Factory
	100	
Very Loud	90	Loud Street Noise, Noisy Factory, Truck Unmuffled, Police Whistle
	80	
Loud	70	Noisy Office, Average Street Noise, Average Radio, Average Factory
	60	
Moderate	50	Noisy Home, Average Office, Average Conversation, Quiet Radio
	40	
Faint	30	Quiet Home or Private Office, Average Auditorium, Quiet Conversation
	20	
Very Faint	10	Rustle of Leaves, Whisper, Sound-Proof Room, Threshold of Audibility
	0	

Figure 2-2. Sound loudness

privacy or increase intelligibility. For example, lowering the attenuation or background noise level by 5 dB can raise sentence intelligibility from 10 to 50 percent—the difference between good privacy and an eavesdropper's paradise. An equivalent change in barrier transmission, reflective surface absorption, or the background masking level will have a similar effect (Figure 2-2). Obviously, there is an upper limit to how much this background sound level can be increased without annoying office occupants or making it hard for them to be understood within their own workplace. A carefully controlled electronic background masking system can provide the proper balance between privacy and intelligibility for both closed- and open-office plans. In fact, it is imperative if speech privacy is to be achieved.

Attainment of Speech Privacy—Closed Plan

Providing acoustical privacy in the closed-office environment involves building barriers along the sound path. Full-height walls, sealed against sound and flanking paths, provide superior attenuation (Figure 2-3). To provide speech privacy, the acoustical envelope (including the ceiling system, floor, and walls) surrounding a closed office must attenuate sound by a 35 to 40 STC (Sound Transmission Class) rating.[3] Conference rooms usually require a 40 to 45 STC rating to accommodate louder sources of sound like audiovisual equipment. To be effective, the envelope must be designed so that there are no flanking paths for sound, such as holes or cracks at wall/ceiling/floor joints, common air ducts and pipes, and back-to-back outlets. In addition, the sound-reflective quality of each room should be reduced through the use of materials such as acoustical ceilings, drapes, and carpeting to reduce echoes or reverberation time. Background masking sound can also be used effectively in closed plans, especially if confidential speech privacy is desired.[4]

Figure 2-3. Closed office

Attainment of Speech Privacy—Open Plan

Since in the open office work areas are not separated by floor-to-ceiling walls, occupants can be easily disturbed by intruding sounds, human or mechanical, from other parts of the office. Figure 2-4 depicts this situation.

Planners have at their disposal many techniques to help them avoid creating a noisy, distracting work environment. Their goal is to reduce the signal-to-noise ratio[5] of office conversation to the point where the needed level of privacy is assured without aborting understandability.

The techniques that will reduce this ratio are as follows:

Figure 2-4. Open-plan office

- Providing a ceiling system that closely approaches an "open sky" acoustical condition. With an effective system, no sound should be reflected.
- Providing barriers that will reduce the direct speech level into adjacent work stations. Barrier surfaces should be highly sound absorbent to avoid sound reflections.
- Minimizing sound reflections from vertical surfaces such as walls, windows, cabinets, and so forth.
- Providing carpeted floors to minimize impact sounds.
- Providing a uniform, controlled background masking system to reduce the signal-to-noise ratio.

When well-designed and well-integrated, these components can cause sounds in an open office to diminish rapidly as they move away from the sources. This diminution may approach the way sound behaves on a beach, where the sky is a perfect absorber, a sand dune is an ideal barrier, and wind and surf act as a natural background masking system. Here, sound diminishes by 6 dB every time the distance from the source is doubled.

It is imperative that all elements—screens, wall treatment, ceiling and background masking—be included to achieve speech privacy. The absence of one or more of these elements may adversely affect the signal-to-noise ratio. For example, an installation with acoustically efficient part high barriers and a highly sound absorptive ceiling system without masking sound may reduce overall sound levels. However, the resultant acoustical environment will actually enhance speech intelligibility in adjoining work stations. In addition, the space may be physically or psychologically oppressive due to the excessive absorption. Masking sound is required to replace the natural masking sounds that are now being absorbed. A similar, but not quite as dramatic, effect will result by installing masking and highly sound absorptive barriers with a poor ceiling system or masking with a good ceiling and poor barriers. Note that the most common failure in designing open-plan offices is to install high-performance ceilings and barriers and omit masking sound. The result is worse speech privacy than if no attention had been given to acoustics. *To achieve speech privacy in an open office all three elements are required: a highly absorbent ceiling system, good barriers with highly absorbent faces, and a background masking system.*

Acoustical Components of the Open Plan

To assure that their open-office design provides an acoustical system that achieves desired levels of speech privacy, planners need to know how each component of the system helps to achieve this goal.

CEILINGS. To emphasize the importance of the ceiling in establishing the acoustical environment in an open plan, imagine yourself at a desk looking at a ceiling and walls made of mirrors. You will soon note that the ceiling is the only surface where the reflected image allows you to see everyone in the room. Unless specially treated, the office ceiling will act like an acoustical mirror, reflecting sounds back and forth across the office and absorbing few or none. This mirror-like quality of a surface is called "specular reflection."[6] Special acoustical treatments such as those shown in Figure 2-5 will minimize the specular reflectiveness of a ceiling.

A variety of options are available for reducing this reflectiveness. They range from flat ceiling panels to baffles and vaulted-ceiling components. Figure 2-6 shows a ceiling with baffles. Flat and vaulted ceilings are illustrated in Chapter 3. Many types of acoustical ceilings and acoustical ceiling materials

No Treatment

With Screen

With Screen and
Acoustical Ceiling

With Screen, Acoustical
Ceiling, and Background Masking

Figure 2-5. Acoustical treatments for open-plan offices

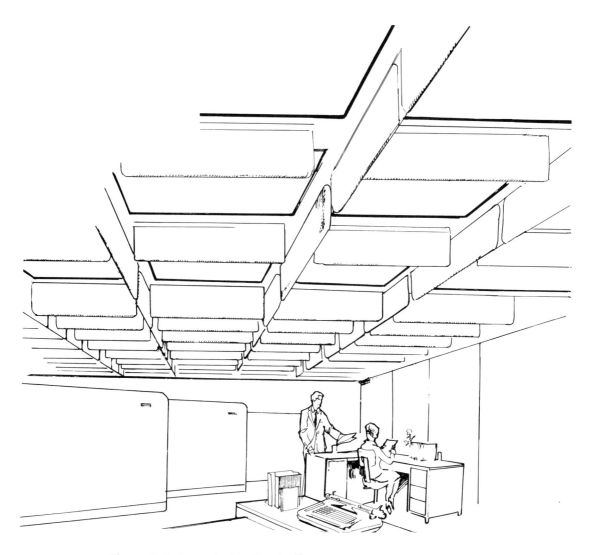

Figure 2-6. Acoustical ceiling baffles

will reduce the reflectiveness of an office ceiling. But planners should recognize that not all ceiling materials are effective in doing so. Tables 2-1 and 2-2 present the findings of two test situations on ceilings differing in materials and type (flat and vaulted). The ceilings tested range in sound-attenuating effectiveness from the open sky, a perfectly nonreflecting ceiling to gypsum board, a highly reflective ceiling. Only four of the ceilings tested provided adequate speech privacy. Clearly, planners must be careful in choosing a ceiling system and ceiling materials.

Table 2-1. Sound Attenuation Performance of Selected Ceiling Materials[a]

Test No.	Description	NIC' 9–12[b]	SPP[c]	AC[d]
XL-1LT[e]	Open sky	23	>60	250
XL-2LT[e]	½″ × 2′ × 4′ gypsum wallboard in suspended grid	11	<60	120
TE-1LT	2″ fiberglass glass cloth faced, TL backed ceiling board in suspended grid	20	>60	220
OC-1LT	1″ fiberglass glass cloth faced, TL backed ceiling board	18	=60	200
OC-2LT	⅝″ mineral fiber fire-rated ceiling board	16	<60	160
OC-3LT	⅝″ mineral fiberboard plus ½″ × 10″ gypsum board baffles in 2′ × 4′ array	16	<60	170
OC-4LT	⅝″ mineral board plus gypsum board baffles, lined each face with 1″ fiberglass ceiling board	19	=60	210
OC-6LT	½″ gypsum wallboard plus 1″ fiberglass lined baffles in 2′ × 4′ array	17	<60	190
OC-7LT	perforated metal pan and pad	17	<60	190
OC-8LT	2″ fiberglass non-TL backed glass cloth	20	>60	220
OC-9LT	1″ fiberglass non-TL backed glass cloth faced ceiling board	19	>60	210

[a] Courtesy of Owens-Corning Fiberglas.

[b] Per PBS C.2 procedure. This is an objective test where NIC' stands for Speech Privacy Noise Isolation Class, a single-number rating of the sound attenuating performance of acoustic materials.

[c] Per PBS C.1 procedure. This is a subjective test where SPP stands for Speech Privacy Potential, a single-number rating that measures the effectiveness of an acoustical system as a whole or combinations of acoustical components. The critical value for open-office acoustics is ≥60.

[d] An estimate of Articulation Class (AC) per American Society of Testing and Materials (ASTM) Standard E-1050-88, *Standard Classification for Determination of Articulation Class.* ASTM E-1111-88, *Standard Test Method for Measuring Interzone Attenuation of Ceiling Systems,* is the usual procedure for measuring AC. Test procedure E-1111 is similar in many respects to PBS C.2. While not directly convertible, these estimates are included to familiarize the reader with the type of test results that can be expected. (See Appendix 2A for a more detailed explanation of the new ASTM Test Standards.)

[e] The procedures for test XL-1LT and XL-2LT which established these maximum/minimum ratings for acoustical ceilings are explained on pages 83–84.

Table 2-2. Integrated Ceiling Systems Acoustical Ratings

Size and Type Luminaire	Type of Ceiling	Thickness of Ceiling Board	Open-Plan Office				Closed-Plan Office			
			SPP[a] Min[b]	SPP Max[b]	NIC'[c] Min[b]	NIC' Max[b]	SPP TL Backed Board	SPP Non-TL Board	NRC[d] Ceiling Board	AC[e]
1' × 2' lensed	Flat	1½', 1", ¾"	<60	≥60	17	20	>70	>65	.95	190
2' × 2' lensed	Flat	1½', 1", ¾"	<60	≥60	15	20	>70	>65	.95	150
1' × 4' parabolic	Flat	1½"	>60	>60	18	19	>70	>65	.95	200
2' × 2' parabolic	Flat	1½"	>60	>60	19	20	>70	>65	.95	210
4' × 4' parabolic	Vaulted	1½"	>60	>60	19	20	>70	>65	.95	210
1' × 4' lensed	Flat	1½"	<60	≥60	17	20	>70	>65	.95	190
1' × 4' lensed	Vaulted	1½"side, ¾" end	<60	>60	15	20	>70	>65	.95	150
2' × 2' lensed	Vaulted	1½"	<60	>60	15	21	>70	>65	.95	150

The numbers in the table were obtained for each ceiling system using an OCF Sound Screen II and an OCF Masking Sound System and Omega II Ceiling Board. (Data supplied courtesy of Owens-Corning Fiberglas.) (a) SPP less than 60 (<60) means that there is no speech privacy. (b) SPP equal to 60 (=60) means that there is minimal speech privacy. (c) SPP greater than 60 (>60) means that there is confidential speech privacy. (d) SPP greater than 65 or 70 means that there is confidential speech privacy between two offices when the voice is raised 5 to 10 dB, respectively, above normal voice level.

[a] Speech Privacy Potential (SPP) is measured and tested in accordance with General Services Administration/Public Buildings Service (GSA/PBS) C.1 procedure II.

[b] The minimum and maximum values were obtained when the screen was centered under a luminaire (minimum value) or between luminaires (maximum value). If a screen is located at a thirty to sixty degree angle with the luminaires, then the maximum values will also be obtained.

[c] Speech Privacy Noise Isolation Class (NIC') is measured and tested in accordance with the GSA/PBS C.2 procedure II. The higher the number, the greater the attenuation.

[d] NRC-Noise Reduction Coefficient measured in accordance with ASTM C-423.

[e] An estimate of Articulation Class (AC) per American Society of Testing and Materials (ASTM) Standard E-1050-88, Standard Classification for Determination of Articulation Class. ASTM E-1111-88, Standard Test Method for Measuring Interzone Attenuation of Ceiling Systems is the usual procedure for measuring AC. Test procedure E-1111 is similar in many respects to PBS C.2. While not directly convertible, these estimates are included to familiarize the reader with the type of results that can be expected. (See Appendix 2A for a more detailed explanation of the new ASTM Test Standards.)

LUMINAIRES. Ceiling light fixtures and other hard-surfaced ceiling components like air terminals and large grid members pose special problems, since they increase the specular reflectiveness of the ceiling (Figure 2-7). The effect of light fixtures—called luminaires by office design specialists—on the sound-attenuating effectiveness of an acoustical ceiling is depicted graphically in Figure 2-8.

These findings indicate the need for the acoustical attributes of the proposed ceiling to be evaluated along with those of hard-surfaced ceiling components such as lights, grid, and HVAC diffusers. Also, consultation between all specialists concerned with ceiling systems should occur before final decisions are made about the acoustical design. See Table 2-2 for examples of complete integrated systems' acoustical ratings.

Only deep cell (i.e., 4″ × 4″ and larger) parabolic fixtures and a specially designed V lens with absorptive side panels have successfully matched the sound attenuation characteristics of a good ceiling material. Flat and small-cell parabolic lenses can be as reflective as a mirror. Up-lighting, in the form of freestanding pedestals or furniture-mounted ambient lighting, is effective because there are no fixtures in the ceiling. Locating reflective materials directly above the sound source may direct the sound back to the source and thereby minimize flanking to an adjoining work station. However, this technique will have an adverse effect on ease of work station relocation, since the reflective material must move every time a new layout is implemented. It is imperative that the acoustical performance of the luminaire match that of the ceiling material. Otherwise, there will be "hot spots" in an otherwise good ceiling system where speech privacy will be totally lacking.

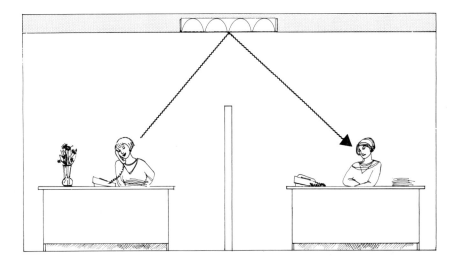

Figure 2-7. Luminaire acoustical schematic

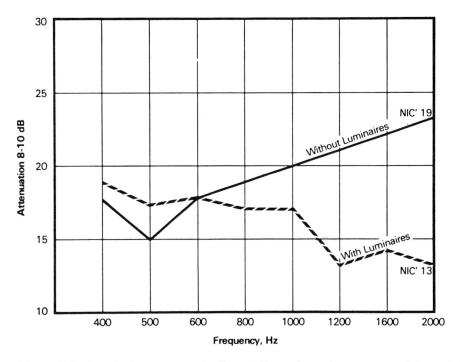

Figure 2-8. Luminaire acoustical effect. Effect of continuous row of 2 × 4 foot luminaires on interzone attenuation at 8 to 10 foot distance. Line of measurement is directly below center line of row. Upper curve is for acoustical ceiling without luminaires.

SOUND SCREENS. The freestanding sound screen, or partial-height acoustical barrier, is one of the basic elements of the open-plan office. It is primarily a sound barrier. When placed in a position where it could reflect sound into an adjoining work station, it must also have highly sound-absorbent surfaces. Such a screen is usually composed of an impervious inner layer called the septum which, as shown in Figure 2-9, is covered with a sound-absorbing layer and finished with an attractive fabric.

   If there were no sound screens in an open office, only distance would reduce speech sounds between work areas (assuming walls and ceilings are highly sound-absorbent). It would obviously be difficult to ensure speech privacy. A screen placed between two work stations attenuates direct sound waves by forcing them to pass through it or around its edges. The heavier the septum material, the greater the transmission loss for sounds attempting to pass through the screen, at least so long as the screen contains no penetrations or leaks. In practice, this transmission loss need only be sufficient to reduce the level of transmitted sounds below that of the sounds that reflect or bend around

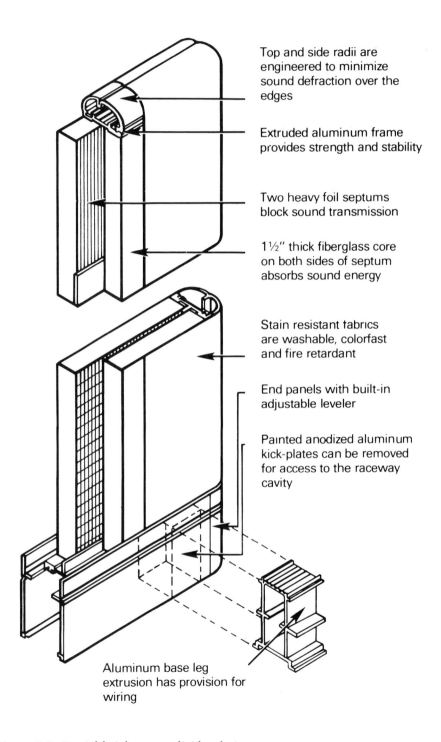

Top and side radii are engineered to minimize sound defraction over the edges

Extruded aluminum frame provides strength and stability

Two heavy foil septums block sound transmission

1½" thick fiberglass core on both sides of septum absorbs sound energy

Stain resistant fabrics are washable, colorfast and fire retardant

End panels with built-in adjustable leveler

Painted anodized aluminum kick-plates can be removed for access to the raceway cavity

Aluminum base leg extrusion has provision for wiring

Figure 2-9. Partial height space divider design

the screen. Usually, one-eighth-inch hardboard or heavy metal foil makes a sufficient barrier.

To be effective sound barriers, screens should be at least 5 feet high and preferably 10 feet wide. Higher screens should be commensurately wider. Acoustical performance as affected by varying screen parameters is shown in Table 2-3. Screens that are curved for aesthetic reasons can also block sound transmission effectively. However, their faces must be highly sound-absorbent to avoid focusing. Office occupants should be discouraged from using screens as tack boards, since most hung materials reflect sounds, defeating the purpose of the screen.

Screens are often located where they could reflect sounds into an adjoining work station. This primary flanking position is illustrated by line *ACB* in Figure 2-10. In a situation such as illustrated here, a hard, acoustically reflective surface must be avoided in position *C*. Table 2-4 details the negative effect on acoustical performance by having hard reflective surfaces instead of highly sound-absorbent screens in this flanking position. For this reason, most screens are covered with a highly sound-absorbent layer, typically a 1 to 1½ inch thickness of low-density glass fiberboard with an acoustically porous covering such as cloth. It is especially important for screens that are frequently moved to be sound-absorbent so that they do not create a flanking path (path *ACB*) for sound when placed in new positions in the office.

Hang-on components used with systems furniture are an additional acoustical concern. Upper cabinets, including the flipper doors, should be rendered highly sound-absorbent in the same fashion as the system panels.

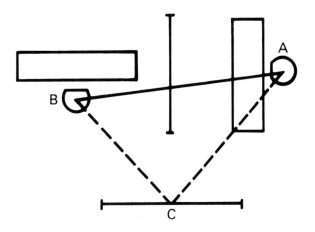

Figure 2-10. Specular reflection. Reflection between work stations via vertical surface *C* (right).

Table 2-3. Comparison of Sound Attenuation Performance of Selected Sound Screens (Direct Sound Path—Interzone Distance 9-12′)

Test No.	Descriptions of Test Specimens			NIC′[a] Difference	AC[b] Difference
XL-1LT	No screen	vs.	5′ × 15′ idealized screen[c]	+15	+150
GSA A2.2	5′ × 8′ idealized screen	vs.	5′ × 15′ idealized screen	+2	+20
GSA A2.3	4′ × 5′ idealized screen	vs.	5′ × 15′ idealized screen	+4	+45
GSA A2.4	5′ × 8′ idealized screen	vs.	6′ × 8′ idealized screen	+1	+10
GSA A2.4 & OCF-10-12FT	5′ × 8′ idealized screen	vs.	Full height 15′ wide partitions	+7 to +20 Est. (depends on ceiling used)	+80 to +220
GSA A2.5	4′ × 8′ idealized screen	vs.	5′ × 8′ idealized screen	+3	+35
GSA A2.6	5′ × 8′ idealized screen 3″ gap above carpet	vs.	5′ × 8′ idealized screen— screen mated to carpet	+1	+10
GSA A2.7	5′ × 8′ idealized screen— hard surfaces both sides	vs.	5′ × 8′ idealized screen— 1″ fiberglass both sides	+1	+10
GSA A2.8	5′ × 8′ idealized screen with hard or reflective screen behind listener	vs.	5′ × 8′ idealized screen with soft of absorptive screen behind listener	+1	+10
GSA A2.9	5′ × 8′ idealized screen with hard walls enclosing listener	vs.	5′ × 8′ idealized screen absorption on side facing listener and hard walls enclosing listener	+ 1	+10

Table 2-3. *(Continued)*

Test No.	Descriptions of Test Specimens			NIC'[a] Difference	AC[b] Difference
GSA A2.1	5' × 8' idealized screen with listener's back to window wall (i.e. hard surface)	vs.	5' × 8' idealized screen with listener's back to drapery-covered window wall	0 to +1	+10

[a] The values are given as an NIC' difference where column one is compared to column two due to the multitude of test conditions possible and each could have an effect on the values. Therefore, an intercomparison of only the specific tested variables are given in the table. This same comment applies to the data in Tables 2-4 and 2-5.

[b] An estimate of Articulation Class (AC) per American Society of Testing and Materials (ASTM) Standard E-1050-88, *Standard Classification for Determination of Articulation Class.* ASTM E-1111-88, *Standard Test Method for Measuring Interzone Attenuation of Ceiling Systems,* is the usual procedure for measuring AC. Test procedure E-1111 is similar in many respects to PBS C.2. While not directly convertible, these estimates are included to familiarize the reader with the type of test results that can be expected. (See Appendix 2A for a more detailed explanation of the new ASTM Test Standards.)

[c] Idealized screens = ½" plywood septum faced with 1" fiberglass. This definition also applies to Table 2-5.

Table 2-4. Comparison of Sound Attenuation Performance of Selected Sound Screens (Flanking Wall Position—Interzone Distance 9-12')

Test No.	Description of Test Specimens			NIC' Difference	AC Difference
GSA A2.11	5' × 8' hard surface screen	vs.	5' × 8' idealized screen	+ 3	+35
GSA A2.12	5' × 8' idealized screen speaker turned 45° and facing flanking screen	vs.	5' × 8' idealized screen speaker facing receiver	+ 2	+20
GSA A2.13	5' × 8' hard surface screen turned 45° and facing flanking screen	vs.	5' × 8' idealized screen speaker turned 45° and facing flanking screen	+ 9	+100

These cabinets are typically located at the approximate height of a standing adult. They will reflect sounds to an adjoining work station directly behind the sound source if they are not sound-absorbent.

VERTICAL SURFACES. Where work stations requiring speech privacy are located near hard vertical surfaces such as cabinets, columns, and perimeter and core walls, surfaces should be covered with sound-absorbing panels to minimize reflections. The negative effects of failing to do so are illustrated by the acoustical performance contrasts shown in Table 2-5. Note that the addition of paintings, photos, or posters to these surfaces will negate their sound-absorption characteristics. Only acoustically transparent materials or art such as open weave cloth materials should be allowed.

From an acoustical viewpoint, the ideal solution would be to cover all these surfaces with an efficient sound-absorbing material. However, practical considerations will not allow this massive use of "soft" material on all reflective surfaces. With the help of the acoustician, planners can identify and treat just those reflective surfaces that create flanking paths for sound. The specialist will need a floor plan of the office that identifies all sound sources, work stations, and reflective surfaces. Potential flanking paths can then be detected for each work station, and offending surfaces can be pinpointed and properly treated. Future office changes may, of course, require a reanalysis of flanking paths and treatment of other surfaces.

As a minimum, sound-absorbing panels should be applied to the region from zero to six feet from the floor. Sound reflected above these panels will be absorbed by the ceiling. Where the finished surface of columns is circular in cross-section and less than 1.5 feet in diameter, treatment is usually not necessary. Objects of this size or smaller serve as convenient sound scatterers or diffusers.

Planners may be tempted to rely on carpeting and drapes alone to reduce the reflectiveness of vertical surfaces. But unless they are extremely thick, carpets and drapes will not be sufficiently sound-absorbent for the needs of an open office. For the same reason, it is ineffective to cover walls with carpeting. Another consideration favoring the use of sound-absorbent panels is the fact that drapes and carpets may not have adequate fire resistance.

FLOORS. Carpeting's prime purpose is to reduce impact sounds such as footsteps, scraping chairs, and shuffling. Although carpeted floors do reduce the sound reflectiveness of an open office, carpeting will not prevent some sound waves from reflecting off the floor. These reflected sounds may be absorbed by the ceiling, furniture, and sound screens.

The special problem of sounds reflecting off the floor and traveling below sound screens into adjacent areas can be solved by resting screens directly on the floor and avoiding the selection of screens raised for the sake of appearance. However, since eliminating the space between the floor and the bottom of the screen may create HVAC air circulation problems, planners should consult the HVAC and acoustics specialists in deciding whether or not to use raised screens in the office.

Another special floor problem for the acoustics system is the hollow or rattling sound some access floors make when occupants walk across the office. Access floors are raised four to twelve inches above the concrete floor to allow passage of electrical and mechanical services. In offices where an access floor is to be used, planners should insist that it be constructed of stiff, heavy materials to avoid the hollow floor effect.

Table 2-5. Comparison of Sound Attenuation Performance of Selected Wall Treatments (Flanking Wall Position—Interzone Distance 9-12′)

Test No.	Description of Test Specimens			NIC′ Difference	AC Difference
GSA A2.13	5′ × 8′ hard surface with speaker facing flanking surface	vs.	Idealized absorptive wall surface with speaker facing flanking surface	+9	+100
GSA A2.10	9′ × 8′ hard "window wall" surface behind listener in receiving zone	vs.	Window wall draped to 9′ height	+0	0
GSA A2.11	5′ × 8′ hard surface with speaker facing screen	vs.	Idealized absorptive wall surface, speaker facing screen	+3	+35
GSA A2.15	Typically landscaped surrounds	vs.	Idealized acoustically absorptive surface	+1	+35

WINDOWS. Windows around the perimeter of the office present a special acoustical challenge, since most acoustical absorbers block the view from the inside and the light from the outside. Here again, draperies are unsatisfactory as acoustical absorbers. To absorb sound reflected from windows, they would have to be lined and heavier than usual and would have to be kept closed. A more satisfactory solution is to tilt the window glass out of the vertical plane, thus causing the unwanted sounds to be deflected to the ceiling. Acceptable results may also be obtained by using vertical louvers or baffles that do not seriously impede vision (Figure 2-11). Other options to prevent windows from creating flanking paths for sound are to place sound screens so that they tightly abut the mullion on the window, or to use a T at the end of a run of screens.

Figure 2-11. Window baffles reduce specular reflection

Background Masking System

Acoustical ceilings, sound screens, and sound-absorbent coverings for vertical surfaces effectively reduce the acoustical reflectiveness of an office. But as Figure 2-12 demonstrates, in an open office they do not by themselves provide more than minimal speech privacy.[7] The reason for this lies in the concept of signal-to-noise ratio. The object of installing acoustical ceilings and screens in an open office is to reduce unwanted signals—in this case, speech sounds and other disturbing noise—that would distract those in adjacent work areas. But by doing so, *all* sounds are attenuated, leaving the direct signals too strong to be masked by existing background office noises. Background masking sound *must* be introduced to provide the proper signal-to-noise ratio and complete the acoustical system.

Planners may be tempted to think that piped-in music or the continuous sound of air circulating through the HVAC system will fill this need. There are substantial reasons why these systems fall short. As a series of transient, pure tones, music masks only those sounds that happen to coincide with the notes

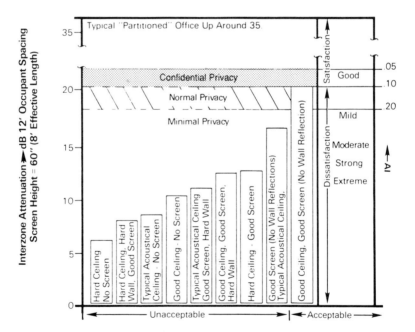

Figure 2-12. Effect of component configuration on open-plan environment acceptability A1. Articulation Index (AI) is a numerical value (0–1.0) of speech intelligibility derived from an analysis of background sound, expected speech effort, and the acoustical qualities of an area and its components. With background sound of approximately 40 dB$_A$. If background sound is less or more, entire scale moves up or down accordingly. Carpeted floor assumed for all conditions.

being played at any given moment. Adjusting the HVAC system so that it provides the proper level and spectrum of background noise has proved difficult to do without simultaneously upsetting its air-handling abilities.

Electronic background masking systems have, on the other hand, proved quite satisfactory. These systems produce an unobtrusive sea of sound that is uniform in quantity and quality throughout the office, and tuned to block out unwanted signals while remaining unobserved by casual listeners. The quality of this sound is reminiscent of ocean surf, whispering pines, or a large water fountain, except that it is very uniform in time and space. It has not been chosen for its soothing qualities, though it may in fact have some soothing effect. Rather, it has been chosen because it contains desirable intensities at frequencies required to mask typical office sounds and speech.

The system that produces this masking sound resembles a conventional music/paging system, and can in many instances be used for music and paging as well as for providing speech privacy. As illustrated by Figure 2-13, the most widely used system consists of a random noise generator, a filter to shape the sound for optimal background masking, a power-amplifying system, and an array of speakers located in the ceiling plenum. A second type of system combines all components into a single, economical unit for the smaller open-plan office.

The loudspeakers should be placed out of sight in the ceiling plenum. The loudspeakers are distributed in a square or triangular array, with approximately a 10- to 20-foot spacing between each unit. Exact distribution of speakers depends on plenum depth, obstructions such as HVAC equipment, ceiling tile properties, and speaker radiation patterns (see Figure 2-14).

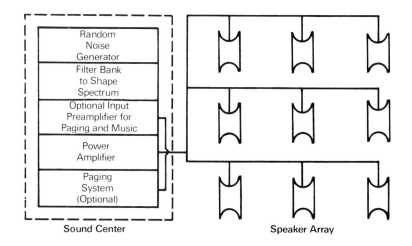

Figure 2-13. Background masking system layout

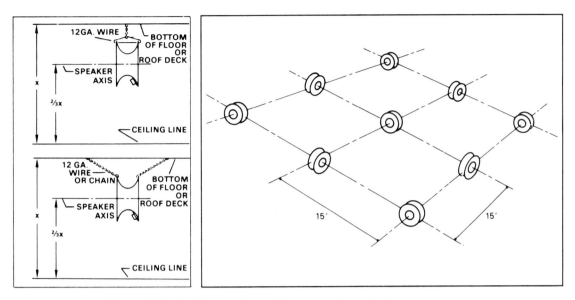

Figure 2-14. Background masking system installation

Once in place and properly tuned by an acoustician, the background masking system must be considered a permanent part of the acoustical system of the office. It is never to be turned off or muted, and it must be allowed to operate at a constant level 365 days a year. To ensure this constant operation, controls should be placed in a locked cabinet. Since the equipment is usually transistorized, this requirement should not create undue energy or maintenance costs. Depending on the size of the power amplifier (see Figure 2-15), energy consumed by the system is less than 300 to 500 watts. Transistorized units normally require only occasional checks to see whether components are functioning properly.

To integrate a paging system with the masking equipment requires that the amplifiers and loudspeakers have sufficient reserve power to make messages audible above the background masking noises. Also, because the ceiling may distort voice sounds, it may be necessary to add a voice filter circuit (usually a tone control) to the system.

Despite their importance as an integral part of open-plan office acoustics, planners must recognize that careful selection and installation of components is necessary if the background masking system is to have a uniform effect throughout the office. To achieve temporal uniformity, the system should produce no more than a 3 dB deviation during any two-second interval (i.e., no surges or clicks in the sound produced). To achieve spatial uniformity, there should be no more than a 3 dB average deviation in the masking sound anywhere in the office.

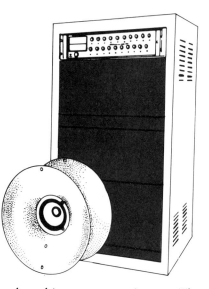

Figure 2-15. Background masking system equipment. The size of a typical masking system control is 18″ × 24″ × 15″ while the speaker size is approximately 6″ thick and 16″ in diameter.

Lack of spatial uniformity is the more common problem. Where spatial uniformity is lacking, the masking sound will seem annoyingly loud in some areas, while in others it does not provide adequate speech privacy. A system is not uniform when it is subjectively possible to point to a source, be it real or preceived. In addition, uniformity in transition from a nonmasking to a masking area is necessary. Otherwise, a negative psycho-acoustic response to the background masking system will be created.

Temporal uniformity is usually a function of the quality of the masking sound equipment. With transistors, temporal uniformity is relatively easy to achieve. Spatial uniformity involves careful integration between the masking system and other ceiling components, and careful placement of loudspeakers. If, for example, a masking system is used with light fixtures that have direct holes in the plenum for air return, the masking sound will pour through these holes and seem obtrusively loud to occupants working nearby. If the ceiling material lacks uniform transmission loss qualities, or if obstructions will not allow speakers to be placed where their radiation patterns overlap, occupants will experience this same annoying variation in masking sound levels.

Planners can avoid this problem by enlisting the help of a skilled acoustician to tune the level and quality of the background masking system to suit their particular office space (see Figure 2-16), and by consulting with all specialists involved in ceiling systems before final decisions are made on office

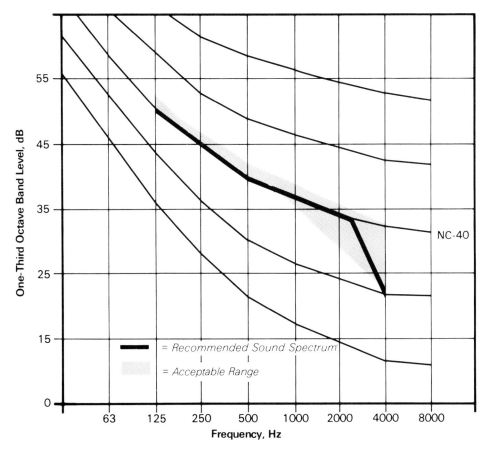

Figure 2-16. Background masking sound spectrum

acoustics. Retuning may be necessary after a move. Thus, each speaker should be fitted with a volume control.

Some masking sound systems promote the concept of multichannel signals. The purpose is to achieve spatial uniformity and to overcome a phasing effect where speaker distribution patterns overlap. Multisource signals are not required by all systems. The dual horn speakers shown in Figures 2-13 and 2-14 do not require multichannel signals. Other offerors recommend that the masking sound be placed on a timer so that the signal will range up or down during the 24-hour period. The only justification for this variance is security. By lowering the masking during off-duty hours, a security checker may be able to hear an intruder who otherwise would be undetected. However, individuals who work late may find this upsetting. Addition of a fire management/paging system as an override to the masking system is effective and economically advantageous.

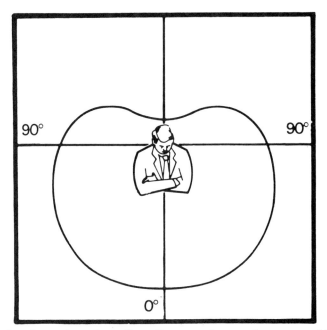

Figure 2-17. Speaker orientation effect. Decrease in speech energy with respect to speaker orientation (approximately 1.5 dB per thirty degrees).

Positioning of Occupants in the Open Office

Acoustical ceilings, sound screens, sound-absorbent wallcoverings, and background masking sound equipment comprise an integrated acoustics system for open offices. However, where space and layout permit, two other elements can be used to enhance speech privacy. One is distance between working areas. In highly absorbent environments, doubling the distance between a speaker and a listener can reduce by 6 dB the strength of the speech signal for that listener. Thus, reasonable privacy could be obtained at approximately 20 feet from the speaker, even without a screen between speaker and listener. The economics of office space clearly limit the number of occasions when distance can be substituted for sound screens.

The positioning of office occupants in relationship to each other is also rarely an adequate substitute for sound-absorbing ceilings and screens. Still, proper positioning can enhance the amount of speech privacy achieved by an acoustical system. Each 30 degrees of rotation away from the straight-ahead position results in a 1.5 dB decrease in speech energy. As shown in Figure 2-17, maximum decrease of 9 dB occurs when the speaker turns his or her back to the listener.

EVALUATION OF PROPOSED ACOUSTICS DESIGN

Achieving an acceptable acoustical environment in an office is essentially a matter of balance and compromise. To be able to perform this feat with any skill requires an understanding of basic principles so that test data may be used intelligently and sensible specifications issued. Hence the need to consult with an acoustician. An acoustician will be in the best position to advise planners if he or she is allowed to test the proposed acoustics design in the field or in a laboratory before final decisions are made. The alternative is for the specialist to use published information about the capabilities of each component.

Performance specifications for acoustical components have evolved rapidly in recent years. The original widely accepted procedures known as PBS C.1 and C.2 were developed and specified by the United States Public Building Services in its *Performance Specifications in Office Buildings and Integrated Ceiling and Background Systems.* PBS Guide Specification Section 13500 was the result of extensive research and testing by Geiger & Hamme Laboratories in Ann Arbor, Michigan, and subsequent testing by Owens Corning Fiberglas. Recently, the American Society for Testing and Materials (ASTM) Committee E-33.02 on Environmental Acoustics, Open Plan Offices, has promulgated a series of test procedures based on the PBS procedures. While the rating system differs, the test procedures are very similar. Data shown in the appendix list results by both procedures where available.

It is evident that by maximizing ceiling absorptiveness it is possible to achieve speech privacy with only sound screens to separate work areas rather than the floor-to-ceiling walls of the closed office (provided there is adequate background masking). As Figure 2-18 indicates, further testing on acoustical materials using the open-plan mockup described here has determined their interzone attenuation performance to range between the maximum level of the open sky and the minimum level established for gypsum wallboard.

Specification Criteria—SPP and NIC'

The GSA specification criteria call for minimum speech privacy potential (SPP) of ≥ 60 or speech privacy noise isolation (NIC') values ≥ 20.

An SPP value is a single-number rating that measures the effectiveness of an acoustical system as a whole or as combinations of acoustical components. An NIC' value is an objective measurement of the degree of speech privacy provided by a screen/ceiling combination. A more detailed description of these values and their usage appears in Appendix 2A. Examples of specification preparations are shown in Appendix 2B.

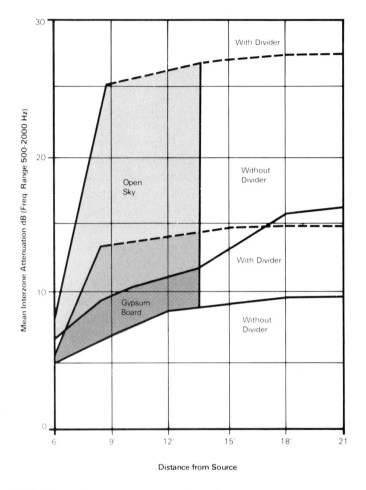

Figure 2-18. Open sky versus gypsum board

COMBINATION OFFICES

Recent developments in office planning have focused on designs that mix the open- and closed-plan office. This design solution has placed unusual demands on the acoustical environment. Conventional solutions that will allow the planner or specifier to use the same subsystem components for both closed- and open-plan offices are not readily available. In fact, a significant dilemma has evolved. Practical solutions for the open-plan office will not work in closed-plan offices. Likewise, conventional systems for closed offices will create poor speech privacy in the open-plan office. The following subsystems are of particular concern:

- Ceiling systems and materials
- Full-height partition systems
- Lighting systems
- Background masking system
- HVAC systems

The integrated ceiling system, composed of grid, board, HVAC distribution devices, light fixtures, and the background masking system, poses the most significant problem. Utilizing highly sound-absorbent (NIC' = 20 or higher) ceiling materials is required for the open office. These materials, when used in a closed office, typically have insufficient sound attenuation. Sound can penetrate the ceiling board and be transmitted via flanking paths created by sound leaks at joints. Significant flanking occurs with the open-backed light fixtures and HVAC outlets commonly used in air-return plenums. The penetrations that allow air movement also provide an easy path for sound waves.

A significant design goal is to provide a ceiling system that need not be replaced in a reorganization from open to closed, closed to open, or a mix of open and closed (Figure 2-19). Since most conventional ceiling systems are designed for optimum performance for only a closed or an open office design, a system and family of products is required. Unfortunately, few manufacturers of ceiling products have yet recognized this need. The design must be flexible for either configuration: It requires a ceiling material and suspended ceiling system that has high sound absorption (NIC' > 20 or AC > 5700) and relatively high sound attenuation (STC > 30). The only acceptable product available at present is a 2-inch thick, 5-pound density fiberglass board with a sound attenuation backing. Sometimes called a TL backing, the attenuation is provided with a gypsum board or heavy-density mineral board backing with the highly absorptive fiberglass exposed to the office space. When utilized with light fixtures that have a closed back (no open-plenum air vents), and in a tight grid with fully ducted air returns, this ceiling system will provide speech privacy in both the open and the closed office.

The ceiling system must contain a background masking system. Masking has proved very effective for both open- and closed-plan offices. For the open-plan office, masking sound must operate close to NC_{40}. In the closed office, masking sound should be turned lower, generally NC_{35} to $_{37}$, to be compatible with the acoustical environment usually expected by most closed office occupants. To achieve these levels, the masking sound system must have a loudness level control on each speaker. As the office environment is changed to closed from open, the masking level must be lowered slightly. By contrast, changing to open from closed requires increasing the sound level at the masking speaker. The masking system should be retuned by a knowledgeable acoustician after these changes.

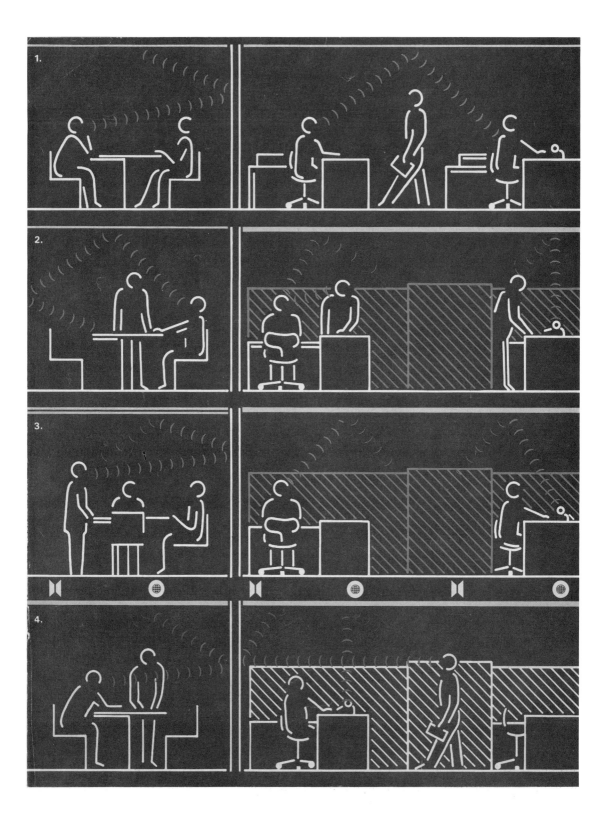

The partition system in a closed office must have highly sound-absorbent faces. When the partition faces the open-plan office area, it will be functioning as a vertical surface. As we saw in earlier discussions, all vertical surfaces should have a NIC' of 20 or greater in the flanking position. Within the office itself, the same highly absorbent facings are necessary to be compatible with the balance of the office acoustical and esthetic environment. Unfortunately, few partition manufacturers have recognized this need. One system that is acceptable utilizes a unique demountable partition composed of steel studs, gypsum board, and 1-inch thick faces of glass fiberboard. In addition to providing excellent sound attenuation (STC up to 50) and sound-absorbing faces (NIC' > 19), this assembly also can achieve a 1-hour fire rating (Table 2-6). Best of all, the system boasts a monolithic appearance, a first for a demountable partition system. But while ideal for the closed/open-plan office and fully researched, this system is not yet being marketed.

The basic conclusion of acoustical control research is that, yes, speech privacy can be achieved in both open and enclosed offices, but it must be done with an integrated system including floor and wall coverings, divider panels, ceiling panels and their luminaries, and background masking sound. The systems approach is essential; there is no single, quick-fix answer to the problems of overall acoustical control.

Figure 2-19. Acoustical options—closed/open: Containing sounds in closed spaces and controlling them in open ones involves tradeoffs that are sometimes self-cancelling or contradictory. New products and techniques are required to provide reliable and economical solutions.

1. A typical office layout mixing open and closed spaces using a mineral board ceiling throughout has a problem: The sound-reflective mineral board effectively isolates the closed office, but allows sound to reverberate freely throughout the open area, making it unworkable.

2. Switching to a fiberglass ceiling and open office dividers in the open area provides the sound-absorbing surfaces the open area needs, but there are still problems. Open-area workers don't have complete speech privacy, and the use of two kinds of ceiling panels compromises aesthetics and relocation ease.

3. Switching to high STC and high NIC' ceiling panels in the closed office with a ceiling having a high NIC' in the open area provides uniform aesthetics at the ceiling and good acoustical control in both the open and closed space.

4. Finally, a ceiling having both a high STC and NIC', coupled with a properly tuned background masking system, provides the ultimate in acoustical control, uniform aesthetics, and flexibility for both the open and closed office.

Table 2-6. STC Values for Typical Partitions and Ceilings[a]

Construction Type	STC
Sound Transmission Class of Metal Stud Wall Construction (1).	
2½″ metal studs, 24″ o.c., ½″ gypsum wallboard both sides	37
2½″ metal studs, 24″ o.c., ½″ gypsum wallboard both sides, with R-8 fiberglass insulation	45
2½″ metal studs, 24″ o.c., 2 layers, ½″ gypsum wallboard both sides	46
2½″ metal studs, 24″ o.c., 2 layers, ½″ gypsum wallboard both sides with R-8 fiberglass insulation	51
3⅝″ metal studs, 24″ o.c., ½″ gypsum wallboard both sides	39
3⅝″ metal studs, 24″ o.c., ½″ gypsum wallboard both sides, with 3½″ R-11 fiberglass insulation	44
3⅝″ metal studs, 24″ o.c., 2 layers, ½″ gypsum wallboard one side, 1 layer ½″ gypsum wallboard other side	45
3⅝″ metal studs, 24″ o.c., 2 layers, ½″ gypsum wallboard one side, 1 layer ½″ gypsum wallboard on other side with R-11 fiberglass insulation	49
3⅝″ metal studs, 24″ o.c., 2 layers ½″ gypsum wallboard each side	50
3⅝″ metal studs, 24″ o.c., 2 layers ½″ gypsum wallboard each side with R-11 fiberglass insulation	56
Sound Transmission Class of Wood Stud Wall Constructions (1).	
2 × 4 wood studs, 16″ o.c., ½″ gypsum wallboard on both sides	35
2 × 4 wood studs, 16″ o.c., ½″ gypsum wallboard with R-11 fiberglass insulation	39
2 × 4 wood studs, 16″ o.c., 2 layers of ½″ gypsum wallboard on one side, 1 layer of ½″ gypsum wallboard on other side	38
2 × 4 wood studs, 16″ o.c., 2 layers of ½″ gypsum wallboard on both sides	39
2 × 4 wood studs, 16″ o.c., resilient channel one side, ½″ gypsum wallboard on both sides	39

Table 2-6. *(Continued)*

Construction Type	STC
2 × 4 wood studs, 16″ o.c., resilient channel one side, ½″ gypsum wallboard on both sides, with R-11 fiberglass insulation	46
2 × 4 wood studs, 24″ o.c., ½″ gypsum wallboard on both sides	42
2 × 4 wood studs, 24″ o.c., stagger construction, ½″ gypsum wallboard on both sides, with R-11 fiberglass insulation	49
2 × 4 wood studs, 16″ o.c., double stud construction, ½″ gypsum wallboard on both sides	47
2 × 4 wood studs, 16″ o.c., double stud construction, ½″ gypsum wallboard on both sides, with R-11 fiberglass insulation	56
2 × 4 wood studs, double stud construction, ½″ gypsum wallboard on both sides, with 2 layers R-11 fiberglass insulation	59
Sound Transmission Class of Miscellaneous Materials	
Sheet metal, 22 gauge	29
Gypsum board ⅝″	27
Aluminum panel	16
Aluminum panel with 2″ insulation, aluminum foil	26
Aluminum panel with 4″ insulation, aluminum foil	31
Aluminum panel with 2″ insulation, sheet lead (1 PSF)	34
3/16″ Steel wall	31
3/16″ Steel duct wall, 4″ TIW insulation, with 16 gauge sheet metal	49

Source: Courtesy of Owens-Corning Fiberglas.

[a] All tests were conducted according to ASTM E90 *Standard Method for Laboratory Measurement of Airborne Sound Transmission Loss of Building Partitions.* The transmission loss for each sample was measured over 1/3 octave bands in order to determine a single number STC rating.

SUMMARY

Important though the acoustician is to the success of an acoustics design, planners should recognize the equal importance of mutual consultation between the acoustician and the other specialists involved in the project. The success of the acoustical system depends on decisions in the realms of:

INTERIOR DECORATING

- Choice of drapes
- Carpeting
- Fabric coverings for screens
- Aesthetic design of the ceiling
- Material

ARCHITECTURAL

- Placement and style of windows
- Beams and pillars
- Use of an access floor
- Shape of the office itself
- Closed or open plan

HVAC

- Shape and size of ceiling fixtures
- Sound characteristics of ventilation systems
- Size and placement of air ducts in ceiling plenum
- Use of light fixtures for air return

LIGHTING

- Size, shape, number, and placement of light fixtures
- Need for good light reflectiveness in ceiling material

FIRE/BUILDING CODE REQUIREMENTS

- Safety features of sound-absorbent materials
- Electronic background masking system

Planners and specialists in each of the other fields must keep in mind the impact of their choices on the acoustical system throughout the process of designing and implementing the office plan. In this way, a pleasant acoustical environment can be created in which employees can work in comfort and without distraction.

Notes

1. A unit expressing the relative intensity of sounds. The zero decibel level represents the average least perceptible sound. 130 dB is the average pain level.
2. A unit of frequency equal to one cycle per second.
3. The sound transmission class is a single-figure rating derived in a prescribed manner from sound transmission loss values.
4. For a more detailed discussion of how to achieve optimum acoustical performances in closed offices and conference rooms, the reader is encouraged to study a document entitled *Acoustical Ceilings: Use and Practice* or other texts listed under Suggested Readings. *Acoustical Ceilings: Use and Practice* is published by Ceilings and Interior Systems Contractors Association, 1800 Pickwick Avenue, Glenview, Illinois 60025.
5. An individual speaker in an average office will modulate his voice so that he will be approximately 20 dB louder than the background level. This assures clear understandability at three to four feet—the average listening distance. By contrast, the voice level in an adjoining work station should be reduced to near zero signal-to-noise ratio for speech privacy.
6. Note that the ceiling must absorb sound at angles between 30 and 60 degrees. Materials with maximum sound absorption at these angles are preferred.
7. Masking sound can be effectively used in closed offices as well as in the open plan. Where confidential speech privacy is desired, the addition of masking will usually provide it even with poor sound barriers. In fact, it has been demonstrated that closed offices having an SPP 70 rating (NIC' = 35 and NC_{40} = 35) provide an equivalent degree of speech privacy as that achieved with an STC = 45 partition and ceiling. Most closed offices are acceptable with SPP 60 or 65. (For an explanation of NC_{40}, see page 71).

Suggested Readings

Acoustical Ceilings: Use and Practice, Ceiling and Interior Systems Contractors Association, 1800 Pickwick Avenue, Glenview, IL 60025.

Acoustical Environment in the Open Office, ASTM Standardization News, Volume 4 No. 8, 1976.

American National Standard Method for the Calculation of the Articulation Index, ANSI S3.5-1969, American National Standards Institute, New York, 1969.

Classification for Determination of Sound Transmission Class, ASTM E-413-73, Annual Book of ASTM Standards, American Society for Testing and Materials, Philadelphia, PA, 1976, Part 18.

Integrated Ceiling and Background (ICB) System, PBS Guide Specification Section 13500, Public Buildings Service, General Services Administration, Washington, D.C., January 1973.

NBS Handbook 119 Quieting: A Practical Guide to Noise Control, U.S. Government Printing Office Catalog (13.11:119), R.D. Berndt.

Owens-Corning Fiberglas Background Masking System, Pub. 1AC-8567A, Toledo, OH, July 1978.

Owens-Corning Fiberglas Integrated Ceiling System, Pub. 5AC-8433, Toledo, OH, May 1978.

Recommended Practice for Laboratory Measurement of Airborne Sound Transmission Loss of Building Partitions, ASTM E-90-75, Annual Book of ASTM Standards, American Society for Testing and Materials, Philadelphia, PA, 1976, Part 18.

Recommended Practice for Measurement of Airborne Sound Insulation in Buildings, ASTM E-336-71, Annual Book of ASTM Standards, American Society for Testing and Materials, Philadelphia, PA, 1976, Part 18.

Sound Control in Commercial Buildings, Owens-Corning Fiberglas Pub. 5CW7654, Toledo, OH.

Standard Classification for Acoustical Ceiling Products, Designation E-1264-88, American Society for Testing and Materials, Volume 4.06, 1988.

Standard Classification for Determination of Articulation Class (AC), Designation E-1110-88, American Society for Testing and Materials, Volume 4.06, 1988.

Standard Guide for Measurement of Masking Sound in Open Offices, Designation E-1041-85, American Society for Testing and Materials, Volume 4.06, 1988.

Standard Practice for Application of Ceiling Suspension Systems for Acoustical Tile and Lay-In Panels in Areas Requiring Seismic Restraint, Designation E-580, American Society for Testing and Materials, Volume 4.06, 1988.

Standard Practice for Installation of Metal Ceiling Suspension Systems for Acoustical Tile and Lay-In Panels, Designation C-636-86, American Society for Testing and Materials, Volume 4.06, 1988.

Standard Specification for Metal Suspension Systems for Acoustical Tile and Lay-In Panel Ceilings, Designation C-635-87, American Society for Testing and Materials, Volume 4.06, 1988.

Standard Test Method for Measuring the Interzone Attenuation of Ceiling Panels, Designation E-1111-88, American Society for Testing and Materials, Volume 4.06, 1988.

Standard Test Method for Objective Measurement of Speech Privacy in Open Offices Using Articulation Index, Designation E-1130-88, American Society for Testing and Materials, Volume 4.06, 1988.

Test Method for Direct Measurement of Speech Privacy Potential Based on Subjective Judgements, PBS C.1 Public Buildings Service, General Services Administration, Washington, D.C., May 1975.

Test Method for the Sufficient Verification of Speech Privacy Potential Based on Objective Measurements Including Methods for the Rating of Functional Interzone Attenuation and NC Backgrounds, PBS C.2, Public Buildings Service, General Services Administration, Washington, D.C., May 1975.

Test for Sound Absorption of Acoustical Materials in Reverberation Rooms, ASTM, C-423-66 (1972), Annual Book of ASTM Standards, American Society for Testing and Materials, Philadelphia, PA, 1976, Part 18.

U.S. General Services Administration Public Service Performance Specifications for Office Buildings, 3rd Edition or later. (Note: Reference Acoustics attribute for all seven subsystems with special emphasis on Section 6, Finished Ceiling, and 7, Space Dividers.)

APPENDIX 2A

Testing Procedures

Maximum/Minimum Sound Attenuation Ratings for Ceilings

An initial test (XL-1LT) developed by Geiger and Hamme Laboratories established a maximum sound-absorptiveness level against which the effectiveness of various acoustical ceiling materials for open offices might be compared. Figure 2A-1 graphically depicts the testing situation on which this maximum level is based.

This testing situation duplicates open-office conditions with the open sky as a perfectly sound-absorbent ceiling; a sound source separated from receiving stations by distance alone or by distance plus a sound-absorbent screen; and a hard, uncovered floor (in actuality, a building roof). The sound source and the receiving stations were all the same height of four feet from the floor.

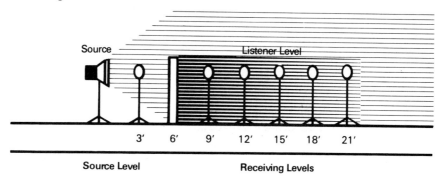

Figure 2A-1. Acoustical test—open sky. Unlimited expanse of open sky above Gieger & Hammer laboratory roof, without carpeting and without side walls, as presumed to represent the attenuation limits of chamber characterizations.

A reference level was established by measuring the volume of sound at a distance of only three feet from the source. This level was compared to readings taken at three-foot intervals on the far side of the screen (at nine, twelve, fifteen, eighteen, and twenty-one feet from the source). The difference between the reference reading and those on the far side of the screen was defined as the "attenuation" of sound at each measuring point. Since the open sky affords no sound reflectiveness, the attenuation of sound measured under these conditions represents the upper limit of sound absorptiveness for acoustical ceiling in open offices.

A second test (XL-2LT) established a minimum sound-absorptiveness level against which the effectiveness of various acoustical ceiling materials for open offices might be compared. Figure 2A-2 graphically depicts the testing situation for test XL-2LT.

Note that the testing situation duplicates that for XL-1LT except in these details: The test was conducted indoors in a space fifteen feet wide by thirty feet long. The eight foot, ten inch ceiling was composed of one-half inch gypsum wallboard. To minimize sound reflections, the floor was carpeted, and the walls were acoustically treated. In short, the situation represented acoustic conditions in an open office with a hard ceiling.

The results of test XL-2LT showed that interzone attenuation (the amount of noise reduction at each measuring station) was lowered from 25 dB for the open sky to about 10 dB for the hard ceiling. This 10 dB value approximated the interzone attenuation obtained under the open sky without the sound-absorbent screen. Figure 2A-3 demonstrates the comparative results of XL-1LT and XL-2LT.

The conclusion was drawn that a range of 15 dB interzone attenuation exists between ceilings having perfect reflectiveness (that is, they absorb none of the sound) and those having zero reflectiveness (that is, the open sky).

The SPP rating was originally developed for open-office designs but it can also be used for closed-office acoustics. The critical SPP value for open-office systems is SPP

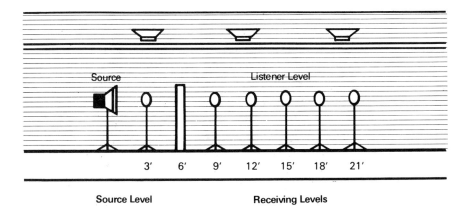

Figure 2A-2. Acoustical test—gypsum wallboard ceiling. Half-inch-thick ceiling boards cut from gypsum wallboard installed in exposed suspension system.

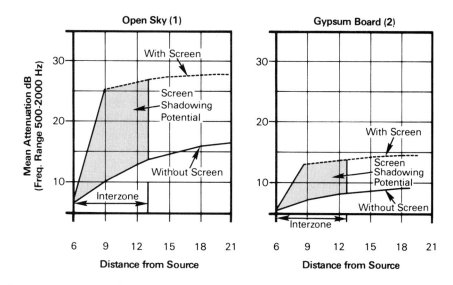

Figure 2A-3. Open-plan shadowing potential for attaining interzone privacy. dB_A is a weighting network that corresponds closely to those sounds actually heard by the human ear.

60 (in other words, a measurement of the system as a whole including the ceiling and background noise systems. SPP $\geqslant$ 60 assumes a background masking system setting in the open office of $NC_{40} = 40$. NC_{40} is a single-number rating system utilized to indicate the level at which the electronic background masking system is set). Closed-office systems and components should be rated at SPP $\geqslant$ 70 with a maximum masking setting of $NC_{40} = 35$.

To interpret the meaning of SPP values properly, one should know which of several procedures were used to produce these values. They are produced by two tests developed for the U.S. General Services Administration/Public Buildings Services written by Geiger and Hamme Laboratories. The subjective test is called PBS C.1; the objective test is called PBS C.2.

The purpose of these tests is to determine whether a particular acoustical system provides adequate speech privacy. Each test is subdivided into three procedures. Procedure I considers the acoustical system as a whole—ceilings, sound screens, and a background masking system as interfaced with the balance of the space to be tested.

Procedure II considers the ceiling, including lights, air terminals, and the background masking system and its uniformity. (This combination of elements is called the Integrated Ceiling and Background Masking System, or ICB.)

Procedure III considers the space divider elements, or screens, and other vertical surfaces. (This combination of elements is called the Integrated Space Divider system, or ISD.)

Procedures II and III can be performed in the laboratory, on the prototype of the acoustical system, or in the field. If the system being tested fails the objective tests of PBS

C.2, GSA provides that the system may still be acceptable if it meets the requirements of PBS C.1 The test facilities for PBS C.1 and PBS C.2 are identical.

PBS C.1 is a subjective measure of SPP. It uses a jury of three or more persons who act as speaker, listener and monitor. The jury should consist of people equal in training and demeanor to those who will occupy the office, or it should be made up of actual occupants. The speaker adjusts his or her speech to 62 dB$_A$ as measured at a distance of three feet. The speaker is monitored to maintain this level during the test.

The listener is positioned at an adjacent work area with controls for the background masking system. The listener adjusts the initial level of the background sound until it provides "confidential privacy" (that is, sounds from the speaker are not understood, but the listener can be understood in his or her own work area). Then, preserving the mask, the listener adjusts the spectrum of the background sound to optimize its acceptability. The level of the optimized background is reduced to the point where the listener judges speech sounds to remain just unobtrusive into his or her concentration on an independent task. This final level is called "minimal privacy." The level of background sound required at this point determines success or failure for the system in terms of the jury consensus.

This test gives a yes-or-no result for SPP at a specified level of speech. The results are highly repeatable so long as comparable juries are used.

PBS C.2 is an objective measure of SPP. Figure 2A-4 shows two laboratory arrangements used to perform PBS C.2 testing.

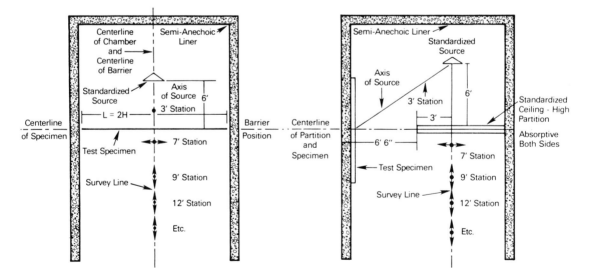

Figure 2A-4. Chamber layout for open-plan applications of Procedure II-S of Test Method PBS-C.2 in barrier configuration (left) and chamber layout for open-plan application of Procedure III-S of Test Method PBS-C.2 in primary flanking configuration (right).

Instead of live speakers and listeners, PBS C.2 testing uses a loudspeaker at a height of four feet above the floor and sound monitoring equipment set at various distances from the loudspeaker along a survey line. The sound is measured at each of these measuring stations. The average of the one-third-octave band sound pressure level values at two, three, and four feet from the loudspeaker provides a reference point of loudness. The loudness at each measuring station on the other side of the barrier is noted and compared to the reference value. Interzone attenuation is calculated and averaged to produce a value called Functional Interzone Attenuation. The NIC' rating is then calculated.

As indicated above, the SPP value for an acoustical system is often accompanied by an NC_{40} value for the background masking system. To find this value, the sound spectrum of the masking system used in PBS C.2 testing is compared with a standard NC_{40} contour. The NC_{40} curve is adjusted up or down so that the deviation between the test data and the contour are no more than 4 dB at any one frequency and a total of not more than 16 dB. A single-number rating is read where the NC_{40} contour crosses 500 Hz. This value is illustrated in Figure 2A-5. Note that the NC_{40} contour crosses the 500 Hz line at 39 dB.

The resultant comparison between attenuation from a screen/ceiling combination and the masking sound level may be expressed as the sum of the NIC' and the background masking level (NC_{40}). This sum is the SPP. The equation for the SPP of an entire acoustics system, then, is

$$SPP = NIC' + NC_{40}$$

Thus, if the NIC' for the ceiling-screen combination was twenty-one and the NC_{40} was thirty-nine, the SPP would be sixty.

The tests described above were developed because earlier tests proved unreliable for predicting the performance of acoustical materials in what was at the time a new concept—the open-office plan. These earlier tests and their ratings were developed by the ASTM and are known as ASTM E-336 (Noise Isolation Class [NIC]), ASTM C-423 (Noise Reduction Coefficient [NRC]), and ASTM E-90 (Sound Transmission Class [STC]).

ASTM C-423 measures the sound absorptiveness of screens, wall treatments, and ceilings. The NRC rating is an average of the acoustical absorption at four frequencies over all angles of incident sound (that is, a diffuse sound field). A typical office situation rarely involves sounds reflecting at grazing angles of incidence. Thus, these data are not really useful to the designer of an acoustical system.

ASTM E-90 measures the sound transmission loss performance of partitions. It specifically excludes flanking paths, a significant problem for the open office. Hence, the STC rating must be used with caution where the open-office plan has been chosen.

By contrast, the PBS and recently published specifications by the American Society of Testing and Materials (ASTM), Committee E-33 on Environmental Acoustics, specifically Subcommittee E-33.02—Open Offices, take the entire environment into account and thereby give a rating scale more attuned to actual field conditions.

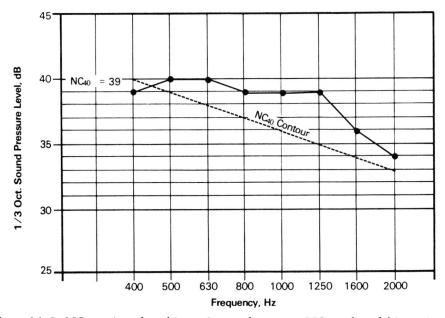

Figure 2A-5. NC$_{40}$ rating of masking noise test data curve. NC$_{40}$ value of thirty-nine is established by 4 dB excess at 1250 Hz.

ASTM Designation E-1111-88, *Standard Test Method for Measuring the Inter-zone Attenuation of Ceiling Systems,* is the first of a series of procedures that are essentially an outgrowth of the PBS procedures. This procedure is essentially the same facility as shown in Figures 2A-1 and 2A-2. The only difference in the procedure is a more detailed description of the source directivity. While data cannot be converted from the PBS C.2 procedure in a strict sense, casual conversions are helpful in understanding the similarities in the procedures.

ASTM Designation E-1110-88, *Standard Classification for Determination of Articulation Class (AC),* provides a "single-figure rating that can be used for comparing building systems and subsystems for speech privacy purposes. The rating is designed to correlate with transmitted speech intelligence between office spaces." AC represents essentially the same acoustical characteristics as the PBS—*Speech Privacy Noise Isola-tion Class (NIC').* The numbering system is quite different and was established by ASTM to avoid confusing results. While there is no direct conversion between NIC' and AC, general equivalency may be achieved by multiplying the NIC' by 11. In fact, this technique was utilized to list estimated values for AC in Tables 2-1, 2-2, and 2-3.

ASTM Designation E-1130, *Standard Test Method for Objective Measurement of Speech Privacy in Open Offices Using Articulation Index,* is designed to evaluate the acoustical performance under actual field conditions. It does not measure the perfor-mance of individual open-office components. Results are in terms of an Articulation Index which is, in essence, a measure of the amount of speech effort required for intelligibility. An AI of 1 typically represents 100% of the words are understood, while an AI of 0 represents total speech privacy. Note that the signal to noise ratio is the key to speech privacy. Consequently, the levels of background sound are a significant element of the evaluation of AI.

ASTM Designation E-1041-85, *Standard Guide for Measurement of Masking Sound in Open Offices*, provides a means to determine the spatial and temporal uniformity of the masking sound system in the actual office or laboratory environment. Measurements are made throughout the occupied space, with results indicating the maximum and minimum sound levels found in the test space over a specified time period. Generally, deviations greater than $+/-$ 2 dB average variance are considered unacceptable.

In the future, ASTM is expected to formulate subjective test procedures, wall treatment tests, and others. When published, it is anticipated that the ASTM procedures will gradually replace those now in use.

APPENDIX 2B

Specification Preparation

General

Specifications for the office can take many forms. They may be product- or performance-oriented, with a wide range of in-between combinations. The following performance specifications for ceilings, walls, floors, screens, and environmental background sound systems are strictly suggestions and may be incorporated by the specifications writer into the format chosen for the particular job. Items such as strength, fire resistance, durability, light reflectance, and color are included, but must be selected to meet job conditions and local code requirements.

Ceilings

The performance criteria shown in Table 2B-1 established the minimum allowance performance requirements for the ceiling in a typical new office environment. These criteria are applicable to both the open-plan and closed-plan office, except where noted. The ceiling herein is defined as that part of the building that is exposed to typical office space including all parts that are required to comply with the criteria when it is complete, installed, and in use (i.e., suspension, grid, and ceiling board). It does not include those criteria that are directly related to HVAC, luminaires, or background sound masking systems unless required for proper interfacing.

Table 2B-1. Ceiling Specifications

Performance Attribute	Criterion	Test Method
Accessible. When necessary to maintain equipment located within the floor-ceiling sandwich, the ceiling panels shall provide the capability of being removed and replaced over 00% (select appropriate value) of the area.	Remove and replace panels twenty times with no change in appearance or performance.	Observation
Acoustics (select category appropriate)		
type 1—Closed plan—elevated voice speech privacy	SPP $\geq$ 70 or NIC' $\geq$ 35 (Masking $\leq$ 35) or AI $\geq$ .01	PBS C.1 proc. II PBS C.2 proc. II ASTM E-1130
type 2—Open plan—normal speech privacy	SPP $\geq$ 60 or NIC' $\geq$ 20 or AI $\geq$ .05	PBS C.1 proc. II PBS C.2 proc. II ASTM E-1130
type 3—Closed plan—normal speech privacy	SPP $\geq$ 60 or NIC' $\geq$ 25 (Masking $\leq$ 35) or AI $\geq$ .05	PBS C.1 proc. II PBS C.2 proc. II ASTM E-1130
type 4—Open or closed plan Nonintrusive (speech privacy not critical)	SPP $\geq$ 57 or NIC' $\geq$ 17 or AI $\geq$ .10	PBS C.1 proc. II PBS C.2 proc. II ASTM E-1130
Control impact-generated sounds from adjoining floors	Masked by NC $\leq$ 40.	IBI 1-1 1965
Control generated noise from lights or HVAC terminals	Masked by NC $\leq$ 35.	USASI S1.2
Dimensions and tolerances shall be controlled to allow proper interfacing with other ceiling components.	Maintain proper fit in the field with normal tools and installation techniques.	ASTM C-635 and ASTM C-636

90

Performance Attribute	Criterion	Test Method
Light reflectance of the ceiling in place.	75%	ASTM E-97
Earthquake resistance. Where local codes require resistance to earthquake loads, the ceiling must be designed to resist lateral forces.	Minimum lateral resistance of .80 lb/sq ft	ASTM C-635, 6
Cohesive strength or interlaminar properties of the facing and core of the ceiling board shall be controlled to avoid peeling.	No delamination under pull five times product weight applied normal to exposed surface.	PBS d.2
Friability. Ceiling board will not be easily chipped or broken.	Not lose more than 50% weight in ten-minute test.	ASTM C-367
Water absorption	Will not absorb more than five times own weight through upper surface.	PBS d.3
Color variation or nonfading	Will not change color more than 1 NBS unit over 1000 hours of standard testing.	Fed. Std. #501a Method 5421
Fire safety Restrict surface burning Characteristics (a) Nonsprinkled buildings	Maximum twenty-five flame spread	ASTM E-84
(b) Sprinkled buildings	Maximum 100 flame spread	ASTM E-84
Restrict—smoke generation	Maximum 150 optical density	NBS Tech. Note #708
Restrict—BTU content or fuel contribution	Maximum 5000 BTU/lb or 2000 BTU/sq ft	ASTM Vol. 61, pp. 1336-47

Table 2B-1. Ceiling Specifications *(Continued)*

Performance Attribute	Criterion	Test Method
Fire Resistance (Note: This rating applies to the entire floor-ceiling assembly. When sprinklers are used, this requirement may be unnecessary.)	0–3 hr (See local code requirements)	ASTM E-119
Will not provide *life support* to vermin, mold, etc., or retain odors.	No life support	Fed. Method TTP 141B Method 627.1
Non-dust-collecting or easily cleanable surface	One year in use demonstration with no significant change in color or appearance.	Observation
Dimensional stability: Ceiling board shall not sag or cause appearance change in normal use	Maximum sag under ten-minute test shall not exceed 1/240 of span.	ASTM C-367 and C-635
Ceiling board	meet spec.	ASTM E-1264
Ceiling grid and installation	meet spec.	ASTM E-635, 6
Seismic restraint (installation)	meet spec.	ASTM E-580

BACKGROUND MASKING SYSTEM

Scope. Table 2B-2 establishes performance criteria guidelines for the background sound masking system. Although most systems are electronic in nature, these criteria are not intended to be so limiting. If the system is electronic, it may be economical to require the system to also provide emergency paging capabilities. The requirements must be satisfied with the complete ceiling system installed in a typical in-use condition. It shall not impair the requirements listed in any other part of these specifications.

Table 2B-2. Background Masking System

Performance Attribute	Criterion	Test Method
Sound level and spectrum	All levels between NC-30–50	PBS C.2 or ASTM E-1041
Spatial uniformity in occupied zone (i.e., 3–7 ft above floor and 3 ft from side walls)	Maximum 3 dB local variance in speech privacy frequencies	PBS C.2 or ASTM E-1041
Temporal uniformity over two-second interval in occupied zone	Maximum 3 dB local variance in speech privacy frequencies	PBS C.2 or ASTM E-1041
Compatibility (with ceiling system and building variables)	SPP $\geqslant$ 60	PBS C.1, C.2
Location	Not visible to occupied space	Observation
Durability: may be covered by automatic backup system or acceptable maintenance/warranty	24 hr/day operation within above parameters (suggest 5 yr minimum coverage with allowance for replacement)	Observation
Control access	Locked cabinet	Observation
Signal distribution (wires, speakers, enclosures, etc.) (National Electrical Code)	Meets local fire and electrical codes	Observation

SCREENS

Scope. Table 2B-3 establishes performance criteria and guidelines for screens or movable part high space dividers and full-height partitions typically used in a closed- or open-plan office. These elements can be a variety of shapes and sizes and combinations provided the in-use elements satisfy these criteria. These units shall not impair the effectiveness of other elements or systems described in any other part of this specification. Full-height barriers or demountable partitions also may be specified by these criteria if desirable. (*Note:* The latter are encouraged if the job has a mixture of closed- and open-office plan layouts.)

Table 2B-3. Screens

Performance Attribute	Criterion	Test Method
Acoustics (select appropriate attributes)		
Type A - Screens. For use with ceiling system having $NIC' \geq 20$ in open plan for "confidential" speech privacy.	$NIC'_B{}^a \geq 20$ $NIC'_F{}^b \geq 25$ or $SPP \geq 60$	PBS C.2 Proc. IIIS PBS C.1 Proc. IIIS
Type B - Screens. For use with ceiling system having $NIC' \leq 20$ in open plan for "normal" speech privacy.	$NIC'_B \geq 20$ $NIC' \geq 21$ or $SPP \geq 60$	PBS. C.2 Proc. IIIS PBS C.1 Proc. IIIS
Type C - Full height partition closed plan for "confidential" privacy with voice raised 10 dB.	$NIC'_B \geq 35$ or $SPP \geq 70$ at $NC_{40} \geq 35$	PBS C.2 Proc. III PBS C.1 Proc. III
Type D - Full height partition closed plan for "confidential" privacy with voice raised 6 dB.	$NIC'_B \geq 30$ or $SPP \geq 65$ at $NC_{40} \geq 35$	PBS C.2 Proc. III PBS C.1 Proc. III
Type E - Full height partition closed plan for "normal" privacy.	$NIC'_B \geq 25$ or $SPP \geq 60$	PBS C.2 Proc. III PBS C.1 Proc. III

Table 2B-3. (*Continued*)

Performance Attribute	Criterion	Test Method
Strength		
(a) Racking load of 150 lb.	No permanent set	ASTM E-72 as adapted to a screen
(b) Vertical load of 200 lb.	No permanent set	Observation
(c) Tipping load of 50 lb.	No permanent set ●	Observation
Weight (Panel May Be Dismantled to Satisfy Criteria.)	150 lb/unit maximum	Standard scale
Fire resistance. (*Note:* Needs will vary in different code jurisdictions. Values given are for worst condition.)		
(a) Flame spread	25	ASTM E-84
(b) Smoke density	150	NBS Tech. Note #708
(c) Potential heat	5000 BTU/lb or 2000 BTU/sq ft	ASTM Vol. 61, pp. 1337-47, 1961
Surface durability. Point impact	1/16″ set with 1/2 lb falling ball at 9″ drop	Fed Std. #406 Method 1074
Light reflectance	10%	ASTM E-97
Color stability	3 NBS units	Fed. Std. 501A Method 5421

[a] NIC′$_B$: Speech privacy noise isolation class—barrier position.
[b] NIC′$_F$: Speech privacy noise isolation class—primary flanking position.

VERTICAL SURFACE TREATMENT

Scope. Table 2B-4 establishes performance criteria and guidelines for any wall, column, filing cabinet, or window wall requiring acoustical treatment in or exposed to an open-plan office. These elements shall not impair the effectiveness of any other elements described in this specification.

Table 2B-4. Vertical Surface Treatment

Performance Attribute	Criterion	Test Method
Acoustical **Sound absorption**	$NIC'_F \geq 25$ or $SPP \geq 60$	PBS C.2, Proc. III PBS C.1, Proc. III
Fire resistance (*Note:* Needs will vary in different code jurisdictions. Values given are for worst condition.)		
(a) Flame spread	25	ASTM E-84
(b) Smoke density	1500	NBS Tech. Note #708
(c) Potential heat	5000 BTU/lb or 2000 BTU/sq ft	ASTM Vol. 61, pp. 1337-47, 1961
Surface durability: Point impact 1/2 lb. falling ball (9″ drop)	1/16″ permanent set using method 1074	Fed. Std. #406
Color stability	3 NBS units	Fed. Std. 501A Method 5421
Light reflectance	10%	ASTM E-97

Chapter 3

LIGHTING

David L. Munson, IALD

Updated by Byron W. Engen, P.E.

Throughout history, humans have needed to find shelter from the elements. As we sought to seal ourselves off from the weather, we also sealed out one of the important elements—light. Until the discovery of a translucent material which allowed natural light in while holding out the elements, humans were forced to provide an artificial light source. The first such source was fire. Over the past 2000 years, humans have progressed from candles, oil lamps, and gas lights to the electric incandescent lamp, which was developed only one hundred years ago.

The earliest uses of artificial light sources were to eliminate darkness and provide illumination to perform basic tasks. Today, with ever-changing environmental demands, our need for improved artificial light sources is even greater. Our use of light as a design tool in architecture has resulted from demands from architects and interior designers to solve their lighting problems with innovative solutions. Lighting no longer functions simply as an aid to visibility, but also serves as a design element to satisfy aesthetic requirements in architectural design.

Lighting should be designed as a combination of art and science. Until recent years, lighting for the majority of office spaces was planned by electrical designers who used a quantitative approach. The emphasis was placed on the use of large quantities of raw illumination, with little or no consideration for the user's comfort, color rendition of the source, or the aesthetics of the system. Lighting layouts traditionally resulted in fluorescent luminaires equally spaced across the room, in an attempt to provide equal illumination for the majority of task positions.

With more emphasis being placed on visual comfort, aesthetics, and energy conservation, this quantitative approach is no longer considered adequate. There has been an emphasis in recent years on a more "qualitative" design approach. An attempt is being made to emphasize the quality of the light being provided, a more pleasing visual atmosphere, and, most important, staying within the bounds of reasonable energy usage.

To accomplish these objectives, an integration of all the disciplines participating in the design of an office project should be involved from the initial design stages. This should include coordination among the architectural, structural, mechanical, electrical, acoustical, fire protection, and lighting designers to analyze the client's needs and to develop goals and objectives as well as specific requirements to be met in the final design. As the design develops, the original schematic ideas will become more specific in terms of actual spatial configurations. By integrating all the systems from the beginning stages, a more functional, energy-efficient, and cost-effective building system can be developed. In essence, one discipline can dramatically affect others. For example, lighting has a major impact on the mechanical, electrical, structural, and acoustical systems of an office. Lighting provides significant portions of the heating and air-conditioning loads; affects the electrical distribution and control system; may affect the interstitial space available for structural members; and affects the acoustical performance of the finished space.

DESIGN CONSIDERATIONS

After an initial evaluation of the total building concept, the lighting designer must do an intensive analysis to determine specific lighting requirements and to ensure a comprehensive and systematic design process. The following factors should be considered:

- Situation
    Human factors
    Functional requirements
    Spatial analysis

- Performance requirements of the lighting system
- Physical constraints
- Flexibility of the system
- Energy usage
- Maintenance
- Cost

1. Situation includes the mixture of human factors, or physiological condition of the occupants, such as age (average age as well as the variation between ages), behavioral characteristics, sex, and the users' psychological relationships to environmental conditions. Situation also includes the functional requirements demanded of a particular space. This involves an analysis of the activities anticipated within the space and the visual tasks to be performed. It also involves an analysis of the space—that is, the composition of an area and its relationship to adjoining spaces. This should include analysis of size, shape, furniture arrangements, availability of daylight, color, textures, and reflective qualities of surfaces.

2. Performance of the lighting system requires that the designer be aware of the visibility levels required for individual tasks and their location, the visual comfort the system affords the user, and the efficiency required of the lighting system.

3. Constraints include all limitations and requirements imposed by the other disciplines—architectural, electrical, mechanical, acoustical. It also includes those imposed by governmental agencies in the form of building codes.

4. Flexibility requirements need to be analyzed to determine the need for future spatial changes that would necessitate task or activity relocations and their impact on the initial design plan.

5. Energy conservation should be considered throughout the design process. The energy code of the jurisdiction in which the building will be located must be consulted and followed. Many codes limit the amount of energy that can be used for lighting as well as other disciplines. A thorough knowledge of applicable codes as well as the availability of energy-conserving lighting products will assist the designer in providing a system that meets all the other constraints as well as energy consumption.

6. Careful consideration should also be given to maintenance of the system to assure design continuity throughout the life of the project. Designing lighting that cannot be easily maintained is not good practice.

7. A cost analysis, including initial life-cycle costs, that takes into consideration budget constraints and operating costs is required in order to evaluate the economic merits of a lighting system.

DEFINING OFFICE TASKS

In today's offices, occupants are exposed to a great variety of visual tasks. The worker must be able to adapt to viewing such diverse tasks as original typed letters, books, magazines, catalogs, duplicated materials, handwriting (both pencil and ink), typed carbon materials, large and fine print, and computer terminals (visual display terminals or VDTs). Visibility for these tasks varies greatly from excellent to very poor. As much attention needs to be applied to improving the quality of the task as is given to improving the lighting system to adapt the human eye to the various tasks.

The visibility of the details of a task is determined by its contrast with the background, by its luminance, by its size, and by the time allowed for observation. As luminance contrast of the task with the background increases, visibility increases. A task must be illuminated to be visible, and the amount of illumination required increases as the age of viewer increases. Within limits, visibility must increase as the size of the task decreases. Eight-point type is the minimum size for good readability, but we prefer larger sizes such as 10 point and 12 point for long-term continuous reading. With low luminance, small tasks, and low contrast, the performance of work is slowed and more time is needed to assimilate the material being viewed. When accuracy is important, all factors must be optimized to assure accuracy and speed of work.[1]

VISUAL DISPLAY TERMINALS

Virtually all offices today have visual display terminals (VDTs). Those offices that do not have VDTs now probably will have them soon. The recent explosion in the use of personal computers in the workplace accounts for much of this trend, but VDTs are also used for access to mainframe computer systems. Computers are used for many functions in the office, such as word processing, spreadsheet analysis, electronic mail, and direct access management information systems. These, and a constantly increasing number of tasks, affect the design of work stations, furniture requirements, HVAC system loads, and lighting system design.

With the introduction of VDTs into the workplace, occupants of offices have become much more aware of the lighting system and its performance. The VDT is very sensitive to veiling reflections, and the performance of the worker is directly affected. Lighting designs with marginal performance are no longer acceptable. The VDT is a very common item that cannot be ignored in the design process. However, many of the same concerns about the overall system design still apply. The lighting design should provide for limitations on veiling reflections; it should control the level of luminance on the VDT screen, the adjacent desk or other surfaces, and the background field of view.

Illuminance

Illuminance may be the easiest to address of the problems associated with lighting for VDTs. Studies have shown that illuminance levels of 75 foot-candles on the face of the screen may reduce task contrast and thus visibility of the screen. Typically, general illumination should be in the range of 20 to 40 foot-candles, with task lighting used where necessary to supplement other tasks. Care should be taken in selecting and placing task lighting to ensure no veiling reflections and controlled brightness of task luminaire.

Luminance

Control of luminance is a bigger design problem when accommodating the VDT. Perceived brightness is more important than calculated illuminance, but they are related. Luminance is determined by multiplying illuminance by reflectivity. Thus, the reflectance of all surfaces in the office have as much effect upon the luminance as illuminance. Selection and placement of surfaces is critical to the lighting design.

It has long been known that luminance ratios are important to good visual performance and visual comfort. Standards in existence since the early 1950s suggest luminance ratios to achieve a comfortable balance in the office and limit the effects of transient adaptations and disability glare.

Measurements of a variety of VDTs show that screen luminance typically ranges from 5 to 25 foot-lambert (fL), with 15 fL being a reasonable average. Some opinions suggest that the IES recommended luminance ratios are conservative, but they provide a useful guideline for design of the illumination system and the room and furniture systems.[2]

DESIGN PROCESS

After consideration of all of these factors, we can begin the steps of the design process:

1. Analyze the composition of the space to determine with the architectural designer the total lighting effect desired.
2. Make decisions concerning the desired appearance of objects or tasks within the space, taking into consideration glare, shadows, and luminance contrast ratios.
3. Plan the location of fixtures in relationship to tasks, and determine the physical parameters required of the luminaires.
4. Select luminaires that meet these performance criteria.
5. Evaluate the total lighting system in conjunction with all other integrated systems.

THE EYE

To understand the relationship between light and how well we are able to see, it is necessary for the lighting designer to know how the eye works. The eye, which is said to be one of the most complicated systems within the human body, can be structurally compared to the parts of a camera. A camera has components that function very much like the lens, iris, retina, and many other parts of the eye (Figure 3-1).

Both the camera and the eye have a lens which focuses images on the retina. The retina is the light-sensitive plane at the back of the eye which relays images to the brain through a network of nerves. In the camera, this light-sensitive plane is the film.

The iris, or colored area of the eye, controls the amount of light which passes through the lens by adjusting the opening called the pupil. The eyelid also, to a lesser degree, controls the amount of light that reaches the retina. Correspondingly, the camera has the iris diaphragm and the shutter.

The ability of the eye to focus on images at varying distances is called *accommodation,* and is a result of changing the curvature or convexity of the lens. This process is stimulated by any shifting of visual attention resulting in blurred vision, which in turn sends a signal to the brain to contract or relax the ciliary muscle which controls the lens. By contracting this muscle, the lens is allowed to assume its natural convex or spherical shape, which is necessary for viewing close objects or tasks. If the lens were too flat, the projected image would be focused behind the plane of the retina and would appear blurred. The lens at its flattest—that is, when the ciliary muscle is relaxed—is focused on infinity or as far as the eye can see.

The eye's ability to adapt to changes in light level involves a two-part process in which both pupil and retina undergo physical changes. This process is called *adaptation.* When the level of brightness is low, the pupil of the eye dilates, or widens, to allow more light to reach the retina, and, conversely, contracts in bright light to limit the amount of light on the retina. This retina is made up of tiny photoreceptors—rods and cones—which send visual messages through a network of nerves to the brain. The cones perceive color and are capable of transmitting very sharp detail to the brain. The rods perceive neither detail nor color, but are extremely sensitive to very low levels of light.

Whenever a change occurs in the level of brightness, a photochemical change or bleaching takes place in the rods and cones. The amount of time required to regenerate varies, but it should be noted that the adaptation process is considerably longer when the change is from light to dark. The adaptation from dark to light requires only two minutes to complete. This phenomenon can be experienced when we enter or leave a movie theater.

The physiological condition that affects the aging eye (generally over age

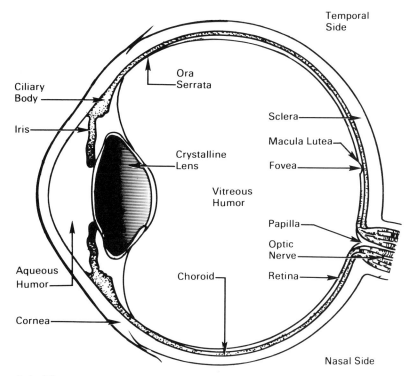

Figure 3-1. The eye

forty) is the loss of elasticity of the lens. This condition restricts the accommodation process of the eye and is referred to as presbyopia. One means of compensating for this inability to focus is to provide higher light levels for visual tasks. Higher light levels allow the iris (aperature) of the eye to narrow, which increases the visual depth of field. Thus, accommodation, or focusing of the lens, is less strenuous. The age of the potential users of any installation should be a major factor when determining appropriate light levels.

As mentioned previously, the eye sees only the luminance reflected from a surface or an object. An example of luminance on a surface would be to compare a black room (0 percent reflectance) having 100 foot-candles to a white room (80 percent reflectance) with the same foot-candle level. (For an explanation of foot-candles, see section "Illumination Measurements and Calculations.") The black room will appear dark even though the same light level is maintained.

Another example would be to compare a 40 percent reflectance room—that is, a room in which all surfaces are a value or color that will reflect 40 percent of the raw illumination that strikes the surface, with an illumination level of 100 foot-candles (fc)—to a room with 80 percent reflectance and 50 fc of illumination. The surfaces of both rooms will appear to be of equal luminance or brightness. As the eye sees only this luminance, the importance of these reflectance values can be critical in designing lighting for the office environment. With today's trend toward using lower foot-candle levels, it is obvious why lighter reflectance values are becoming a necessity if the atmosphere of the office is not to be dark and gloomy.

CONTRAST

Contrast refers to the variations between high and low areas of brightness. The eye can adapt quite well to normal contrast. However, extreme contrast can cause a strain on the muscles of the eye which will slow the visual process, particularly if these conditions persist. On the other hand, a certain amount of contrast is essential (both physiologically and psychologically) if seeing is to be comfortable and effective. In an office situation, three zones of contrast in the visual field are of prime importance (Figure 3-2).

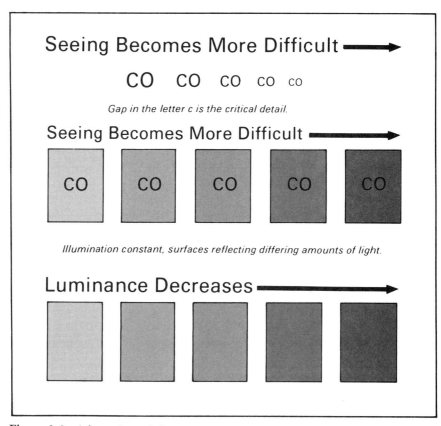

Figure 3-2. Adaptation of the eye to contrast and luminance

First Zone

The first zone is the task itself, sometimes referred to as the primary task. The writing on a paper is an example of a primary task. The primary task has contrast within itself, the contrast of the pencil line to the paper. Increasing this contrast between the pencil line and the paper will increase visibility. The converse is also true. For example, it is easier to see black ink on white paper than it is to see black ink on gray paper.

Second Zone

The second zone refers to the surfaces immediately surrounding the primary task, such as the desk top or work surface. It is suggested that to achieve optimum visual comfort the primary task (zone 1) should be slightly lighter than the surface immediately surrounding it (zone 2). It is generally recommended that the ratio be no greater than 3 to 1.

Third Zone

The third zone is defined as the value of distant surfaces such as walls, ceilings, and floors. The contrast relationship between zone 1 and zone 3 should not be less than one-fifth of the task brightness, or no more than five times the task brightness under normal conditions. For example, if the task brightness is 50 foot-lamberts, zone 3 should be no less than 10 foot-lamberts or no greater than 250 foot-lamberts. Changes greater than these will usually result in eye strain.

These ratios of contrast relationships should be regarded as maximums. Reductions of contrast ratios are generally beneficial.

Glare

If the contrast relationship between any of these zones becomes too great, it will produce an effect called glare. Glare is defined by the IES as "the sensations produced by illuminance within the visual field that are significantly greater than the luminance to which the eye is adapted, and which causes annoyance, discomfort, or loss in visual performance and visibility."[3] Glare can be categorized into two types. One is direct glare, which refers to excessive brightness coming directly from a light source or a bright exterior exposure such as a window. The second is reflected glare, which occurs when a light source produces reflections of high luminance from a polished or glossy primary task surface (a desktop or a printed magazine; see Figure 3-3).

Most glare encountered in the office environment can be controlled. Direct glare from the fixture can be controlled by shielding the source emitting

Figure 3-3. Reflected glare

light in the direction of the viewer's eye, or by decreasing the contrast in the zone surrounding the direct glare source. For example, unshielded lights in a white ceiling will appear less glaring than the same fixtures in a dark ceiling. Low brightness fixtures such as those utilizing a parabolic louver reduce glare by minimizing the light emitted above 50 to 60 degrees from a point directly below the fixture (Figure 3-4).

Reflected glare severely reduces visibility on the task. It can be controlled by reducing the specular quality of the task or by relocating the luminaire out of the offending zone. Where is the offending zone? Usually for any given task location, there may be one or more luminaires that cause a reflection on the task material. This is generally referred to as veiling reflections. Because the same luminaire in an open-office area may be providing very beneficial light to another task location, it is generally difficult to eliminate luminaires in an offending zone.

In an office situation, this zone is above and in front of the task. Since most tasks are viewed at an angle of 25 degrees from vertical, a luminaire emitting light at this angle will cause veiling reflections because the angle of reflectance is equal to the angle of incidence. It is also helpful to select a luminaire that emits less light at this angle and more light at angles above or below 25 degrees. It should be noted that light above 60 degrees will cause direct glare from the fixture, which can also have a serious effect on the user's visual comfort.

ILLUMINATION MEASUREMENTS AND CALCULATIONS

A quantity of light is measured in foot-candles, which is defined by the IES as "the unit of illumination when the foot is taken as the unit of length. It is the illumination on a surface one foot square in area on which there is a uniform distributed flux of one lumen, or the illumination produced on a surface one foot square in area on which there is a uniform distributed flux of one lumen, or the illumination produced on a surface all points of which are at a distance of one foot from a directionally uniform point source of one candela."[4] (See Figure 3-5.)

In designing a lighting layout, we must be able to calculate the quantity of illumination for each particular space. This may be done by manual methods using the zonal cavity or point-by-point methods (for details, see Appendix 3A) or by any number of computerized calculation methods available on both mainframe and personal computers. The designer must use experience and design ability to evaluate the results of the calculations. The manual methods typically result in an overall *average* illumination level that probably will not give the actual illuminance on the task. The average level does not account for variances in illumination caused by furniture, partitions, screens, and varying surface reflectances. Some computer programs are beginning to address this inconsistency, but many of the commercially available programs do not have subroutines to account for all the variances, especially the effects of partitions, screens, furniture, and other obstacles to direct light. Field measurements have shown that the resulting illumination at a task may vary by a factor of 2 to 4 from the predicted average value when the variances are not considered.

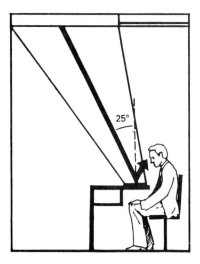

Figure 3-4. Reflected glare in the offending zone

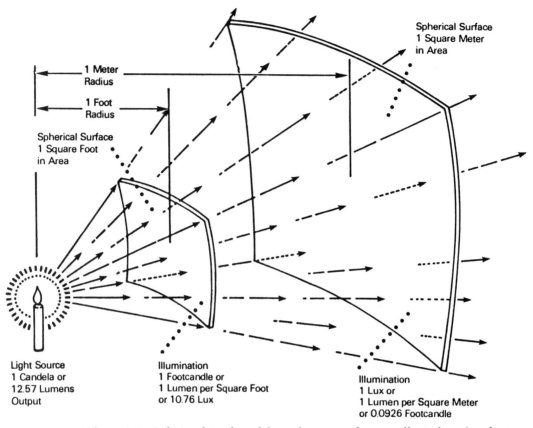

Figure 3-5. Relationship of candelas or lumens to foot-candles or lux. One foot-candle is the illumination on a surface one foot in area that is one foot from a "standard" candle. (Reprinted by permission, from General Electric TP-118.)

Task Visibility and ESI

The fact that veiling reflections have a serious effect on task visibility is not a new discovery, but until recently it was impossible to calculate the level of visibility of a task. Visibility is the ease of performing a visual task and is generally dependent upon contrast and background luminance. This can be calculated or measured by a technique or method referred to as equivalent sphere illumination, or ESI.

Equivalent sphere illumination is a method for evaluating the visibility of a task as it is measured inside a uniformly lighted sphere. One of the first devices for measuring ESI depended on the ability of an observer to visually compare the appearance of the two task locations by adjusting the light level on task position 2 (see Figure 3-6) in a sphere. When equal visibility was obtained, the measurement of illumination (foot-candles) in the sphere (at task position 2) was used for determining the ESI on the task position (position 1). For example, if the visibility of both task positions are equal and the illumination level on the task position inside the sphere (position 2) is 50 foot-candles, then the ESI of the task position outside the sphere is 50 foot-candles, regardless of the level of illumination on position 1. This procedure proved to be very time-consuming and because the outcome was based on observer evaluation, it also proved to be rather inconsistent.

The visual task photometer (VTP) was a further advancement of this theory. The VTP eliminated the observer as a determining factor and by use of a photometer was able to measure contrast of a task in order to calculate ESI. This method proved to be more accurate, but the equipment necessary to perform the test was too bulky and sensitive for field application.

Portable ESI meters are available which allow the designer to evaluate the installed system for ESI. However, the designer must be aware that the ESI meter readings are applicable only to the specific task for which the meter is designed. This typically is the No. 2 pencil task. The ESI for this task does not give an indication of visibility of other tasks such as the VDT and should not be used for their evaluation. Other methods of evaluation and analysis must be utilized for these tasks.

Visual Comfort Probability

A method of predicting the visual comfort a group of people will experience in a given room is known as visual comfort probability (VCP). This method takes into consideration fixture brightness at different viewing angles, fixture size, room size, fixture mounting height, illumination level, and room surface reflectances. This calculation will predict the percentage of people in a room who will find it acceptable if seated in the worst location for direct glare in the

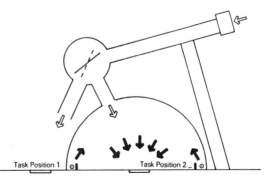

Figure 3-6. Visual Task Photometer (VTP)

room. This prediction of VCP can be used only for lighting that is located in a uniform grid. VCP tables cannot be used for predicting visual comfort in a task-oriented, nonuniform layout or with indirect luminaires.

However, new computer programs that take into account fixture locations and room reflections can predict VCP at any given point within a room. It should be noted that VCP cannot be determined for indirect luminaires since the light coming directly out of the fixture cannot be seen from normal viewing angles.

Most major lighting manufacturers have VCP tables for fluorescent lighting fixtures which are based upon IES methods of calculation. Using these tables, the designer can predict the number of viewers out of 100 who would find the lighting comfortable. For standard office tasks, the IES recommends a VCP level of 70 or above. For VDT tasks, the VCP level should be at least above 80 and preferably above 85. While these levels do not guarantee that all workers will be comfortable, going below these levels will usually result in some degree of excessive brightness, with resultant discomfort for a percentage of viewers.

ILLUMINATION REQUIREMENTS

In order to determine the necessary levels of illumination required to perform a particular task, the designer will usually refer to a set of guidelines published by various agencies. The most widely used are the guidelines set by the Illuminating Engineering Society.

Prior to 1982, the IES published illumination recommendations based on an averaging of data and assumptions about user eyesight, age, and task demand. This averaging led to a single-number system of recommendations.[5] In the 1970s, research was performed on a new method for specifying illumination levels.[6] This resulted in the IES publishing a new standard that included more flexibility for the unique applications found in actual field conditions.[7]

The recommendations are divided into nine ranges of illumination. The first three categories A through C are levels to be used over an entire area in which the visual task remains constant over time and space. An example would be a task involving a person walking through a lobby.

Categories D through F involve tasks that remain relatively fixed at one location in the majority of work situations. The illumination of these task locations should be applied to the task areas only. At the same time, a minimum of 20 fc should be maintained in the nontask location.

Categories G through I are for extremely difficult visual tasks and may be difficult to illuminate properly. These extreme tasks will require careful analysis of all considerations in order to arrive at a well-developed overall illumination system, as well as a system for specific task illumination (see Tables 3-1 and 3-2).

While this approach may be more time-consuming than the single-number system, the designer will be more informed as to the peculiarities of each space as far as function, observer, and task variations. It is recommended that the designer consult the *American National Standard Practice for Office Lighting* published by the Illuminating Engineering Society of North America for complete details on using this method of specifying illumination requirements.[7]

Table 3-1. Illuminance Categories and Illuminance Values for Generic Types of Activities in Interiors

Type of Activity	Illuminance Category	Ranges of Illuminance		Reference Work Plane
		Lux	Foot-candles	
Public spaces with dark surroundings	A	20–30–50	2–3–5	
Simple orientation for short temporary visits	B	50–75–100	5–7.5–10	General lighting throughout spaces
Working spaces where visual tasks are only occasionally performed	C	100–150–200	10–15–20	
Performance of visual tasks of high contrast or large size	D	200–300–500	20–30–50	
Performance of visual tasks of medium contrast or small size	E	500–750–1000	50–75–100	Illuminance on task
Performance of visual tasks of low contrast or very small size	F	1000–1500–2000	100–150–200	
Performance of visual tasks of low contrast and very small size over a prolonged period	G	2000–3000–5000	200–300–500	

Table 3-1. Illuminance Categories and Illuminance Values for Generic Types of Activities in Interiors (*Continued*)

Type of Activity	Illuminance Category	Ranges of Illuminance		Reference Work Plane
		Lux	Foot-candles	
Performance of very prolonged and exacting visual tasks	H	5000–7500–10,000	500–750–1000	Illuminance on task, obtained by a combination of general and local (supplementary lighting)
Performance of very special visual tasks of extremely low contrast and small size	I	10,000–15,000–20,000	1000–1500–2000	

Table 3-2. Weighting Factors[a] to Be Considered in Selecting Specific Illuminance within the Ranges of Values for Each Category in Tables 3-3 and 3-4

Task and Worker Characteristics	Weighting Factors		
	−1	0	+1
Workers' ages	Under 40	40–55	Over 55
Speed and/or accuracy[b]	Not Important	Important	Critical
Reflectance of task background	Greater than 70%	30 to 70%	Less than 30%

Source: Reprinted from ANSI/IES RP-1-1982 by permission of the Illuminating Engineering Society of North America.

[a] See ANSI/IES RP-1-1982 for use of table.
[b] In determining whether speed and/or accuracy is not important, important, or critical, the following questions need to be answered: What are the time limitations? How important is it to perform the task rapidly? Will errors produce an unsafe condition or product? Will errors reduce productivity and be costly? For example, in reading for leisure there are not time limitations and it is not important to read rapidly. Errors will not be costly and will not be related to safety. Thus, speed and/or accuracy is not important. If, however, prescription notes are to be read by a pharmacist, accuracy is critical because errors could produce an unsafe condition and time is important for customer relations.

ARTIFICIAL LIGHT SOURCES

Incandescent Lamps

The incandescent lamp produces light by passing an electric current through a filament which acts as a resistor and heats to the point of incandescence, thus producing light. One of the major advantages of the incandescent lamp is the color of the light source. Most people have come to accept incandescent lighting as a standard for color rendition, to which all other light sources are compared.

Due to its inefficiencies, compared to some of the more recently developed sources such as fluorescent or high-intensity discharge sources, the incandescent lamp no longer serves as a source for general illumination for most office space. However, the filament is quite small and can easily be controlled with the use of reflectors or in a reflectorized lamp such as a par lamp. In this form, it can be used quite successfully as accent lighting, or to highlight specific activities within the office.

The major disadvantage of the incandescent lamp is that it typically has a relatively short life (750 to 2000 hours), and is generally inefficient as far as light output compared to wattage consumed.

Fluorescent Lamps

Since its introduction in 1940, the fluorescent lamp has been widely accepted as the general light source for office application. The fluorescent lamp consists of a glass envelope that contains mercury at low pressure and a small amount of inert gas (argon). The inner walls of the bulb are coated with energy-activated powders, called phosphors. When voltage is applied, an arc is produced by the current flowing between two electrodes through the mercury. This generates a small amount of visible light, but mainly produces invisible ultraviolet radiation which activates the phosphors, thus producing visible light.

When the fluorescent lamp was first introduced, the color of the light emitted was not satisfactory. Due to advances in phosphor coatings, its color rendition has been greatly improved and is now generally accepted as a color-corrected light. A large variety of lamps allow the designer freedom of choice in color selection. However, lamps of different colors should not be mixed on the same installation.

The fluorescent lamp, in comparison to the incandescent lamp, has a considerably longer lamp life (18,000 to 20,000 hours) and is more efficient as far as light output in relation to wattage consumed. What is generally considered a disadvantage is that fluorescent lamps, like most electric discharge lamps, must be used in conjunction with an auxiliary apparatus called a ballast.

The ballast starts the lamp and limits the passing current to the value for which the lamp is designed. The disadvantages are that the ballast increases power consumption, which increases the heat buildup in the fixture. The ballast also increases the size of the fixture and the cost. Noise is also contributed by the ballast.

Recent developments in lamp and ballast technology have resulted in more efficient choices. Lamps with greater light output (lumens/watt) can be coupled with high-efficiency ballasts to reduce energy requirements. New developments in solid state ballasts have improved their efficiency as well as allowed some dimming capability. The designer must make certain that the selected lamps and ballasts are compatible.

As the fluorescent lamp is not a point source, meaning that the light is not emitted from a single point but a linear source, the reflector systems used with this lamp must be carefully designed to utilize light output efficiently.

High-Intensity Discharge (HID) Lamps

HID lamps have grown in popularity in the past few years due to their efficiency, and have been used in many office lighting systems. However, they are usually found in indirect lighting applications rather than ceiling-mounted downlight systems. HID sources include mercury vapor, metal halide, and high-pressure sodium lamps.

MERCURY VAPOR. The mercury vapor source was first thought to be more efficient than the fluorescent lamp. Its relatively small size made it easier to control (as far as reflector systems) than the fluorescent lamp.

The mercury lamp is constructed of two glass envelopes. The inner envelope contains mercury vapor and a small amount of argon under pressure. The outer envelope acts as a shield from drafts and temperature changes and produces a surface for the phosphor coatings that help correct the source color. An electric current striking an arc creates heat which causes the mercury to vaporize, producing ultraviolet energy which then activates the phosphors. The lamp does not reach its full light output until the mercury is entirely evaporated. This slow start ranging from 7 to 14 minutes should be a major consideration in its application.

Today, with the use of advanced color-correcting phosphor coatings, the mercury lamp has been used successfully as a general light source, providing the luminaire in which it is used is properly designed for its particular application.

METAL HALIDE LAMP. The metal halide lamp is a modification of the mercury vapor lamp. In addition to mercury, the arc tube contains metallic vapors which are responsible for its improved color rendition. Phosphor-coated or color-corrected lamps are available for areas requiring more improved color qualities.

The metal halide lamp has considerably higher initial light output than the mercury lamp, but light output decreases at a faster rate and the lamp generally has a shorter life. Due to heat problems, the lamp also has restrictions on the positions in which it can be used.

Because of the small size of the metal halide lamp, and the fact that it is not always a phosphored lamp, precise optical control is more easily attained with the use of properly designed reflector systems.

HIGH-PRESSURE SODIUM (HPS). High-pressure sodium, the latest addition to the high-intensity discharge sources, is also constructed of two glass envelopes, but light is produced by electricity passing through sodium vapor. Its very thin arc tube provides excellent optical control capabilities.

The high-pressure sodium lamp is the most efficient of the HID sources. However, its severely distorted color output limits its use in office applications. This color distortion can be overcome by the use of high-pressure sodium in conjunction with other sources, such as daylight and/or metal halide.

LIGHT SOURCES

Color

Since the apparent color of a surface depends on the color characteristics of the light source under which it is viewed, the selection of a light source can be critical. The lighting designer should always be consulted before a color scheme is decided upon. As far as color characteristics, one of the main objectives when selecting a light source is to make people look attractive in their surroundings. This can be facilitated by using a light source that is complimentary to skin tones and therefore makes the occupants of the space look healthier.

Decisions concerning finishes and materials should be made after the selection of the light source. These selections must be made under this same light source at the correct intensity for proper selection of reflectance values and for the avoidance of color distortion. For example, if the finishes and colors were selected under 600 fc of daylight (north sky) for use in an office being lighted with 60 fc of warm white fluorescent, the colors in place would appear darker in intensity and warmer in hue.

In order to evaluate color characteristics of sources, the designer may refer to published data from manufacturers (see Figures 3-7, 3-8, 3-9, and 3-10). One method of evaluating refers to color temperature, which is expressed in degrees Kelvin (°K), and refers to the absolute temperature of a theoretical radiator (the black body radiator) which color matches that of the source being evaluated. This theory applies only to sources of continuous spectral composition, such as incandescent. Electric discharge sources such as fluorescent or high-intensity discharge emit an uneven spectral distribution. These lamps have mixed energy peaks which give the visual appearance of white light. In these types of sources, the color is expressed in "apparent" degrees Kelvin.

The Kelvin system is a convenient single-number index that deals only with the apparent color of the source but does not give an accurate description of the way the source affects the colored environment. One method of evaluating the way a source affects a colored environment is by use of a spectral distribution chart which shows the amount of relative energy (microwatts) over each wave length. The variation in relative energy is what determines the color a light source will produce.

The color-rendering index refers to the degree to which the perceived colors of objects illuminated by a source conforms to those same objects illuminated by a reference source under specified conditions. The higher the color rendering index (100 being the reference point), the better one can distinguish proper colors when viewed under that source. For sources under 5000° K, a tungsten filament, which has a continuous spectrum, is the reference source. For sources over 5000° K, typical daylight, as defined by the International Commission of Illumination,[8] is the reference source. Note that the color-rendering index should be used only when associated with its color temperature (Table 3-3).

Light Source and Luminaire Efficiency

The selection of an appropriate light source for the office environment should take into consideration not only the initial efficiency of the source (lumens/watt), but also its efficiency in combination with the selected luminaire. For example, it has been shown that the incandescent lamp, when used in specific applications, can be considered a very efficient source, even though its lumen/watt efficiency is low. Source selection should also be based on the color of the source, lamp life, and energy efficiency.

SELECTION OF A LUMINAIRE

After the initial architectural design decisions have been made and preliminary layouts have been drawn showing the possible locations of light sources, the designer is faced with the selection of the proper luminaire.

Table 3-3. Comparison of Lamps Commonly Used in Office Lighting

Lamp	Type	Wattage w/Ballast	Approx. Lumen/ Watt	Corre- lated Kelvin	Color Red. Index	Appearance on Complexion[a]	Appear- ance on Neutral Surface[a]
150A21/IF (Frosted)	Incandescent	150	16	2800	100	Excellent	Yellow white
F40T12/CW (Cool white)	Fluorescent	50	64	4200	66	Fair	Blue white
F40T12/CWX (Cool white deluxe)	Fluorescent	50	44	4200	89	Good	White
F40T12/WW (Warm white)	Fluorescent	50	64	3000	52	Good	Pink white
F40T12/WWX (Warm white deluxe)	Fluorescent	50	44	3000	73	Excellent	Pink white
H37KC-250/DX (Deluxe white)	Mercury vapor	280	44	3900	48	Poor	Blue white
H37KC-250/WDX (Warm deluxe white)	Mercury vapor	280	35	3300	48	Fair	Pink white
H37KC-250/N (Warm tone)	Mercury vapor	280	44	3300	52	Good	Yellow white
M250/BU-HOR (Clear lamp)	Metal halide	300	66	4250	66	Poor	Blue white
M250/BU-HOR/C (Coated lamp)	Metal halide	300	66	3900	72	Fair	Blue white
LU150/55 (Clear lamp)	High- pressure sodium	200	80	2100	13	Poor	Yellow
LU250 (Clear lamp)	High- pressure sodium	310	88	1950	20	Poor	Yellow

Source: Data based on available lamp manufacturer's data.

[a] Author's opinion. User evaluation suggested.

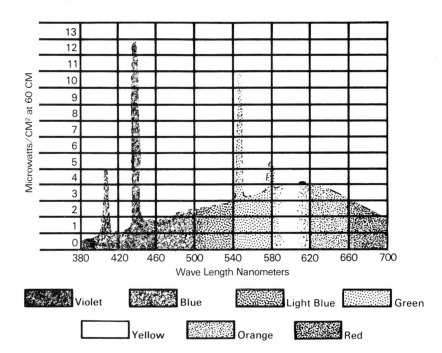

Figure 3-7. Spectral distribution of F40 cool white lamp (Reproduced by permission from Westinghouse Electric Corporation, Lamp Division)

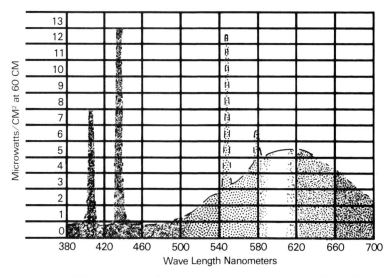

Figure 3-8. Spectral distribution of F40 warm white lamp (Reproduced by permission from Westinghouse Electric Corporation, Lamp Division)

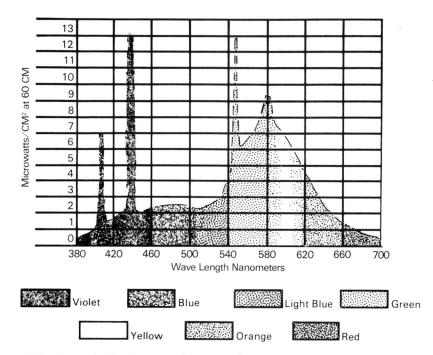

Figure 3-9. Spectral distribution of F40 cool white deluxe lamp (Reproduced by permission from Westinghouse Electric Corporation, Lamp Division)

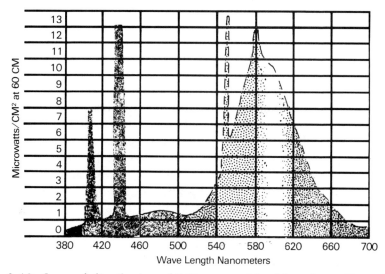

Figure 3-10. Spectral distribution of F40 warm white deluxe lamp (Reproduced by permission from Westinghouse Electric Corporation, Lamp Division)

Most luminaires can be categorized into two basic classifications of photometric distribution with variations in mounting the luminaire:

1. Direct
    a. Recessed
    b. Surface-mounted
    c. Pendant-mounted
2. Indirect
    a. Pendant
    b. Furniture-integrated
    c. Freestanding

The selection of the proper luminaire should take into consideration a number of factors.

Luminaire Appearance

The appearance of luminaires—their size, shape, and finish—should be coordinated with the architect or interior designer early in the design process, since light fixtures have an important visual impact on the space. Some architectural constraints that should be considered are building module size, space limitations, and fixture proportions in relationship to space.

Luminaire Component Analysis

Careful investigation of all component parts incorporated in a luminaire should be undertaken to determine fixture reliability. The designer should review drawings showing component parts, or should visually inspect a working sample.

A luminaire's optical system, or the method by which light is controlled, determines its photometric performance, and can be accomplished by three general methods. The first method is *reflection*. This is the process of collecting and redistributing light from the source into more useful zones by the use of specular or semispecular surfaces. A properly designed reflector system is considered to be the most efficient way to control light distribution.

In recent years, there has been growing popularity in the use of low-brightness fluorescent luminaires. These luminaires use parabolic reflectors which eliminate the high-angle brightness of the fixture by redirecting the light into more useful zones. An advantage of this type of design is that the parabolic reflectors are electrically grounded and do not build up a static charge that will attract dust. Some test data have shown that the parabolic design can remain 95 percent clean over a period of five years. The parabolic design also has special acoustical properties. The louver, due to its shape, collects and traps the sound or randomly distributes the sound. Thus, sound waves striking the luminaire are not directly reflected into adjoining spaces. The selection of the parabolic luminaire should be done in concert with the acoustician for the project.

The second method is *refraction*. Refraction is defined by the IES as "the process by which the direction of a ray of light changes as it passes obliquely from one medium to another in which its speed is different."[9] This is usually accomplished in luminaires by use of glass or plastic prismatic lenses. The use of prismatic lenses in luminaires is most successful when wide photometric distribution is desired for general illumination. An important disadvantage in using lenses in fluorescent luminaires is that the plastic lens tends to build up a static charge, thus attracting dust, which changes the photometric distribution and necessitates more frequent cleaning.

It must also be noted that although the overall efficiency can sometimes be higher with a lensed fixture, some portion of the light may not be within the useful zones and can cause excessive brightness and discomfort to the occupants due to direct glare.

The third method is *reduction*. Reduction uses bladed louvers, baffles, or light shields to block out light in offending zones, but allows the intensity of light in useful zones to remain unchanged. The use of this reduction method, due to its subtractive approach, reduces the efficiency of the luminaire. This type of optical control is no longer considered appropriate for general illumination when energy efficiency is required.

In order to ensure that the luminaire and its electrical components, including the ballast, are safe, they should bear the label of a reputable testing laboratory. The list that follows contains more information on ballasts. The ballast, which is the auxiliary equipment required for electric discharge sources, should be labeled with the following information:

1. Lamp designations (such as HID, fluorescent, etc.).
2. The type (auto transformer, constant wattage, etc.).
3. Sound classification (quietest being A; with B, C, and D being progressively louder).
4. Power factor (rating to determine power consumption and start-up performance. High power factor being the most efficient; low power factor being a cheaper component and less efficient).
5. Class P (automatic resetting thermal protection).
6. Minimum starting temperature.
7. CBM (ballast meets performance specification of the Certified Ballast Manufacturers Association).

Photometric Performance in Relationship to Energy Efficiency

In order to determine the photometric characteristics of a luminaire, a manufacturer will have an independent testing laboratory test the fixture. This testing will provide information on the candlepower distribution, which is measured at certain degrees for each particular plane. It also includes such information as the number of lumens for each zone, luminaire efficiency, foot-lambert brightness of each zone, and spacing-to-mounting ratios. Calculations are also provided for visual comfort probability and the coefficient of utilization. This combination of information provides the designer with the ability to calculate foot-candle levels in a number of ways outlined in the appendix to this chapter.

If the fixture is an air-handling unit, data for heat extraction, air supply, and air return are also available. Some manufacturers will also provide average maintained illumination charts. However, since this information is based on averages, the designer should rely on his own calculations (Figure 3-11). The designer should never assume that because two fixtures appear to be of the same design, they will perform equally. Tests are necessary to show each fixture's particular photometric characteristics.

Quality of Construction

Due to spiraling inflation rates, some manufacturers have been known to take cost-cutting measures which can result in a reduction of quality. Visual inspection of a luminaire should be made to check for quality of workmanship and to see that paint or reflector surfaces are free of flaws and scratches, and that all moving parts are aligned and function as intended.

Ease of Installation

If a luminaire is properly designed to allow for ease of installation, time savings for the electrical contractor can result in cost savings for the client. Contractors have been known to take this into consideration when bidding a job.

The same applies to maintenance of a system. An efficiently designed system that allows for easy replacement of lamps and access to all surfaces that collect dust can result in cost savings for the client for the life of the luminaire.

Cost

Since the total cost of lighting fixtures in relationship to the total cost of an office building amounts to between 1 and 3 percent of total construction costs, major cost-saving attempts should be considered in other areas during the early design stages.

Report of Candlepower Distribution

Luminaire - Aluminum reflector-louver unit.
  Specular aluminum finish.
Lamps - Two F40CW/U/3, each rated 2900 lumens, 2290 fl.,
  Mounting Recess Shielding, Parallel 30° Normal 40°.

Candlepower

Deg.	Parl.	45	Norm.	Zonal Flux
0	1791	1791	1791	
5	1784	1806	1824	171
15	1714	1844	1911	518
25	1602	1837	2009	847
35	1305	1589	1574	943
45	932	1077	1274	855
55	594	562	143	414
65	77	63	37	62
75	23	20	14	20
85	5	4	3	5
90	0	0	0	

Zonal Summary

Zone	Lumens	Lamp	Fixt.	Deg.	Avg. Fl. Parl.	Avg. Fl. Norm	Max. Fl. Parl.	Max. Fl. Norm	Fl. Ratio Parl.	Fl. Ratio Norm
0-40	2480	42.8	64.7	45	1219	1665	2447	2583	2.0	1.6
0-60	3749	64.6	97.7	55	957	231	782	1325	0.8	5.7
0-90	3836	66.1	100.0	65	168	82	170	136	1.0	1.7
				75	82	48	102	68	1.2	1.4
				85	54	33	68	34	1.2	1.0

S/MH = 1.4 IES Class Spread   CIE Type Direct

IES Visual Comfort Probability

REFLECTANCE 80/50/20

100 FC. Room		Luminaires Lengthwise				Luminaires Crosswise			
W	L	8.5	10.0	13.0	16.0	8.5	10.0	13.0	16.0
20	20	85	80	72	76	91	87	84	76
20	30	86	81	76	72	91	89	86	79
20	40	87	83	78	74	92	90	88	82
30	30	89	85	79	72	93	90	86	78
30	40	89	86	81	75	93	91	88	81
30	60	90	86	82	77	93	92	89	83
40	40	91	88	84	78	94	92	89	82
40	60	91	88	84	79	94	92	90	83
40	80	91	88	85	80	94	93	91	84
60	40	92	89	85	80	94	93	90	84
60	60	92	89	86	81	94	93	91	85
60	80	92	89	87	82	94	93	91	86
100	60	93	91	88	84	95	94	92	87
100	80	93	91	88	85	95	94	92	88
100	100	93	91	89	85	95	94	92	88

Figure 3-11. Photometric test report. Testing the photometric characteristics of a luminaire will provide information on the candlepower distribution, number of lumens for each zone, luminaire efficiency, foot-lambert brightness of each zone, and spacing-to-mounting ratios. (Reprinted by permission of Owens-Corning Fiberglas Corporation)

Average Maintained Illumination

RCR	25	32	40	50	64	80	100
	Area in Square Feet Per Luminaire						
1	142	111	89	71	55	44	35
2	130	102	81	65	51	41	33
3	118	92	74	59	46	37	30
4	108	85	68	54	42	34	27
5	99	77	62	49	39	31	25
6	89	69	55	44	35	28	22
7	81	63	51	40	32	25	20
Watts Per Sq. Ft.	3.5	2.8	2.2	1.8	1.4	1.1	0.9

1. Uniform Illumination - IES Zonal Cavity Method
2. Reflectances - 80/50/20
3. Maintenance Factor - .85
4. Standard F40 U/3 Lamps - 2900 Lumens
5. Work Plane Height - 2 Ft. 6 In.
6. RCR - Room Cavity Ratio

$$RCR = \frac{5h\,(L + W)}{(L \times W)}$$

Where: h = height of cavity
L = length of space
W = width of space

Coefficient of Utilization Table
Effective Floor Cavity
Reflectance 0.20
Effective Ceiling Cavity
Reflectance 0.80

RCR	Wall Reflectance		
	70	50	30
1	74	72	70
2	70	66	63
3	65	60	56
4	61	55	50
5	56	50	45
6	53	45	40
7	49	41	36
8	45	37	32
9	41	33	28
10	38	30	25

**Heat Removal
Relative Light Output**

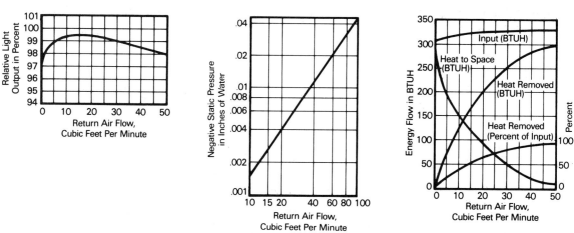

Figure 3-11. Photometric test report (*Continued*)

Value judgments of comparison costs of various fixtures in relation to the total cost of the lighting system can be seen in minor variations in a life-cycle cost analysis. It is recommended that a life-cycle cost comparison be done and fixture substitutions considered.

LIGHTING SYSTEMS

After determining what levels of illumination will provide adequate visibility for occupants, the lighting designer must determine the kind of lighting system he or she wishes to use. The options, as far as fixture types are concerned, include direct, indirect, and task/ambient, which is a combination of both.

Direct Lighting

In a direct lighting system, light comes from its source to the work space without first being reflected from other room surfaces. Direct lighting is the most commonly used system for offices, and is often applied as a blanket solution, using a grid or row pattern throughout the entire ceiling of an office. This system provides equal levels of illumination across large spaces, which is necessary when the activity or task location within a space is unknown.

Another application of direct lighting is the task-oriented approach. With this method, fixtures are located only over work areas to provide the proper general illumination level. Areas other than work stations, such as corridors, reception areas, and lobbies, are illuminated to a lower illumination level. Task-oriented lighting is a direct response to a need for optimum lighting and energy conservation. Coordination with the architect and/or interior designer as well as the owner is needed to assure acceptance of a ceiling pattern that does not look uniform.

A recent application of direct lighting is the system developed for use with high amounts of VDTs in the workplace. With this application, a uniform pattern of low-brightness ceiling luminaires is used to provide a low level of uniform illumination throughout the space—typically in the range of 15 to 30 foot-candles—which provides illumination for traffic and large, noncritical tasks. Task lighting is installed at each work station to provide illumination for the local task. Low-brightness ceiling luminaires are usually chosen to reduce the potential for veiling reflections on the VDT screens. The individual work stations can be customized by task lighting to provide optimum user comfort and productivity. Energy savings are possible with this system as well, provided that a coordinated design is developed in conjunction with owner, architect, space planner, and HVAC engineer.

Direct lighting offers the designer the option of using an integrated ceiling package, which consists of modules with a luminaire in the center and provisions for sprinklers, sound masking systems, and air distribution. These modules are designed for use with a variety of luminaires in both flat and vaulted ceiling configurations (Figure 3-12).

A strong architectural design statement can be achieved by the use of a three-dimensional vaulted system, which also provides improved acoustical

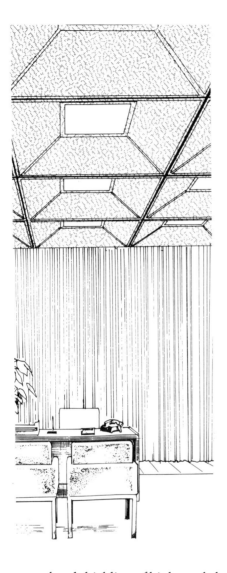

Figure 3-12. Integrated ceiling system

control and shielding of high-angle brightness (Figure 3-13). (It should be noted that standard calculation methods for determining ESI or VCP cannot be applied to vaulted-ceiling systems due to their unique shape.)

The flat ceiling configuration creates a monolithic appearance and can accommodate minimum plenum clearance. Concealed air distribution units and/or movable partitions can be located on modular lines with access provided through the luminaire (Figure 3-14).

The integrated ceiling package also has the advantage of facilitating the coordination of ceiling components and their installation by making it the responsibility of one contractor.

Figure 3-13. Three-dimensional vaulted ceiling lighting system

Indirect Lighting

Indirect light is reflected from a secondary surface, such as the ceiling or the walls or a combination of both (Figure 3-15). The use of totally indirect lighting in the office provides a near shadow-free environment similar to conditions under an overcast sky. The ESI or visual clarity aspects of the task are generally greater with the use of indirect lighting than with the use of typical direct systems.

In evaluating an indirect lighting system, the designer must be careful when using computer calculation programs. Many of the programs are not designed to perform calculations for indirect lighting systems, even though they may give an answer. This is especially the case when calculating ESI and VCP.

In providing this near shadow-free environment, objects such as partitions and desks tend to lose definition due to a lack of contrast. What generally occurs in indirect lighting systems is that the task brightness will appear dark in comparison to the ceiling brightness. Due to the process of phototropism, the eye adapts to the brightest object or surface in the visual field, in this case the ceiling. The eye will adapt quickly to this brightness, but will take noticeably longer to adapt to the task brightness, since its luminance value is less.

Figure 3-14. Flat ceiling integrated system with low brightness luminaires

Figure 3-15. Indirect ceiling-mounted lighting system

Probably one of the most important and least understood components of the indirect system is the ceiling, or the surface from which the light is reflected. The ceiling tile is expected to satisfy requirements that are in direct conflict with each other. An acoustical function of the ceiling tile is that it should absorb as much sound as possible, but it is also expected to reflect as much light as possible. Since the physical properties of light and sound are primarily the same, this task becomes very difficult.

It is an assumption in most calculations for indirect sources that the ceiling surface is of a flat, diffuse nature with cosinal characteristics. In reality, the acoustical tile that is commonly used has a porous surface that does not reflect light in the same way. In order to maintain the necessary light levels, heavily textured and low-reflectance surfaces should be avoided. The designer should also be aware that the excessive ceiling contrast ratios created by the indirect fixture could lead to visual discomfort.

The sources most commonly used for indirect lighting are fluorescent and HID. Indirect fluorescent luminaires are used in linear and grid arrangements, preferably with ceiling heights 10 feet or higher, depending on luminaire photometric characteristics. Indirect HID sources can be pendant-mounted, wall-mounted, freestanding, or furniture-integrated. Unless there is adequate shielding of the source, these luminaires should be located above eye level to avoid glare.

Task/Ambient Lighting

Another lighting method sometimes used—primarily in open-office designs—is task/ambient. The purpose of this system is to provide sufficient levels of illumination on work surfaces by the use of task lights and generally lower levels of illumination by other supplemental luminaires in nonwork areas, or areas surrounding the immediate task (Figure 3-16). Low-level illumination is required in order to provide the necessary contrast between the task (zone 1) and the environment (zone 3).

Furniture-integrated lighting provides ambient light by indirect luminaires located either within the furniture system or in freestanding units. Sources presently used for this application are fluorescent or HID.

The need for task lighting has been generated by the growing trend toward open-office planning and modular furniture systems. These systems consist of work surfaces surrounded by acoustical partitions and overhanging shelves and storage units. The workstations cannot be effectively illuminated by overhead lighting alone due to the shadows caused by partitions and shelves.

Flexible or fixed luminaires can be used to provide task lighting. Flexible luminaires, such as swing arm lamps, can be adjusted to a user's requirements by the user. This allows the user to control veiling reflections on the task by removing the fixture from the offending zone. Fixed luminaires used for task lighting are surface-mounted fluorescent lamps either incorporated directly into or attached to the furniture system. These fixtures tend to create veiling reflections on the task.

Such reflections can be minimized by the use of refractors or lenses with a "batwing" distribution. This lens splits downlight into right and left components, which produces a minimum of direct downlight and lights the task from oblique angles in an attempt to reduce the veiling reflections. Another solution to this problem would be to light the task from two sides. However, this has not been successfully accomplished because of the large source size usually required to illuminate the task properly.

Some areas within open-office plans do not lend themselves to task lighting. These areas include secretarial stations, reception areas, or conference rooms, where freestanding partitions are not located adjacent to the task. These areas can be illuminated by direct lighting located above task areas or by freestanding indirect luminaires. The use of direct sources for lighting these areas limits spatial flexibility, since the ceiling-mounted luminaires must be moved when office relocations take place.

Lighting these areas with freestanding indirect luminaires faces restrictions of floor space and luminaire location in relationship to the task location. If no task lighting is used and proper illumination on the task surface is to be maintained, the ceiling brightness must be two to three times greater than the

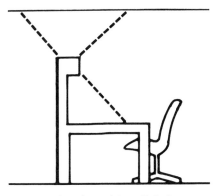

Figure 3-16. Furniture-mounted task-ambient lighting

value of the ceiling over normal work stations. The indirect components are used only for general illumination and are usually supplemented by task lights.

Although most manufacturers of furniture systems will advertise tremendous energy savings with task/ambient systems, a careful analysis of each application should be made. The determining factor in energy consumption is the number of square feet per task. For example, if an ambient light source (250 watt, HID uplight, 18'-0" on center) consumed 1.0 watts per square foot to maintain 30 foot-candles, and the total lighting system consumed less than 2.0 watts per square foot, then a 4-foot task light consuming 50 watts could be used every 50 square feet. If each work station averages 80 square feet (8' × 8' work area with a shared 4' corridor) and requires two 50-watt task lights, the resulting energy consumption would be 2.25 watts per square foot for both task and ambient lighting.

One disadvantage of task/ambient lighting is that all the sources are located within a space. Heat extraction, which is available with ceiling-mounted luminaires, cannot be accomplished, and thus cooling costs are increased.

To evaluate this type of system, one must weigh the disadvantages against the advantages:

- Complete flexibility of lighting in relationship to task locations
- Ease of maintenance
- Tax advantage due to faster depreciation allowed on furnishings
- Lower initial base building costs since no general lighting is required

Daylight

Until recently, the application of daylight for illumination in office design has been considered solely as part of the architectural design with which the lighting designer has not been involved. Its application has been reintroduced in attempts to design more energy-efficient lighting systems.

Careful analysis of the architectural design should be made to determine the type of exposure as well as the location and orientation of the site. An investigation of the heat gain/loss transmission of windows or skylights versus the light contribution should be made. In such a comparison, glazing is sometimes found to be energy-inefficient relative to the energy used in heating or air conditioning needed to bring the temperatures back to the comfort range.

Sunlight is not considered to be a stable light source for illumination, since its orientation, intensity, and color is constantly changing. However, sky brightness or daylight striking surfaces can be used quite effectively in perimeter or single-story offices. The control methods of daylighting should be designed properly to allow maximum use while maintaining brightness control and contrast ratios, as discussed earlier. These control methods may include reflectors and/or light shelves for redirecting light into more useful zones, shading devices such as blinds or draperies, and special light-transmission glazing. In any method using reflectors and/or light shelves, the ceiling may play a critical role in providing satisfactory illumination. Careful coordination with other professionals is required to ensure that proper reflectivity and texture of ceiling is provided.

Sophisticated computer programs are now available for use on personal and mainframe computers to assist the designer in planning for the use of daylight. Designers should consider using these aids to design, and also consider the use of models or even full-scale prototypes. In any application of daylight, however, the creativity of the designer is needed to ensure a satisfactory operating system. Control of the total lighting system, including daylight, is needed for this application to be effective. The use of dimming devices on the luminaires should be considered to provide for optimum energy utilization as well as occupant comfort. Control of the intensity of the daylight may be needed so that the radiant heat from daylight does not cause discomfort. Evaluation of the radiant aspect should be carried out with the space planner and the HVAC engineer.

CONTROLS

The use of controls can play a major role in energy conservation. They help the designer in the office where varied illumination levels are possible or where contributions of daylight are used. The need for control is dictated by rising electrical costs due to depleting natural resources used in producing electrical energy.

Artificial illumination can be manually controlled by the user or by recently introduced automatic systems. In the latter, the illumination level of a task will automatically be adjusted to accommodate light depreciation factors or the supplements of daylight. The use of manual control systems, where the occupant is responsible for energy conservation, is not as effective as automatic systems, since slight variations in illumination levels are not easily detected.

Due to recent advances in direct digital control, computers may be used to control the entire building system, including lighting, through twisted pair lines to the space. This eliminates the need for individual switching for office spaces. Changes in office layouts can be programmed into the controlling computer. Daily variations in the operating schedule can be programmed into the controller. In some systems, individual sequence changes can be programmed as special circumstances. When individuals work late, they can call the computer by telephone and enter specially coded messages using the telephone touch-tone pad.

This system is activated by the use of multiplex switching devices located in each light fixture or the circuit breaker, which is assigned a code number. The code numbers are then combined in the computer into lighting groups and are switched when the user code numbers are called. The computer can also be assigned to control lighting as required for cleaning crews, or when load shedding is needed to control peak electrical demands.

A life-cycle analysis that takes into account projected electrical costs should be evaluated to determine if the use of controls is appropriate for each installation.

PROJECT EVALUATION

Upon completion of the project, it is important that the lighting designer review the design to analyze the success of the actual installation and to determine whether the original design intent was met. This analysis will make the designer aware of problems and can provide valuable information that can be used for reference on future projects.

The lighting designer, working with the other professionals on the project, should ensure that a complete building commissioning is performed by the design group or by a special building commissioning firm. Commissioning assures that the installed systems operate and perform as designed. Commissioning entails checking the operation of every component in the lighting system. Special attention should be paid to the automatic control systems to be sure they provide the control the designer required for occupant comfort. The designer should also make the owner and operator of the installation aware of all functions and capabilities of the lighting system to ensure that they will be used effectively and, just as important, will be maintained properly.

SUMMARY

Lighting should be designed as a combination of art and science to provide illumination for tasks performed in the office. This requires integration of all the disciplines involved in the office design. Integration of all the systems from the beginning facilitates a more functional and efficient, as well as an energy- and cost-saving, lighting system.

Lighting has a major impact on mechanical, electrical, and acoustical systems of an office in terms of heat loads, energy consumption, and acoustical absorption of the fixtures. Therefore, a comprehensive and systematic design process is important to achieve visual comfort, aesthetic appeal, and energy conservation. This means that the design team must place greater emphasis on the quality of lighting, as well as the quantity of illumination.

Notes

1. *American National Standard Practice for Office Lighting*, ANSI/IES RP-1-1982. New York: Illuminating Engineering Society of North America.
2. Kohn, Mitchell, 1988. Lighting offices containing VDTs. *Lighting Design and Application* 18(12):9–11.
3. Kaufman, John E., and Christensen, Jack F., eds. 1984. *IES Lighting Handbook: 1984 Reference Volume*. New York: Illuminating Engineering Society of North America, pp. 1–11.
4. Kaufman and Christensen, pp. 1–14.
5. *American National Standard Practice for Office Lighting*, ANSI A132.1-1973. New York: Illuminating Engineering Society of North America.
6. Flynn, John. 1979. The IES approach to recommendations regarding levels of illumination. *Lighting Design and Application* 9(9):74.
7. ANSI/IES RP-1-1982.
8. CIE Committee. 1965. *Method of Measuring and Specifying Color Rendering Properties of Light Sources*. CIE Publication No. 13-1965:E-1.3.2.
9. Kaufman and Christensen, pp. 1–26.

Suggested Readings

Ballman, T. L., and Levin, R. E. 1987. Illumination in partitioned spaces. *Journal of the Illuminating Engineering Society* 16(2):31–49.

Cahana, Michael Z. 1989. The use of computers by lighting designers. *Lighting Design and Application*. June 1989:2–9

de Boer, J. B., and Fischer, D. 1978. *Interior Lighting*. London: Macmillan.

Evans, Benjamin H. 1981. *Daylight in Architecture.* New York: McGraw-Hill.

Flynn, John E., Segil, Arthur W., and Steffy, Gary R. 1988. *Architectural Interior Systems,* second ed. New York: Van Nostrand Reinhold.

Helms, Ronald N. 1980. *Illumination Engineering for Energy Efficient Luminous Environments.* Englewood Cliffs, NJ: Prentice-Hall.

Hentschel, H. J., Klein, E., Leibig, J., and Roll, K. F. 1987. Energy-effective direct/indirect office and VDU-lighting systems: test and application. *Journal of the Illuminating Engineering Society* 16(2):89–105.

IES Recommended Procedure for Lighting Power Limit Determination, LEM-1-82. New York: Illuminating Engineering Society of North America.

IES Recommended Procedure for Lighting Energy Limit Determination, LEM-2-84. New York: Illuminating Engineering Society of North America.

IES Recommended Procedure for Design Considerations for Effective Building Lighting Energy Utilization, LEM-3-84. New York: Illuminating Engineering Society of North America.

IES Recommended Procedure for Energy Analysis of Building Lighting Designs and Installations, LEM-4-84. New York: Illuminating Engineering Society of North America.

Kaufman, John E. (ed.). 1987. *IES Lighting Handbook: 1987 Application Volume.* New York: Illuminating Engineering Society of North America.

Nuckolls, James L. 1983. *Interior Lighting for Environmental Designers.* New York: Wiley.

Orfield, Steven J. 1987. Open-plan office lighting. *Lighting Design and Application,* July: 17.

Parent, M. D., and Murdoch, J. B. 1988. The expansion of the zonal cavity method of interior lighting design to include skylights. *Journal of the Illuminating Engineering Society* 17(2):141–173.

Peterson, David. 1988. Integrated lighting management. *Lighting Design and Application.* September 1988:14.

Robbins, Claude L. 1986. *Daylighting—Design and Analysis.* New York: Van Nostrand Reinhold.

Recommended Practice of Daylighting, RP-5-79. New York: Illuminating Engineering Society of North America.

APPENDIX 3A

Methods for Calculating Illumination

Zonal Cavity Calculation Method

This type of calculation is used primarily to determine foot-candle levels in large areas with an equally spaced grid of fixtures throughout, and will compute an average foot-candle level for the space. The zonal cavity method is only applicable to empty rectangular spaces. It does not account for furniture, modular systems, screens, and partitions. Using standard methods, it does not account for nonuniform surface reflectances. The zonal cavity method should be used with caution, as the actual illuminance at any point in the space may vary considerably from the average value calculated using this method.

One of the keys to the calculation is the coefficient of utilization (CU) which is an index of how well the fixture can be expected to perform within a particular space. The CU value varies with the size and reflectance values of the room and can be obtained from manufacturer's testing data.

The light loss factor (LLF) is a percentage of the light still available from a system after a given period of time before lamp replacement and luminaire cleaning. The LLF is a combination of lamp lumen depreciation (LLD), which accounts for loss of efficiency with the age of the lamp, and luminaire dirt depreciation (LDD), a loss of efficiency due to dirt accumulation on the fixture. Since each type of luminaire has its own characteristics for dirt depreciation, it is necessary to check manufacturer's test data for recommendations.

The computation uses the following equation:

$$\text{Average foot-candles} = \frac{(\text{number of luminaires}) \times (\text{lumens per luminaire}) \times (\text{CU}) \times (\text{LLF})}{\text{area in square feet}}$$

Point-by-Point Method

This is a more involved method of calculating illumination which can be used for nonuniform layouts or task-oriented lighting. It uses the following equation:

$$\text{illumination} = \frac{\text{candlepower} \times \text{cosine of angle of incidence}}{\text{distance}^2}$$

Candlepower is a measurement of light emitted from the luminaire at a particular angle. This information can be obtained from the manufacturer's test data. With this method of calculation, all contributing luminaires must be added together to find the total foot-candles on a task. This method is more accurate than the zonal cavity method. However, it does not include illumination reflected from the surfaces within the room. It should be noted that with point-by-point calculation, the distance of the source must be at least five times the maximum luminous dimension away to obtain accurate results.

Interreflected contributions of light from each surface within the room can also be calculated using the point-by-point method. The interreflected calculation is a long and tedious procedure and should be attempted only with a computer program and when more accurate values are required. There are numerous other calculation methods available for lighting, and these are published in the latest *IES Lighting Handbook*.

Chapter 4

HVAC

Gershon Meckler

Updated by Byron W. Engen, P.E.

A heating, ventilating, and air conditioning system (HVAC) should provide office users with an environment that is free from drafts and cold surfaces, that has a controlled indoor air quality (IAQ), and in which the air is neither noticeably hot or cold, too humid, or too dry. At the same time, the HVAC system should minimize the use of energy and minimize life-cycle costs. While these last two requirements combine to constrain HVAC design in some ways, they also present new opportunities for creativity and innovation. They require that the various building elements and environmental systems be coordinated through close teamwork among the planning team specialists who are responsible for their design. The building envelope, office spaces, lighting, acoustics, fire safety, electrical power distribution, and HVAC systems all must be designed as an integrated whole (Figure 4-1).

In the past, the technologies of these environmental systems have been developed and applied to the building design more or less separately. The result has been a collage of independently functioning, energy-inefficient systems. Interdisciplinary team planning seeks not only to identify the organization's and users' needs comprehensively, but also seeks to resolve them through

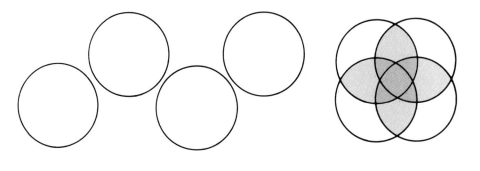

Conventional Design   Integrated Design

Figure 4-1. Building envelope, office spaces and acoustics, lighting, fire safety, and HVAC systems

integrated design. In contrast to the conventional approach in which systems have been layered, integrated design produces an environment whose elements function as a whole and as efficiently and economically as possible. Such an environment satisfies the office users' health and comfort needs and supports their individual activities, allowing them to perform their tasks with maximum effectiveness and minimum strain.

To understand the current objectives of office HVAC design, it is helpful to be familiar with some of the changes that have occurred in HVAC design over the last few decades. In the past, heating systems were directly fired by fossil fuels and were designed to offset heat losses through the building envelope during the winter. Space cooling was considered a luxury and was only installed in some special-use facilities such as theaters and retail stores. When air conditioning was provided, it was designed separately and independently from the heating system. It was operated only during the summer to offset outside climatic conditions.

After World War II, offices began to be subdivided for leasing to tenants. This introduced the need for a flexible HVAC system so that individual tenants could plug into the system as needed. In 1952, the dual duct system was introduced to satisfy this need. It provided the necessary flexibility and control through separate cold and hot primary-air supplies which were then mixed as necessary at the point of use. At the same time, low-cost electricity made refrigeration economical for cooling and dehumidification. Inexpensive electricity also allowed lighting levels in offices to increase, and, in the 1960s, heat-of-light systems were introduced to use the waste heat from lighting to heat the building perimeter during the winter.

The 1970s presented the challenge of conserving energy without sacrificing the benefits that increased environmental control had brought over the years. After the Arab oil embargo in the winter of 1973–74, the American Society of Heating, Refrigerating, and Air Conditioning Engineers (ASHRAE) developed a basic standard for energy conservation in new buildings.[1] The direction was to increase the thermal efficiency of the building envelope, reduce the intake of outside air, improve the sealing of the building, recover waste heat, and broaden the temperature criteria for comfort.

The 1980s brought us into the computer age, with sophisticated control of the environmental system by personal or mainframe computers. Precise control of the entire building from a central point was now possible. Direct digital controls (DDC) were introduced. These allowed integration of the control function with the computer. A greater awareness of indoor air quality and the need for refinements in the design process to ensure healthy environments presented new challenges to the planning team. Recent findings of the relationship between chlorofluorocarbons (CFCs) and the ozone layer will present new challenges and new systems as alternate refrigerants are introduced to reduce the effect on the global environment. The 1980s was also marked by continuing concern for conserving energy. ASHRAE revised its energy standard in 1980[2] and 1989[3].

At present, the need remains for the HVAC system in an office building to provide a quality environment and, simultaneously, through innovative, integrated design, to conserve the resources required to construct, operate, and maintain the services necessary to that environment.

A quality office environment protects the health of the users, ensures their comfort, and aids their productivity. Air circulating in a space provides fresh air and removes stale air, excess moisture, and smoke. It cools heat sources such as people, lighting, equipment, and infiltrating air, and reduces summer envelope gains. In winter, it heats cold surfaces and cold infiltrating air, and replaces heat lost through the envelope. The outside air brought in to supply the space has to be conditioned in terms of temperature and humidity. Part of the displaced air is exhausted from the building and part is recirculated so that the combined volume of fresh and recirculated air is sufficient to handle thermal, moisture, and pollution loads without the high cost of a complete air change.

Figures 4-2 and 4-3 show the principal loads on and needs for heating, ventilating, and air conditioning in summer and winter. As these drawings indicate, the demands placed on the HVAC system by people, equipment, and luminaires are relative to the occupancy of the space. The loads on the building envelope, and the temperature and humidity of the outside air brought into the system, on the other hand, are determined by external conditions.

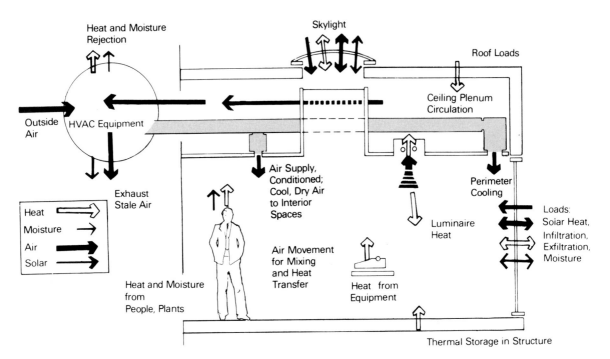

Figure 4-2. Summer need for ventilating and air conditioning

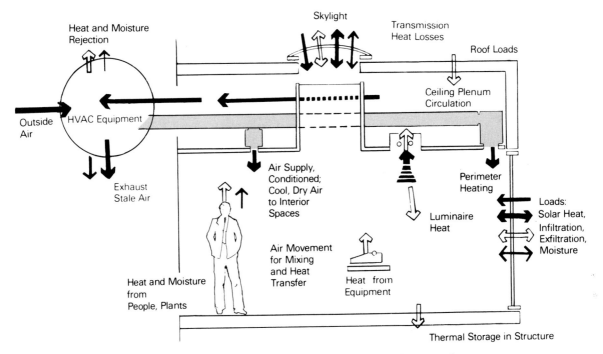

Figure 4-3. Winter need for heating, ventilating, and air conditioning

COMFORT

In the context of heating, ventilating, and air conditioning, providing comfort for the office users is fundamentally a matter of controlling the rate at which heat flows from their bodies; the rate, in other words, at which their bodies are cooled. By heating the air and surfaces around people, this rate is slowed, and therefore they feel warmer. Cooling the air and surfaces around them increases the rate at which they lose heat, causing them to feel cooler.

People give off heat and moisture by the metabolic conversion of food into energy, and the thermal power they generate is directly related to their activities. For comfort, the air and surfaces around them should create the conditions necessary for a flow of body heat appropriate to their activities. The flow of body heat to the surroundings depends upon the temperature, humidity, and movement of the air, radiation and abduction characteristics of surfaces, and user traits.

To provide thermal comfort, a combination of factors are necessary. Control of temperature, radiation, humidity, and air movement are important. The occupant can affect thermal comfort by the type of clothing worn and by the amount of activity. ASHRAE has provided standards[4,5,6] over the years to address thermal comfort requirements. These standards have been refined as research into thermal comfort has provided more answers. The current standard, ANSI/ASHRAE 55-1981[6], includes adjustments for clothing, activity, air movement, and temperature drifts to give greater flexibility and energy-saving potential. See this standard and later revisions for more details on determining conditions for occupant comfort.

Radiation to and from surfaces within the office space should be controlled in order to maintain the users' heat gain and loss balance in the environment. Proximity to cold surfaces, for example, even without direct contact, causes discomfort due to loss of the body heat radiated to those cold surfaces. Conversely, hot surfaces such as sun-heated windows radiate heat to the body and may create discomfort. Thus, windows heated by the sun and radiation from high-intensity illumination must be balanced by introducing cooler air into the space. Similarly, warmer air is needed in the winter to balance the radiant attraction of cold windows and cold perimeter floors.

Direct contact with hot or cold surfaces causes heat to be conducted to and from the body. Surface temperatures, therefore, should be about equal to the air temperature. This means that wood, fabric, and plastic feel neutral to the touch, and metal feels slightly cool.

Clearly, the HVAC specialist must design the system in accordance with average office-user needs as far as temperature, humidity, air movement, and so on are concerned. Although the designer knows the users' general levels of activity, he or she cannot design for the particular characteristics and unique comfort needs of each individual. The clothing, health, body size, and sex of the user are obviously beyond the designer's control. One important point is that people can adapt to the office environment by adjusting the weight of their clothing and, to a certain degree, by arranging their workplaces to suit their personal needs.

FRESH AIR, AIR MOVEMENT, AND FILTERING

Proper ventilation within the office space is a function of fresh air intake and air movement. Outside air is introduced into the space through ducts, windows, or infiltration, and is circulated by fans. Outside air must be mixed with the air in the office space in order to replenish the oxygen supply, to dilute the particulates, toxic pollutants, pathogens, and odors in the space, and to control humidity and ionization. Clearly, fresh air intake is necessary to protect and ensure the users' health and comfort.

Criteria for replenishing office air with fresh outdoor air have been reduced to minimum levels to conserve energy. ASHRAE recommends minimum flows for various activities,[7] but local building codes must be consulted because they may present requirements different from industry standards. However, these flows alone are generally insufficient to handle the cooling loads of the spaces. Consequently, part of the air within the space needs to be recirculated and mixed with the outdoor air so that there is enough conditioned-air volume to satisfy the cooling and heating loads of the occupied space. Because this inside air has already been conditioned, substantially less energy is required to recondition it than is required for outside air.

A minimum for air movement in the office space has not been established for ventilation or comfort requirements. Air movement is not a comfort determinant in itself, as long as drafts are avoided, so separate criteria need not be established for it. However, it should be sufficient to distribute heat loads, moisture, and fresh air within the space, and to dilute pollutants. Air movement should also prevent thermal gradients greater than 4 to 6°F from developing within the space; with higher gradients, natural convection will cause users to feel a temperature imbalance. Natural convection, as a result of gradients of less than 4°F, is negligible.

The ASHRAE standard does not require any minimum air movement for thermal comfort. The maximum average air movement allowed in the occupied zone is lower in winter than in summer. For winter conditions, ASHRAE specifies that the average air movement shall not exceed 30 feet per minute (fpm). During summer conditions, the specified maximum average air movement shall not exceed 50 fpm. However, during summer operation, increased air movements can be used to offset the effect of higher temperatures in the occupied zone while still maintaining comfort. Caution is required, because loose paper, hair, and other light objects may start to be blown about at air movements of about 160 fpm.

As the air within the office is recirculated and outside air is brought in, the particulates they carry are removed by filters. The degree to which the air is filtered—that is, the amount and size of the particles collected—depends on several factors: the cleanliness needed for users' health and the operation of office equipment, the amount of soiling created within the space, and the pollution of the outside air. Recirculated air in offices is usually low in particulates; those it does carry are generally from tobacco smoke, dry skin, hair, and clothing. Adequate filtering is important to the health of the users and affects the cleanliness and appearance of the office. One noticeable effect of insufficient filtering is the formation of dark areas on surfaces surrounding the diffusers that supply air to the space.

Exhaust air from office spaces, toilets, and parking garages contains concentrations of the internal pollutants. This air is discharged into the external environment for dilution. The point of discharge should be well removed from, down wind of, and higher than the outside-air intake of the building and adjacent properties.

HUMIDITY CONTROL

With too little moisture in the office space, the movement of people over carpets may cause electrostatic charges to develop. The discharge, whenever a person touches a metallic object, can be quite disconcerting. Electrostatic charges have dramatic and damaging effects on electronic equipment such as personal computers. Special grounding pads may be needed at the computer, or grounded carpeting may be required. Further, an insufficient humidity level can dry the mucous membranes. High humidity, on the other hand, can create damp conditions when the surrounding surfaces are below the dew point of the air. Condensation on windows in winter is a common situation. If moisture remains in a poorly ventilated area, fungal growths and corrosion may result.

Humidity is an important factor in the user's thermal comfort, but materials and equipment may also be sensitive. Paper, for example, is particularly susceptible to absorbing water vapor when the relative humidity (RH) exceeds about 80 percent. In drafting offices, tracing paper crinkles if humid conditions develop when the HVAC system is turned off for an evening or a weekend. Drafting pens tend to clog in hot, dry air and smudge in humid conditions. The quality of reproductions from and paper handling capability of copiers can be affected by moisture in the air.

People, plants, coffee makers, and food preparation are sources of moisture and increase the humidity of the air in the space. The air supplied to the space, then, must be dry enough to absorb this moisture, and the air and humidity exhausted from the space must be sufficient to maintain users' comfort. This drier air is achieved by dehumidifying the outside and recirculated air in a central or zone air-conditioning process. As an example of how much moisture is generated within the space and how much must be removed by a dehumidification process, consider an office with a user density of one person per 100 square feet. Each person gives off latent heat equal to 2.5 Btus per hour per square foot (Btu/h · ft²); this requires the removal of 0.0023 pounds of moisture per hour per square foot. If the air supply to the space is 0.9 cfm/ft² and the humidity ratio of this supply air is 0.006 pounds of water per pound of dry air (lb/lb), then after the air has been circulated in the space, its humidity ratio is raised to 0.0102 lb/lb. This means that, for a 100,000 square foot office area, 230 pounds of moisture per hour must be removed with 90,000 cfm air movement through the space.

One of two processes may be used for dehumidifying outside and recirculated air. Conventional dehumidification by condensation passes the outside and recirculated air over refrigerated cooling coils. The air is chilled below its dew point to condense moisture. Then the air is reheated to the proper supply temperature. In this process, the air is dried to a humidity ratio of 0.008 to 0.009 lb/lb, or about 60 grains per pound (gr/lb). Desiccant dehumidification absorbs moisture directly from the air. This process uses a much lower volume of air than the conventional condensation process, but it also removes more moisture from the air, drying it to a humidity ratio of 0.005 lb/lb, or 30 gr/lb. Because of this low humidity ratio, dehumidifying the outside-air volume alone is often sufficient to handle the humidity load. In this case, recirculated air does not require dehumidification, and local space recirculation may be used. This, in turn, means that primary- and return-duct sizes and fan power may be reduced.

In dry climates, the humidity generated within the office space may not be sufficient for the users' comfort. Moisture may be added to the air by water sprays or steam nozzles, as required.

INTERNAL THERMAL LOADS AND INTERIOR SPACE

In order to maintain office environmental conditions that are within the comfort zone, the HVAC system must condition the outside and recirculated air supplied to the space. It must provide cool air to handle the heat in the space, and warm air to offset heat losses. As far as internal thermal loads are concerned, the demand for thermal power depends directly on the activities of people and the operation of equipment within the office. Generally, these are fairly stable for any particular organization (Figure 4-4).

Although the internal cooling loads—that is, the thermal loads created by activities and operations within the occupied office space—are more or less

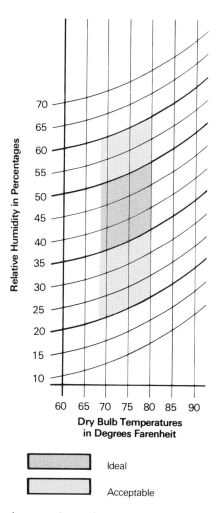

Figure 4-4. Comfort envelopes for air conditioning

constant, and in most offices user densities are light, allowances must be made for congregations in such areas as conference rooms, lecture rooms, and cafeterias. Separate controls may be necessary to accommodate intermittent and variable loads in these areas.

Movable pieces of equipment, such as typewriters, personal computers, coffee makers, and table lamps, add to the overall cooling load of the space and, because of their portability, usually do not require special consideration in the design of the HVAC system. Fixed items of equipment, however, generally do require special attention because they are both fixed in the space and often add substantially to the cooling load (Table 4-1).

Table 4-1. Internal Cooling Loads

Source of Load	Load
People	
Sensible heat—sitting, walking	2.5-3.2 Btu/h•ft²
Latent heat—moisture evaporation, respiration	2.5-3.3 Btu/h•ft²
(Density = 1 person/100 square feet)	
Movable office machines	
Office equipment	0.5-3.0 Btu/h•ft²
Fixed equipment	
Variable	
Luminaires	
Energy efficient, 50–70 fc	5.0-7.0 Btu/h•ft²
Air distribution fans	
Ventilation supply and recirculation (depends on cooling load)	3.0-16.5 Btu/h•ft²
Total space load range	13.5-33.0 Btu/h•ft²

There is a trend in many offices to computerize routine work while maintaining the same number of personnel. Manual operations are being increasingly replaced by mechanized systems such as word processors and copiers. Records traditionally stored in the office space are being removed to a remote computer storage facility and linked to the office by a terminal display console. The consequence of this trend is to introduce more electronic and mechanical equipment into the space, and thereby to increase cooling loads on the HVAC.

The heat generated by the lighting system within the space is a major portion of the cooling load. Most often, this load is spread throughout the space whether the lighting is located in the ceiling or integrated with the furniture, and so may be considered as a general load. If there are areas that require special lighting, the additional load produced should be taken into account in the HVAC system design. Loads generated by the fan power required to circulate air through the building and its spaces depend on the primary and recirculation arrangement for the HVAC.

The occupancy also determines the period of operation in the HVAC system. Most offices are closed on weekends, but many businesses extend their weekday hours to accommodate the preferences of users. Thus, building services are likely to be required for ten hours a day, five days a week. For organizations that have adopted a four-day week, HVAC services may be needed from ten to thirteen hours in each of the four days.

During unoccupied periods, the primary-air supply and many of the luminaires are usually turned off. Generally, perimeter heating is supplied during the winter in order to avoid the possibility of freezing temperatures and condensation on windows. After hours, cleaning staffs use the lighting as needed, but the residual conditioned air in the space is sufficient for their work.

The internal thermal loads the HVAC system must handle are generated throughout the office space. However, in HVAC design, the office is divided into interior space and perimeter space. The interior space has no interface with the building envelope, whereas the perimeter space is influenced both by the interior space, in terms of occupancy loads, and by the envelope, in terms of varying climatic conditions. This distinction is made in HVAC design because the two kinds of space represent different sets of conditions to which the HVAC must respond. Because the interior space relates only to internal thermal loads, it is discussed in this section. Perimeter space is discussed in the following section, in conjunction with external thermal loads.

In the interior space, there is no daylight, no view, no street sounds, no walls with varying temperatures. The activities and operations of users and equipment constitute the major thermal loads. This means that the interior space presents a continuous cooling load throughout the year, and that the HVAC must remove the heat generated by people, equipment, and lighting. The quality of the environment, in this case, centers around the tasks performed in the space rather than around those tasks performed in combination with any external influences.

Air movement takes on special importance in the interior space because it is a major source of environmental variation and can be used to stimulate people's perceptions. Air motion can move such objects as mobiles and plant foliage, and so add to the variety of user perceptions of the space. Another special consideration in HVAC design for the interior space is that, because this space is relatively quiet, low-frequency vibrations and airborne noises from mechanical equipment are more perceptible to users. Odors, too, are more noticeable in the general ambience of sensory adaption to the interior space.

PERIMETER SPACE AND EXTERNAL THERMAL LOADS

The envelope of the building defines the outer boundary of the perimeter space. In HVAC, the inner boundary is often determined by the pattern of air induced through perimeter terminal units. This may be on the order of fifteen feet or the depth of perimeter rooms, whichever is less. In the perimeter space, external loads on the envelope are added to the loads created by occupancy of the office space.

In designing the HVAC for the perimeter space, and in designing the envelope itself, many external factors must be considered. The most important are: the conductive transfer of heat between the inside and outside of the envelope through walls and windows; infiltration and exfiltration of air through the envelope; and heat gains to the perimeter space as a result of solar irradiation.

The thermal loads created by the external environment vary according to the time of day, the season, the overall climate, and the degree of control afforded by the building envelope. Daily humidity ratios are roughly constant, with a slight midday rise. At night, however, relative humidities rise toward saturation, causing condensation on colder surfaces.

During any operating period, the HVAC system must condition the outside air to meet the supply criteria for the space. When the outside air is mixed with reconditioned, recirculating air, the combination must provide the comfort conditions described earlier. Whenever the outside air conditions satisfy the thermal supply requirements, the central HVAC air system equipment would utilize outside air, thus eliminating the need to energize the central plant heating and refrigeration equipment.

The infiltration and exfiltration of air through the envelope should also be considered in the intake of outside air, and in thermal loads placed on the space. However, in tight modern buildings, infiltration and exfiltration rates are low. An additional thermal load on the envelope is solar irradiation, which heats the building's external surfaces and penetrates glazing.

Because dealing with the issues involved in the perimeter space and external thermal loads requires considerable integration between the architectural and HVAC systems, these issues are discussed further in the section entitled "Integrated Systems Design."

FLEXIBILITY, CONTROL, AND ZONING

Changes that occur within the office over time can alter air-distribution needs and thermal loads. New requirements for the HVAC system may result from workplace rearrangement, increases or decreases in user density in the space, and/or functional changes in user activities and equipment operations. If the building is leased to various tenants, altered HVAC requirements may arise from a turnover of tenants and/or modifications by individual tenants.

In the case of a leased building, flexibility is built into the HVAC system by designing for alternative layouts and by broadening the range of operation of the HVAC components. Ceiling distribution systems are generally constructed by the tenant and are independent of the primary-air distribution and perimeter systems.

If user density increases or if equipment is added to a particular area, both of which are fairly common occurrences in offices, the cooling and dehumidification loads for that area are increased. The trend toward installing more and more electronic equipment in offices suggests the use of local fan-coil terminals, or water- or air-cooled equipment.

Regardless of the nature of what the occupancy of the space is to be at the time of move-in, then, if changes are projected, the HVAC system must be designed with the flexibility to accommodate these changes. This ensures that user requirements and comfort needs can continue to be met in the future.

Variable thermal loads may be handled by varying either the volume or the temperature of the air. An all-air system, however, may need excessively large primary ducts to provide the necessary cooling or heating for the space. A broad thermal range can be achieved by the use of terminal coils, which can control the degree of temperature drop across the coils. In addition, terminal fans can maintain a constant air movement within the space by recirculating air locally in amounts proportional to the variable air volume received from the primary supply. Thus, a fan-coil arrangement provides both a broad flexibility in handling thermal loads and a constant air supply to the space.

In the open-plan office, visual/acoustical screens and partitions leave an open layer throughout the space. This layer usually extends from about five feet above the floor to the ceiling. The air-mixing zone created by the ceiling diffusers is therefore uninterrupted by any arrangement of the screens or any workplace layout. Return air, which is taken past the luminaires into the ceiling plenum, also remains uninterrupted with any workplace configuration.

Ceiling terminal units may be placed anywhere in the ceiling to handle local thermal loads. Control is sensed at the terminal return, providing a good aggregation of the local conditions. In large open-plan offices, the major limitation is in the size of the primary-air supply to the terminals.

For an all-air system in an open office, the central plant usually provides all the cooling, heating, dehumidification, and humidification. The size of the primary duct must be very large to handle the thermal and humidity loads in the space, and therefore may increase the depth of the ceiling-floor sandwich. Further, the fan power necessary for central air handlers is high.

An alternative arrangement is to process only outside air through the central plant. Terminal systems then handle the sensible cooling and heating as needed. This arrangement allows the primary ducts to be reduced in size by as much as half, and to supply the terminals with a sufficient amount of cool, dry air to handle the basic interior load.

Figures 4-5 through 4-10 illustrate a large open office in which the HVAC layout incorporates a very small primary-air system in the floor-deck cavity. Fan-coil terminals cool the interior spaces and cool or heat the perimeter spaces. To save space and costs, the terminal coil piping is integrated with the sprinkler system.

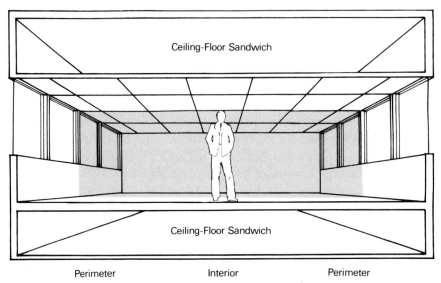

Ceiling-Floor Sandwich

Ceiling-Floor Sandwich

| Perimeter | Interior | Perimeter |

The perimeter space is affected by the infiltration and exfiltration of air and humidity through exterior walls and by solar irradiation, as well as by thermal loads from risers/equipment.

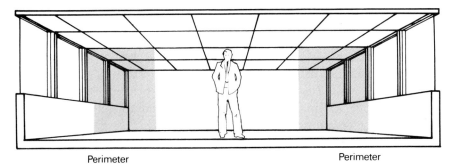

| Perimeter | Perimeter |

No daylight, no exterior view, no steel sound, no walls with varying temperatures. Users and equipment constitute major thermal loads of interior space.

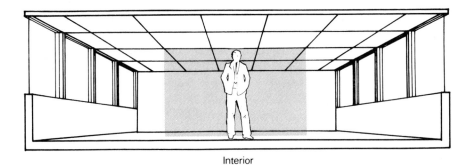

Interior

Figure 4-5. Characteristics of perimeter and space

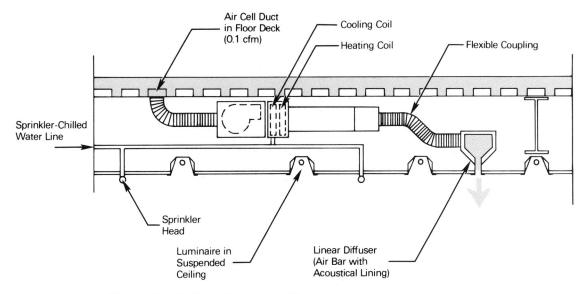

Figure 4-6. Ceiling-floor sandwich

In the closed-plan office, the floor-to-ceiling partitions require that air be distributed to each office separately to ensure air movement within every space. A desirable solution would be simply to plug in ceiling diffusers as needed. The dual duct system came closest to this by mixing air in a terminal that was supplied by hot and cold air from separate ducts. This system, however, is highly space- and energy-consuming. In general, HVAC flexibility tends to be limited in the closed plan, particularly in situations where occupancies may vary over time and change thermal loads.

HVAC zones are also more difficult to control in closed offices than in open offices. A thermostat in the return-air stream, either along a corridor or in the ceiling plenum, does not sense the variations in individual offices. Perimeter-wall induction units with cooling and heating coils, however, do offer independent control of conditions in perimeter rooms. If ceiling fan-coil terminals are used, adjacent perimeter rooms may be zoned for the same exterior wall exposure. Separate terminals may be used to provide the proper comfort conditions for spaces with widely varying thermal loads.

In all cases, regardless of whether the office is a closed or an open plan, and regardless of the degree of flexibility required for the HVAC system, control of the environment is the key issue. Designing the system according to zones enhances this control. A zone is a space or series of spaces whose thermal loads vary similarly and therefore call for similar control. Within the zone a thermostat sensor controls the air to the spaces of the zone. This sensor is placed in the return air stream for an aggregated assessment of the conditions in the spaces so that the air supply can satisfy the thermal loads properly.

Zones in an office building are defined first in terms of floors and then, within each floor, in terms of interior and perimeter spaces. Spaces with variable occupancies, such as conference rooms, require separate control zones. The perimeter areas are further divided into zones according to orientation toward the sun. For a rectangular building facing east and west, the perimeter zones become the east and west sides of the building. In this case, each zone's cycle of solar exposure is reasonably consistent throughout the year. With a rectangular building that faces north and south, however, the south façade is subject to high solar variations through different seasons, while the north façade is shaded fairly consistently.

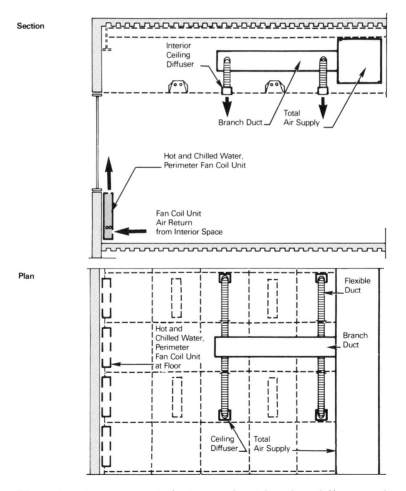

Figure 4-7. Low pressure/velocity supply with ceiling diffusers and separate system, hot and chilled water, perimeter fan coil units at floor

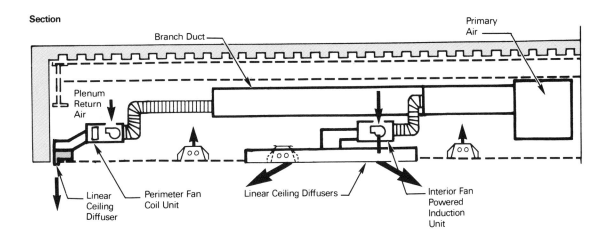

Branch Duct

Primary Air

Plenum Return Air

Linear Ceiling Diffuser

Perimeter Fan Coil Unit

Linear Ceiling Diffusers

Interior Fan Powered Induction Unit

Plan

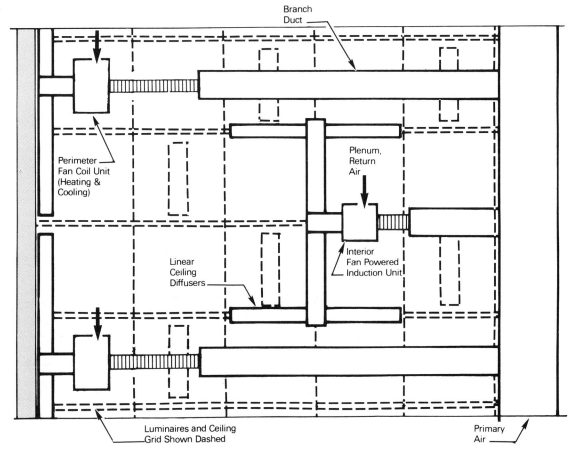

Branch Duct

Perimeter Fan Coil Unit (Heating & Cooling)

Plenum, Return Air

Interior Fan Powered Induction Unit

Linear Ceiling Diffusers

Luminaires and Ceiling Grid Shown Dashed

Primary Air

Figure 4-8. Medium velocity supply with interior fan-powered induction unit, perimeter fan coil unit, and linear ceiling diffusers

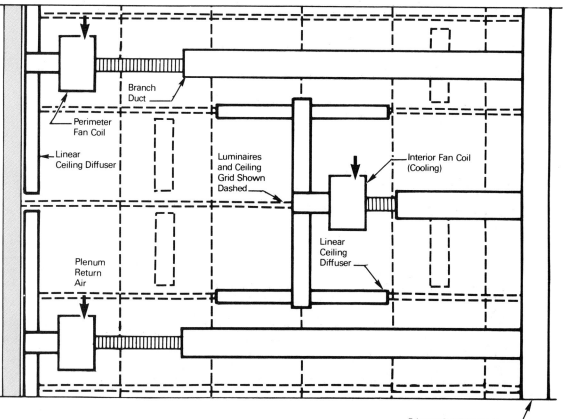

Figure 4-9. Medium velocity supply with interior and perimeter fan coil units and linear ceiling diffusers

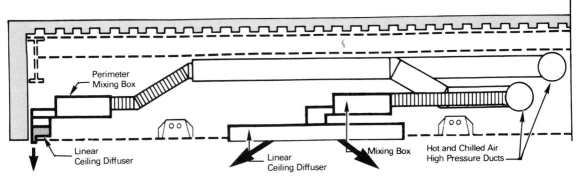

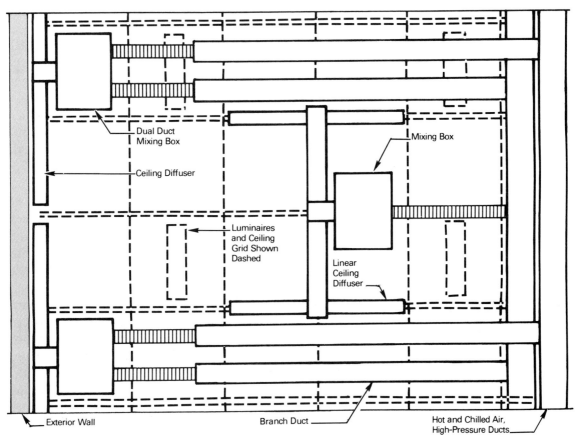

Figure 4-10. Dual duct with ceiling and perimeter linear diffusers

ENERGY CONSERVATION AND LIFE-CYCLE COSTS

During the 1960s, there was competition between electric and gas utilities to energize buildings. Electrical utilities promoted the use of high lighting levels and integrating the lighting's waste heat with the HVAC system. This encouraged the insulation of the building envelope and recovery of the interior heat to reduce the heating load. Gas utilities promoted total energy systems for co-generating on-site electricity and absorption refrigeration. These systems required somewhat lower lighting levels than the electrical systems so that the electrical demand could be reduced. However, they provided ample heat for offsetting envelope losses, and no recovery of interior heat was necessary.

Office buildings during this period were energy-intensive. The performance of any energy-conserving system was viewed relative to the system's productivity, with little regard for the amount of energy productivity required. Equipment was oversized to cover any contingency. Even in gas-fueled systems, lighting levels were high, placing a significant cooling load on the HVAC during the summer. Heat gains and losses through the building envelope, the percentage of outside air used in ventilation, and fan power were also higher than necessary.

The 1970s brought a dramatic change in energy consciousness in general, and specifically in energy consciousness related to HVAC systems in buildings. This change arose in part from a growing concern over environmental pollution, and from the culmination of that concern in environmental regulations in 1970. One result of these regulations was an escalation in the price of electricity and an intensified usage of oil. Then, in the winter of 1973–74, the Arab oil embargo occurred, marking a pivotal point in the historical development of energy-related systems. This event greatly accelerated the movement toward conserving energy, increasing the efficiency of systems, and seeking alternative energy sources. In a national quest to reduce energy consumption, the federal government has developed regulations to mandate the conservation of resources and to provide alternatives in more abundant energy sources.

The initial direction of conservation measures after the oil embargo was to limit the demand for energy by curtailing the use of equipment. In government offices, lamps were removed from luminaires, ventilation was cut back, thermostats adjusted, and overtime restricted. In some cases, those measures degraded productivity and made offices less comfortable for the users.

The 1980s brought continued emphasis on energy conservation and new concerns about improved indoor air quality. With the explosion of personal computers and the electronic office, the planning team must consider the impact on the environment from these elements. The development of DDC for computer control of the environment allows for sophisticated energy conservation by operation. These devices provide opportunities to conserve energy, stabilize costs, and sustain production by providing a quality office environment.

The summer energy flows for a typical office are shown in Figure 4-11. This diagram helps us to visualize where power is being used and rejected. In design, this knowledge assists in interfacing demand profiles with the loads on individual systems and the utility supply. The previous sections on internal and external thermal loads described the power demands on the HVAC system. These demands set the base case from which we can propose conservation alternatives.

The questions are: what can be done to reduce energy waste, and who has the expertise to guide the organization in saving energy? These questions are addressed in Figure 4-12, which indicates measures for conserving energy and divides these measures into building-use management and design issues. Architectural, mechanical, electrical, and electronic systems are included. Each idea may or may not be feasible in regard to a particular office, but in combination, these ideas do provide a basis for investigating alternatives with consultants.

The motivation to conserve energy comes first from a need to reduce the escalating annual costs for energy, and then from a need to comply with regulatory requirements to conserve energy and to use renewable resources such as solar, geothermal, and hydro- and refuse-derived fuels. Escalating energy costs are responsible for an increasing portion of the operational expenses for buildings. And as annual operating costs have grown, capital costs have also grown. Together, these two factors have brought new attention to life-cycle costing.

In designing and evaluating energy-conserving systems, then, it is important to determine the energy-cost savings both for the capital investment in equipment, and for the annual operation of the systems. Further, any additional benefits a particular design may have, such as in its interface with other systems, should be ascertained and considered as advantages and disadvantages are weighed.

In assessing the life-cycle costs of an energy system, its interrelationships with other systems must be considered, because the operation of one component often depends on the operation of another. For example, if waste heat from lighting is to be recovered, the fact must be considered that the waste heat is only available when the lighting is in use. And in terms of cooling, for instance, removing heat loads not only saves refrigeration, but can also reduce duct size and fan power. Maintaining air movement over people by recirculating air locally provides similar reductions.

A minimum expenditure of resources requires considerable integration of systems in design, in packaging of components, in simplicity of site installa-

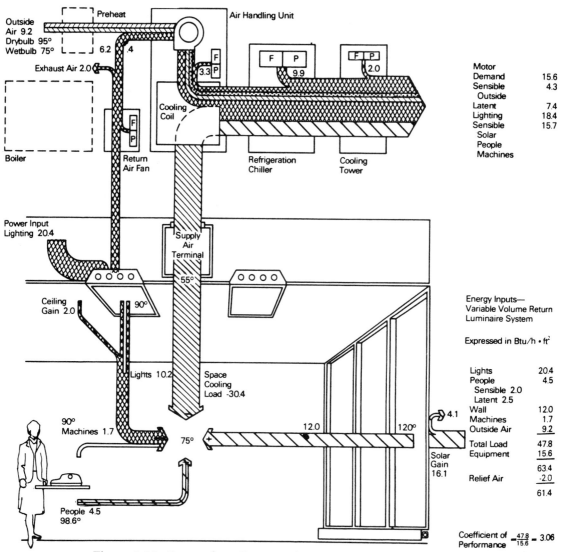

Figure 4-11. Energy flow diagram of an energy integrated system

tion, and in operation to achieve the intended performance. The rational process of putting this all together is called a systems approach. Various professional disciplines and experiences are brought together to achieve the interactions between the systems. With an integrated system design procedure, all interested parties (owner, designer, financier, manufacturer, contractor, local authority, utility, and user) can identify and contribute to the design of a successful office.

In general, through integrated design, the power and space required to move and process air will be minimized. This is reflected in a lower cost for construction. An effective HVAC system should also minimize the annual consumption of energy supplied by utilities so that annual operating costs are lowered. In addition, the design should seek to use utilities during time periods when the lowest rates are in effect.

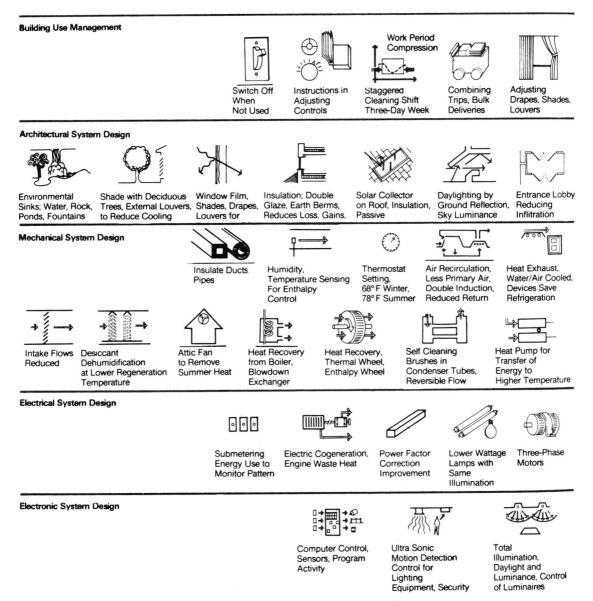

Figure 4-12. Alternate systems for possible energy conservation (*Construction Specifier,* June 1978, John Hallidane)

INTEGRATED SYSTEMS DESIGN

The HVAC system in an office must minimize both the usage of nonrenewable energy resources, and expenditures for capital and operational costs. It must fulfill users' general and specific heating, ventilating, and air conditioning needs, and, in combination with other office systems, provide a healthful, comfortable, stimulating environment that supports user tasks and facilitates their performance. Fulfilling these requirements necessitates not only considerable integration of the components of the HVAC system itself, but also the integration of each office system with all others.

This means that the HVAC, acoustical, lighting, fire safety, power and signal distribution, architectural, and interior design systems must be planned and designed through a coordinated team approach, and that the designs themselves must be functionally coordinated and integrated. In Chapter 1 on office planning, matrices indicated some of the general areas in which integration is required among disciplines and systems in regard to office subsystems and tasks. The relationship of the HVAC system to office subsystems and tasks is identified more specifically in the matrices shown in Figure 4-13.

If the planning and design project involves constructing a new building for the organization, then, as the building design begins to take shape in terms of configuration, number of floors, and rough square footages, possible schematic solutions for the HVAC system can be developed. As planning and design continues, and user requirements for each floor become more specific, the HVAC system design can be developed in greater detail. This is accomplished with constant input from system integration so that possible solutions may be evaluated for overall effectiveness in fulfilling *all* user and organization requirements.

The implementation of a design needs integration to conserve time, materials, and energy. Traditionally, the manufacturer has provided a range of products from which a contractor selects. A designer has rarely met with the manufacturer, but has relied on trade literature and sample products. In an integrated approach, the manufacturer does not just provide components, but becomes part of the design team. The owner can be assured that the whole system will function properly. Figure 4-14 illustrates the interface of those involved in the implementation of a design.

A physical integration must occur between the separate systems not only by allowing for space, but also by preserving the continuity of energy and material flows between the subsystems. The HVAC system works in conjunction with other building systems to control heat, moisture, air movement and quality, energy consumption, and costs. The interactions within and between the systems involved in controlling the office environment must be carefully integrated to reduce the consumption of utility-supplied energy (Figure 4-15).

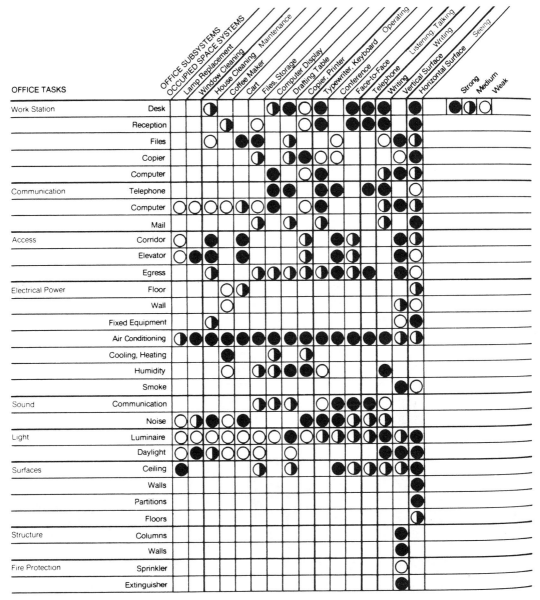

Figure 4-13. Matrix—disciplines/subsystems for HVAC interface

This allows, for example, the waste of one system to become the source for another.

A few possibilities in this regard are as follows: Energy may be recovered from exhaust air to transfer heat from the interior to the perimeter space in winter. This may be accomplished through the use of terminal heat

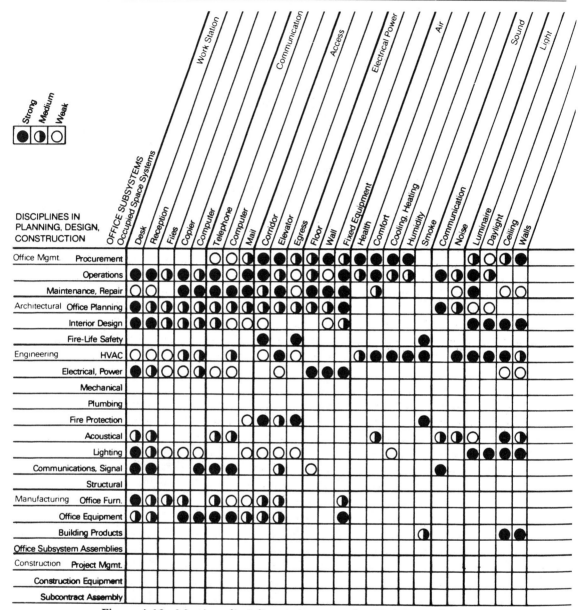

Figure 4-13. Matrix—disciplines/subsystems for HVAC interface (*Continued*)

pumps connected by a closed water loop. Another method is to install a coil water loop between the air streams of the exhaust and the outside air intake. Waste heat from system components may also be used to heat water, lessening or eliminating the need for additional utility-supplied energy for this purpose. An additional means of conserving energy is co-generation, which both provides electrical energy through a generator and uses the heat from the engine that

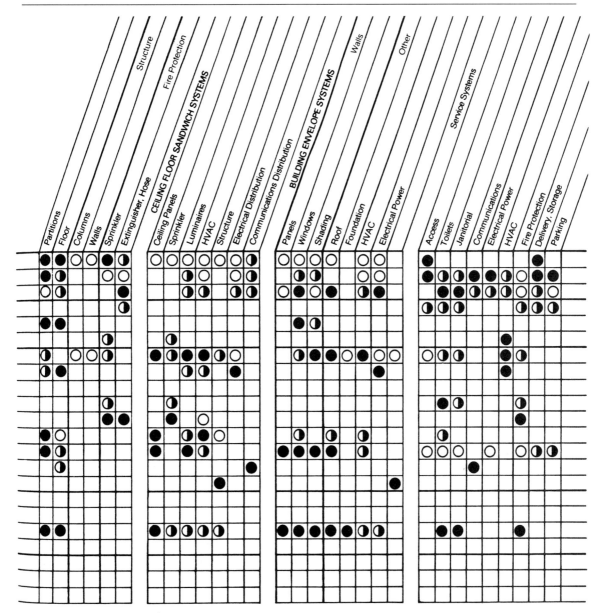

Figure 4-13. (*Continued*)

drives the generator. An apparently inefficient generator thus becomes an efficient component of an integrated system.

The following sections describe major areas of systems integration, including the ceiling-floor sandwich, partitions, the building envelope, lighting, acoustics, and fire safety. Some additional discussions related to specific HVAC components are included in the appendix to this chapter.

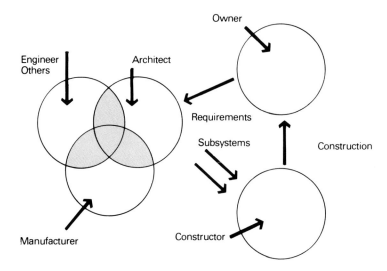

Figure 4-14. System integrators

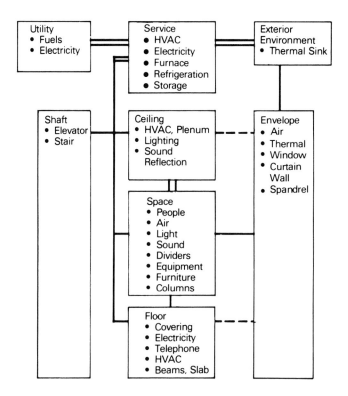

Figure 4-15. Integration of energy and material flow between spatial systems

Ceiling-Floor Sandwich

The space required for the ceiling-floor sandwich should be minimized to reduce costs for its construction and to allow more floors within a given height restriction. Reducing the ceiling-floor sandwich means that all services and clearances must be compressed in height. One way to do this is to decrease the size of the primary-air supply ducts. By moving the cooling or heating normally achieved by coils in a central plant to local fan coils or zone air handlers, the dimensions of primary-supply ducts may be reduced by as much as one-half. In addition, this reduces the size of the central plant fans and coils. The primary ducts may become small enough to pass through lattice beams without affecting the structural continuity of the space.

Structural beams govern the basic depth of the ceiling-floor sandwich. Usually, primary-air ducts parallel the primary structural beams and pass under the secondary beams. Where there are lattice beams or reinforced penetrations in the web, small ducts may be passed through them (Figure 4-16).

In the main, HVAC equipment can be accommodated in a space 18 to 24 inches deep. Clearly, the center lines of separate systems should not coincide or

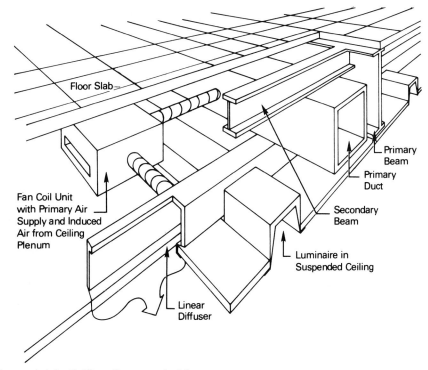

Figure 4-16. Ceiling-floor sandwich

height requirements will be increased. Systems may be combined, however, as in a ceiling grid that incorporates linear diffusers, or sprinkler piping that is used for terminal-coil circulation, or steel decking cavities that also function as primary ducts.

The incorporation of a ceiling plenum offers considerable flexibility for the layout of branch ducts and terminal units, and is therefore useful both in closed and open offices. Access to the plenum for equipment maintenance is simplified by a grid-supported ceiling with removable panels. Terminal units generally have side access for maintaining fans, coils, and dampers; some units have bottom-hinged service panels.

Partitions

The partitions in an office space greatly affect the distribution of air within that space. The full-height partitions in closed offices define rooms in which air must be separately supplied, recirculated, and exhausted. The degree of flexibility allowed for the layout patterns of ceiling air diffusers depends upon the ceiling construction, and the ducting to a branch duct or terminal. Perimeter fan-coil units may be used to circulate and condition the air in each room. Recirculation may be done through partition vents, through the ceiling plenum, or through terminal fans. Exhaust and central recirculation are done through corridors or the ceiling plenum.

In open-plan office spaces, the air-mixing zone of the space is not affected by visual/acoustical screens. This allows for maximum flexibility in the HVAC layout.

Building Envelope

The design of the building envelope has a direct impact on the HVAC system and therefore requires the architect and the HVAC specialist to work closely together on all aspects of envelope design. Energy conservation criteria now dictate design concepts which point to an energy-integrated architecture sensitive to the energy potential of natural sources. Central to this goal is the evolution of the building envelope from a static barrier to a dynamic skin through which natural energy sources provide a portion of the energy required in the buildings of the future. Issues that should be considered include heat flow through walls, roof, and windows; direct solar heat gain; infiltration and exfiltration of air through cracks; and the permeability of the building's skin to moisture.

Thermal transmission through walls, windows, and roof depends on the difference between inside and outside temperatures. The outward flow of energy is determined from the product of the temperature drop, surface area, and the thermal transmittance or U-value. The conductive transfer of heat is almost independent of building orientation. Wind on external surfaces, for example, brings the temperature of those surfaces nearer that of the outside air.

High thermal resistance is desirable to reduce the effects of variations in the outside air on the inside space. Thermal insulation should be placed in the walls and in the roof, the continuity of metal should be broken where possible, and windows should have thicker-than-normal glass or double glazing.

For a new building, the requirements of the governing energy code may determine the thermal performance required. The ASHRAE standard on energy-efficient design should also be consulted. Tradeoffs should be considered for daylight and the consequent reduction in power needed for luminaires and cooling when appropriate.

Solar irradiation places an additional thermal load on the envelope and the office's perimeter space by heating external surfaces and penetrating glazed areas. Figure 4-17 shows the monthly solar intensity through a good venetian blind for 30 to 40 degree latitudes, which covers the United States. It is interesting to note that whether we are in the southern or northern part of the country, the north wall is thermally stable with respect to solar gain. In other words, we get no variation throughout the year anywhere in the United States in terms of solar input on the north wall. However, during the so-called winter season, the solar gain through eastern and western exposures may vary from 70 to 90 Btus per square foot of glass, depending upon whether we are in the north or south. As spring and summer approach, solar intensity from the east and west reaches a maximum of around 140 Btus per square foot.

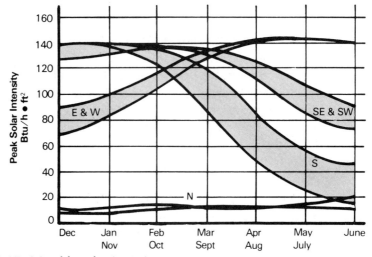

Figure 4-17. Monthly solar intensity

But it is the southern exposure which is subject to the greatest variance in solar intensity. It is particularly interesting that in the southern part of the United States, the solar gain from the south reaches its maximum during the winter months and its low point during the summer months. This means that during the so-called winter season, depending upon the amount of glass we have, the outdoor conditions, and the energy level inside the building, we could very well have a reversal of load—a demand for cooling due to sun gain on the south side.

It's this interaction and this variation of sun input on the walls of a building, coupled with the level of lighting in the interior, that creates the serious problem in terms of environmental control. Because this solar load is radiant by nature, it can only be removed after it enters the space and is absorbed by objects within the space. It is the interaction of this kind of energy, plus the energy input within the space, that really affects our comfort because it affects the thermal balance. Because of these balance problems, systems are often overcontrolled, resulting in aggression between different components of a same system attempting to respond to a partial heating and cooling situation.

The major issue concerning solar irradiation and the building envelope is control. External sunshading devices such as overhangs, projections, louvers, grilles, and screens can be effective in intercepting radiation (Figure 4-18). These solutions have the advantages of being air-cooled and minimizing reflection to adjacent buildings. Further, they may be designed to intercept solar radiation during certain seasons and allow it to penetrate glazing in others. For example, automatic louvers designed to track the sun exclude direct sunshine while admitting daylight and providing a glareless view.

Reflective coatings on windows may reduce radiation gains and lessen daylight glare, but the radiation reflected onto adjacent buildings and grounds may be excessive. Tinted, heat-absorbent glass does absorb radiation and prevent it from entering directly into the perimeter space. However, the window itself heats, producing radiant heat within the space which might not be accounted for in the balance of comfort conditions in the space (Figure 4-19).

Outside shading by trees, screening, ivy, landforms, and other buildings are other means of solar control. Deciduous trees provide shade in summer and allow the sun to penetrate in winter (Figure 4-20). Infiltration and exfiltration of air through a loosely constructed envelope add to the heating and cooling loads of the space and generally should be minimized. In mild climates, however, the use of operable windows for ventilation should not be overlooked. Hopper or awning windows are a simple means of directing fresh air upward and mixing it with the air in the space. The possible drawbacks to operable windows are that they afford no filtering or control over humidity. The HVAC system is usually nominal in mild climates, often only heating by convection under the windows in winter.

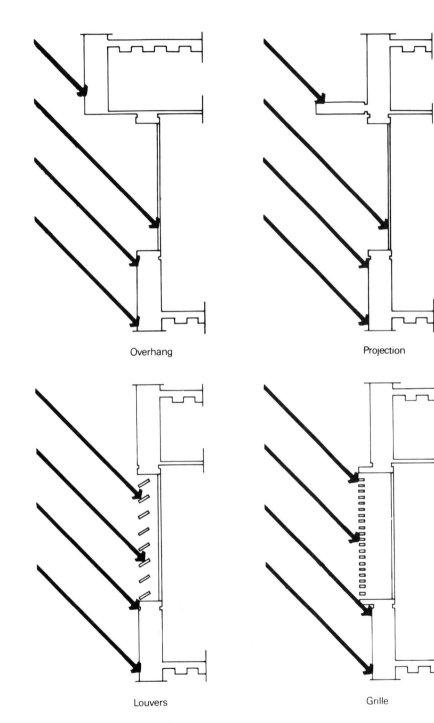

Overhang

Projection

Louvers

Grille

Figure 4-18. Sun control

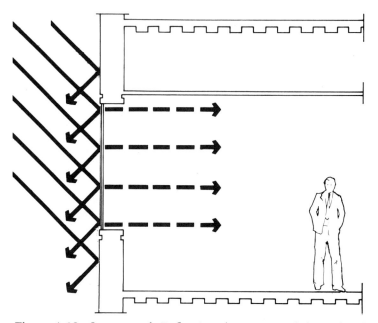

Figure 4-19. Sun control. Reflective glass or tinted, heat-absorbent glass reflects or absorbs solar radiation. Radiant heat from the window may penetrate the space.

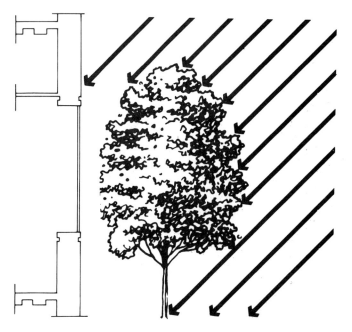

Figure 4-20. Sun control

HVAC equipment that allows little arrangement flexibility, such as fan-coil units under windows, should also be considered in the envelope design. In situations in which fan-coil units are to be installed, for example, internal full-height partitions are generally aligned with the window mullions. This arrangement then reflects back on the layout of ceiling diffusers.

Recently, the building envelope has received new attention in relation to heat and light control. Results of this attention include window diffusers, glazing, coatings to reduce solar heat gain, and special blend blinds that reflect light toward the ceiling. Experiments with natural illumination promise substantial energy savings through sophisticated use of atriums, light shelves, clerestory windows, and multiple sources of reflected and diffused daylight.

It is clear that the building envelope is the key mediator between a continuously fluctuating external environment and the desired stability of the interior environment. This new emphasis on the building envelope has spurred interest in passive solar design and has encouraged efforts to integrate passive strategies with advanced technologies to minimize energy use. Ideally, the building envelope would emulate the life model by responding instantly to external thermal variations by activating a sophisticated response mechanism to maintain an appropriate thermal balance.

In many instances, however, passive systems alone cannot provide the flexibility and responsiveness required for adequate thermal control. In those cases, sensitive design handling that blends passive concepts with advanced technology yields the most rational and effective results. Figure 4-21 illustrates an interior thermal window louver based on energy-conscious design criteria that uses the building envelope as a passive solar collector. The interior thermal louver can best be described as a building envelope system which responds passively to external stimuli to maintain interior thermal stability. It is passive in the sense that it responds and makes use of natural energy flows rather than actively initiating change.

Figure 4-22 shows the effectiveness of the thermal louver as a shading device intercepting solar radiation, in contrast with (1) exterior sun louvers, (2) reflecting glass, (3) clear glass with venetian blind, and (4) unshaded clear glass. A space load imposed by the solar radiation is drawn on a radial scale in the chart for the various solar orientations. The center represents a maximum thermal transfer through the envelope. Unshaded clear glass presents the highest load with the greatest orientation variation.

Thermal louvers not only significantly reduce interior space heat gain, but also fulfill the following functions:

- Reducing direct glare while admitting daylight and view
- Supplementing winter heating by collecting solar energy and distributing it to other areas within the building

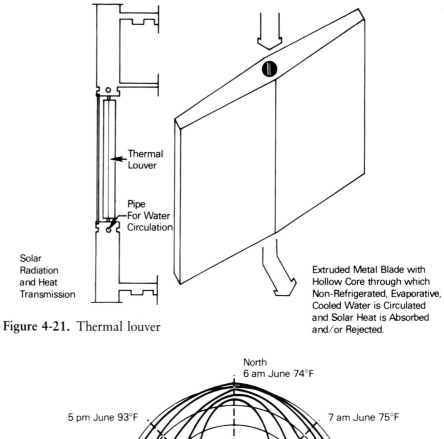

Figure 4-21. Thermal louver

Thermal Louver

Pipe For Water Circulation

Solar Radiation and Heat Transmission

Extruded Metal Blade with Hollow Core through which Non-Refrigerated, Evaporative, Cooled Water is Circulated and Solar Heat is Absorbed and/or Rejected.

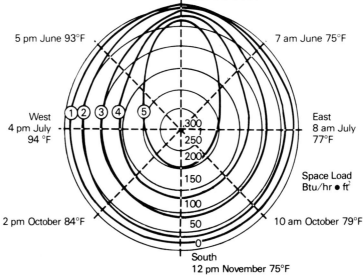

North
6 am June 74°F

5 pm June 93°F

7 am June 75°F

West
4 pm July
94 °F

East
8 am July
77°F

Space Load
Btu/hr • ft²

2 pm October 84°F

10 am October 79°F

South
12 pm November 75°F

Figure 4-22. Effectiveness of various shading devices in intercepting solar radiation. Curve 1, thermal louver; curve 2, exterior sun screen; curve 3, reflecting glass; curve 4, clear glass with venetian blind; curve 5, clear glass.

• Offsetting winter perimeter heat losses and maintaining the thermal balance for comfort near windows

Acoustics

The speech privacy needs of the users and the overall acoustical balance of the office space generally require control of the noise produced by the HVAC system's components. The continuous airborne noise from building equipment, including HVAC terminal units, diffusers, fans, luminaires, and transformers, when under full load, should be less than the noise criteria (NC) curve generally described for an acceptable background noise level. On the average, the HVAC system needs to be about NC_4 below the NC curve for the space. However, the acoustical control required for HVAC components relates to the particular organization's situation and the needs of its users, and therefore necessitates strong input from the acoustical specialist.

Lighting

The lighting system places a direct load on the air conditioning system. Lighting systems account for about 30 to 50 percent of the air conditioning load. Careful planning by the team is required to ensure that proper lighting utilizing energy-conserving luminaires is chosen and that the air conditioning designer works with realistic values for the lighting load.

Daylight through windows or skylights, as a source of light within the office space, requires integration of the lighting and HVAC systems and the design of the building envelope. The issues to consider are the degree to which light can be provided and solar irradiation can be controlled and used to advantage; the amount of light provided versus any additional loads on the HVAC system caused by radiation and conduction through the windows; and construction and annual costs for the windows over the costs for installing and operating a more extensive lighting system.

Fire Safety

The interface of the HVAC system with fire safety is mainly related to maintaining the compartmentalization of space required for fire safety, reducing the spread of smoke, and combining the piping for the two systems. The last of these represents a significant opportunity for systems integration. A 1979 provision by the National Fire Protection Association permits sprinkler piping to be integrated with the HVAC system.[8] In large open offices, such combined piping can afford substantial savings in construction costs.

Because fire can spread between fire compartments through HVAC ducts, the ducts are equipped with dampers that have fusible links. In order to avoid the spread of smoke within the office, air recirculation must be closed down. Therefore, it is important for the HVAC system to be controllable through the fire-safety communication system.

SUMMARY

HVAC systems provide environmental comfort to office users. This comfort is achieved by controlling fresh air, air movement, air filtering, humidity, and internal/external thermal loads.

Using the team planning concept, integration with other technical disciplines makes the finished project more efficient. Such efficiencies help meet required goals in energy conservation and life-cycle costing. Attaining user comfort, yet meeting those required goals, takes creativity and innovation. It is not an easy task and requires a team planning effort.

Notes

1. *ASHRAE Standard for Energy Conservation in New Building Design*, ASHRAE 90-75. New York: American Society of Heating, Refrigerating, and Air-Conditioning Engineers.
2. *ASHRAE Standard for Energy Conservation in New Building Design*, ANSI/ASHRAE 90A-1980. Atlanta: American Society of Heating, Refrigerating, and Air-Conditioning Engineers.
3. *ASHRAE Standard for Energy Efficient Design of New Buildings Except Low-Rise Residential Buildings*, ASHRAE 90.1-1989. Atlanta: American Society of Heating, Refrigerating, and Air-Conditioning Engineers.
4. *ASHRAE Standard for Thermal and Environmental Conditions*, ASHRAE 55-66. New York: American Society of Heating, Refrigerating, and Air-Conditioning Engineers.
5. *ASHRAE Standard for Thermal Environmental Conditions for Human Occupancy*, ASHRAE 55-74. New York: American Society of Heating, Refrigerating, and Air-Conditioning Engineers.
6. *ASHRAE Standard for Thermal Environmental Conditions for Human Occupancy*, ANSI/ASHRAE 55-1981. Atlanta: American Society of Heating, Refrigerating, and Air-Conditioning Engineers.
7. *ASHRAE Standard for Ventilation for Acceptable Indoor Air Quality*, ASHRAE 62-1989. Atlanta: American Society of Heating, Refrigerating, and Air-Conditioning Engineers.
8. *Standard for the Installation of Sprinkler Systems*, NFPA 13, 1978. Quincy, MA: National Fire Protection Association.

APPENDIX 4A

HVAC Component Options

The HVAC air/water distribution to occupied space consists of a series of interfacing components that filter, condition, move, and control the temperature of the air throughout a building. These may be grouped into filters, central-plant or zone air handlers and conditioners, fans, ceiling terminals, and perimeter terminals. Each component plays a particular role in the distribution process, but the compatibility of components is dependent upon the overall integration required to meet the demands for an economical, quality environment.

Filters

The outside air brought into the space is generally filtered to remove particulates. Systems include dry throwaway or cleanable filters, roll filters, bag filters in cartridges, and electrostatic precipitators for the finer particles. Face velocities for the air through a filter are about 500 fpm with 0.4″ to 0.5″ water gauge (wg) pressure drop or 0.2 lb/ft². Particulates are caught in the fibers of the filter, which is then discarded or cleaned at regular intervals (Figure 4A-1).

Electrostatic precipitators positively ionize the air through a high-voltage wire at about +12,000 volts direct current (DC). The air passes through plates which are alternately at about +6,000 volts DC and a ground. Positive ions move to ground where they adhere to particles in the air. This causes the charged particles to move to a grounded plate where they are held by a viscous coating. Plates are washed in a preset cycle to remove deposits.

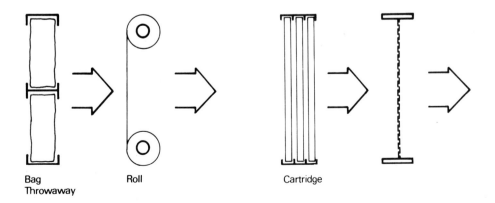

Bag
Throwaway   Roll   Cartridge

Figure 4A-1. Filter types

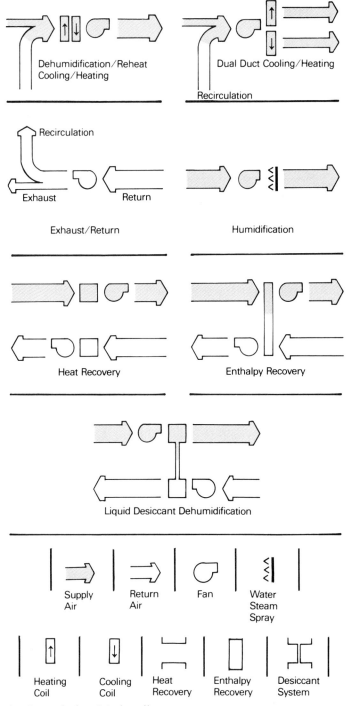

Figure 4A-2. Central plant/air handlers

Central-Plant or Zone Air Handlers and Conditioners

Outside air and air recirculated from conditioned spaces is cooled or heated, and dehumidified or humidified to provide primary air to the office space. Cooling and heating of the air is generally by coils circulating chilled and hot water, respectively (Figure 4A-2). Dehumidification is conventionally achieved by cooling air below its dew point to condense the water vapor. Alternatively, desiccant systems may be used in which liquids such as lithium chloride and solids such as silica gel absorb moisture directly from the air. Here the heat gained through absorption is removed, often with unrefrigerated cooling water, and the desiccant is reconcentrated in a heated regenerator. Because the cooling is at an elevated temperature, the efficiency of the system is increased and less energy is consumed. The desiccant regeneration process, by which the absorbed moisture is removed, may be done at a low 140 to 180°F. This also increases the efficiency of the system as a whole, and these temperatures interface well with solar flat-plate collectors and waste-heat sources.

Humidification can be done by simple sprays of water which simultaneously cool the air. A spray of steam may be used where the air has to be heated.

Cooling for coils is done conventionally by a refrigeration process using a centrifugal chiller. Where heat is readily available above 200°F, an absorption chiller may be used. Heat is transferred from the evaporator to the condenser in the chiller. The heat of compression in a centrifugal chiller is passed to the condenser, whereas in an absorption process, it is divided between the condenser and an absorber. Heat from the condenser is usually rejected to the outside environment by a cooling tower. This tower cools by a water spray and a draft of air induced by fans. More innovative and energy-conserving systems are evolving in which this low-temperature energy is used for preheating or, with a heat pump, is brought to a useful temperature for water heating, perimeter heating in winter, or possibly for desiccant regeneration.

Exhaust air from the space represents a waste of energy in the conditioning of the air to that space. This air may be recirculated to the central plant or zone conditioner, or within a terminal unit. Energy may also be recovered from the exhaust air by a runaround loop between coils in the exhaust and outside-intake air streams, or by an enthalpy wheel.

Fans

Fans are used to move air about the building. The largest ones are associated with the central plant or zone air-handling and conditioning equipment. Low-pressure fans deliver through large ducts, whereas high-pressure systems use smaller, often round, ducts. The fan power required increases with higher pressures, velocities, and air volumes. Constant-volume distribution used to be the basic arrangement, but nowadays a variable air-volume (VAV) system is often used to conserve fan power and the volume of air.

Centrifugal fans are the general type used in HVAC. Here, rotating vanes throw air outward from the center into the duct. The vanes may be backward-curve or forward-curve. Higher efficiencies are usually achieved with backward-curve blades.

Because the tip speeds are greater, there is less flow, static pressures are higher, and stability is better with varying volume. Centrifugal fans are usually used in central plant systems, ranging in volume from 700 to 500,000 cfm and static pressures from ¼" to 15" of water.

Axial flow fans are mounted directly in a duct and, as the airfoil blades rotate, impart an axial velocity to the air. This velocity is very sensitive to the pitch of the blade, which has led to the development of a variable-pitch blade for variable-volume control. Axial flow fans are characteristically high-velocity, low-static pressure systems ranging in volume from 2,000 to 125,000 cfm and static pressures up to 3" of water. Figure 4A-3 shows a two-stage fan arrangement in series with contrarotating impellers. These reduce the rotation losses of the air in the duct and consequently reduce the static pressure. Wave guides provide another acceptable method of reducing this air rotation. With high blade-tip velocities, the sound/power levels tend to be higher than with centrifugal fans. This means that acoustical attenuators should be used in the duct after the fan, and in the recirculation duct, because sound carries in all directions.

Propeller fans are simple axial fans used for high-volume exhaust at a low-pressure head, less than 0.5" of water.

Ceiling Terminals and Diffusers

The terminal units may control, recirculate, mix, heat, cool and distribute air between the primary supply and the supply to the space. The usage of the ceiling-terminal arrangements shown in Figure 4A-3 depends on the cooling, heating, recirculation, and distribution needs of the space. Their historical development can be seen from

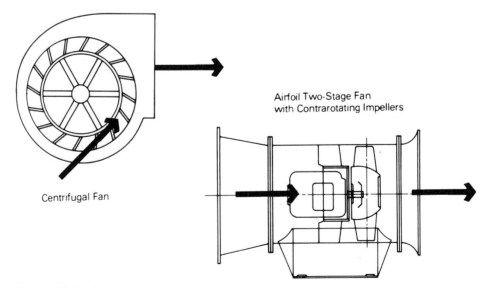

Airfoil Two-Stage Fan
with Contrarotating Impellers

Centrifugal Fan

Figure 4A-3. Fans

constant-volume all-air systems, to variable air-volume systems, and fan-coil arrangements that recirculate the air locally, taking heat from the luminaires through the ceiling plenum.

Constant-volume terminals provide a simple means of delivering air to the space from a central or zone air-conditioning plant. They interface with a conventional cooling/heating system and satisfy a steady space load.

Reheat terminals are used to reheat the air in a zone when temperatures drop too low. These terminals reheat the air by means of coils. Clearly, reheating refrigerated air is an energy-wasting practice. Usually, reheat terminals are used with systems which supply refrigerated air at a constant volume and temperature. A damper system for providing a variable volume of primary air can, however, be used to modulate the refrigerated air produced, thereby decreasing the need for reheat terminals.

Dual duct systems consist of separate cold and hot primary-air distribution ducts throughout the building. Terminals mix these air streams in the appropriate proportions for the local space, providing a constant volume of conditioned air to the space. The dual duct system was developed in the period of 1952–62, during the New York construction boom, as a flexible HVAC arrangement for tenants. Additional ductwork for the all-air system is space-consuming, costly, and requires considerable fan power to maintain the air supply. Control and flexibility are its main merits. It has a low static load and excellent reduced noise characteristics.

A central plant or zone air handler provides the cooling/dehumidification and the heating/humidification for the respective air streams. It should be noted that the cooling loads produced by the lighting were not excessive during this period.

Variable air-volume control uses a damper to vary the volume of primary air through the terminal to the space. Under reduced thermal load, the air volume is throttled back, and the fan power is reduced to save energy. Unfortunately, a variable air volume to the space reduces the discharge velocity at the diffuser, which reduces both the throw and mixing of the air in the space.

Nozzle induction terminals recirculate warm air from the luminaires through the ceiling plenum for use in winter perimeter heating. In these terminals, dampers throttle the primary air through the nozzle and combine it with air induced from the plenum to provide a near-constant volume to the space under variable load. They have the characteristics of VAV control, but limit the range for induction. Heating coils may be added to supplement the plenum heat if necessary.

Fan induction terminals maintain a constant circulation of air to the space. This ensures a steady air movement regardless of the thermal load. In offices, air is induced for the plenum to take advantage of the heat from the luminaires. A significant advantage is that the VAV primary supply can be throttled down under reduced thermal load to conserve fan power. Centrifugal fans or blowers are used. Noise is kept to a minimum by isolation and careful selection of fans.

Fan-coil induction terminals have features of fan induction, but also control the local thermal loads. A low-volume, constant primary supply satisfies the basic outside-air and humidity load requirements. Induced plenum air is cooled or heated by separate coils to handle the sensible space loads. This is particularly suited to large open-plan

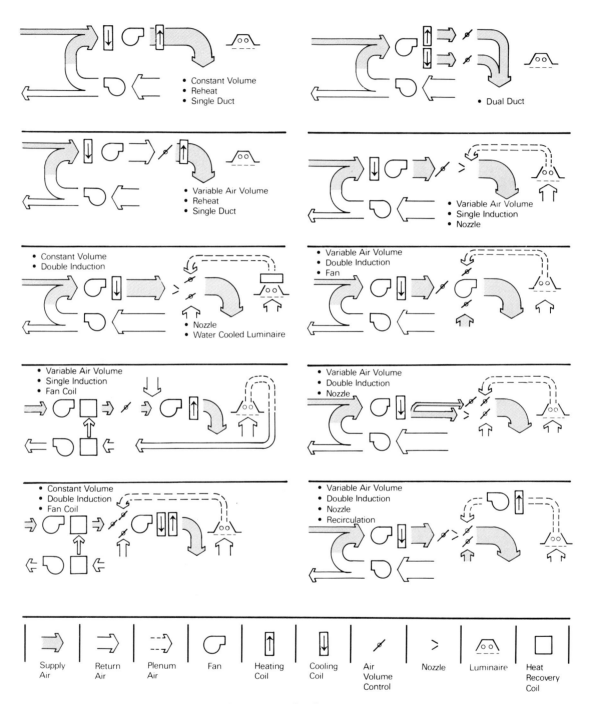

- Constant Volume
- Reheat
- Single Duct

- Dual Duct

- Variable Air Volume
- Reheat
- Single Duct

- Variable Air Volume
- Single Induction
- Nozzle

- Constant Volume
- Double Induction

- Nozzle
- Water Cooled Luminaire

- Variable Air Volume
- Double Induction
- Fan

- Variable Air Volume
- Single Induction
- Fan Coil

- Variable Air Volume
- Double Induction
- Nozzle

- Constant Volume
- Double Induction
- Fan Coil

- Variable Air Volume
- Double Induction
- Nozzle
- Recirculation

| Supply Air | Return Air | Plenum Air | Fan | Heating Coil | Cooling Coil | Air Volume Control | Nozzle | Luminaire | Heat Recovery Coil |

Figure 4A-4. Seasonal operation for fan coil

182

offices in which large primary ducts would be difficult to accommodate. Where there is a sprinkler system, the same piping may be used for a line to the coils in the terminal unit. As shown in Figure 4A-4, a unitary heat pump may be included in the fan-coil terminal as a source of cooling or heating. The heat pump is connected with a closed water loop as a sink for the cooling or heating. This removes the sensible load from the central or zone plant. Also illustrated is a variation in which the cooling is by fan induction with VAV control, and the heating is through a fan coil on the plenum recirculation. Nozzle induction for VAV control of the cooling may be combined with fan-coil heating on recirculation. This is suitable for variable cooling and heating loads that may occur in perimeter areas.

The seasonal operation for a fan-coil terminal arrangement is as follows: In summer, the outside air is dehumidified in a central plant. Air is recirculated and cooled centrally or in a zone to handle the heating load. As the cooling load decreases in the fall, central circulation is reduced. Then, when the outside conditions are right, just the outside air is used, as an economizer cycle. In winter, air is recirculated through the warm plenum and into the space. Heating coils in the perimeter terminals provide additional heating.

Air-terminal unit connections to the ceiling diffusers may be direct, by flexible ducts. For larger units with larger distribution, a header duct may be provided. Air to each separate diffuser needs to be balanced in terms of required air flows. Butterfly or louver dampers are inserted at the diffuser or terminal unit to enable manual adjustments to be made. Where there are penetrations through a fire compartment, a fusible link is incorporated to close the duct automatically when there is a fire. A proportioning damper also projects into the airstream of the duct to divide the appropriate air volume.

Diffusers may have circular, rectangular, or linear distributions. The controlling vanes are adjustable to alter the distribution of air in the space. Conical sections of circular diffusers may be raised or lowered, or, in linear diffusers, retractable slot sections can be adjusted to set the level and direction of mixing air in the space. A variety of linear diffusers can be incorporated within the ceiling panel system and as boots on luminaires. In installing linear diffusers, it is important to attenuate the noise from terminals and the primary supply by lining them with sound-absorbing materials. This also insulates a cool air supply from a warm plenum.

Perimeter Wall Terminals

A convector is a heater installed below windows to offset winter heat losses. Hot water or low-pressure steam is passed through coils or cast-iron sections. Electrical elements may also be used. Heating is by natural convection, and the area around the unit must be free to allow the air to circulate (Figure 4A-5).

Perimeter terminal units may supply air to the window through ceiling diffusers or through wall induction units. Ceiling units have the advantage of leaving the perimeter wall area free. Individual tenants can then arrange for their own HVAC distribution under separate contract.

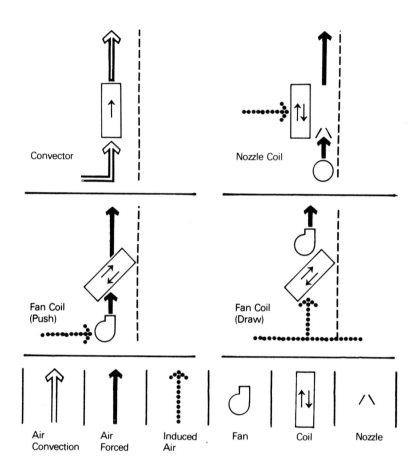

Figure 4A-5. Perimeter wall units

Chapter 5

FIRE SAFETY

Ralph Gerdes

Updated by William E. Fitch

The previous chapters have discussed acoustics, HVAC, and lighting and the special interrelationships they share. In order to complete the planning and design process, the element of fire safety must be considered. The organization and the planning and design teams must assume the responsibility of providing an environment that will serve the needs of the users and that will protect them under emergency conditions.

Consideration of fire problems is not only a moral obligation on the part of the planning and design teams, but is mandated by law as well. A fire safety program which protects the lives of occupants and firefighting personnel, minimizes property damage, and maintains continuity of operations needs to be established. Program objectives must be defined and the level of need determined, with problem areas recognized and solved. The application of fire protection principles reduces the possibility of danger to life and financial investments.

The losses of a fire-damaged company can be devastating. The most obvious and tragic loss is that of life. However, companies may also suffer from the loss of property, the mental and emotional stress of employees, the loss of customers, the loss of a return on capital investment, the costs of retaining key personnel during a shutdown and of replacing equipment, and the inability to defend against unjust claims.

There are precautions that a company can and must take which will provide a fire-safe environment. Building codes and standards, which we discuss later in the chapter, give planning teams mandatory points of reference for the safety aspects of design. The systems concept gives planning teams guidance for alternate ways of meeting the safety needs of their organization. It does so by assuring maximum fire protection, while not unduly limiting planning options.

THE SYSTEMS CONCEPT

The systems concept for fire protection integrates all services and safety features to form a total system. This is based on the understanding that one fire protection feature does not necessarily work alone or independently and is affected by the operation of other features. The integration of features can result in a more efficient, safe and economical structure.

The steps within a systems approach for fire protection are as follows:

- Determine the desired level of safety (goal).
- Examine each occupancy hazard (problems).
- Identify problem areas.
- Meet fire safety goals by limiting fire potential (solution).

This goal-oriented systems approach has several advantages over the approach of merely meeting code requirements. It provides a quantitative measure of fire safety goals. It enables the planning team to evaluate the entire design with its built-in safety features for size, cost, aesthetics, degree of protection and, above all, relationship to the needs of the particular organization. It therefore enables the planning team to provide a level of protection often beyond code minimums at the lowest possible cost.

In working with a fire protection engineer to integrate a safety system into their office design, planning teams need to consider how the following elements will be handled:

- Building construction
- Fire detection
- Occupant response
- Notification/communications
- Exiting
- Smoke control
- Fire control/suppression
- Fire department response
- Emergency power

BUILDING CONSTRUCTION

The type of construction classification for a building is a function of the use of combustible or noncombustible elements and their degree of fire resistance. Building codes define when a material is noncombustible, although the definition may vary from code to code. Aesthetics, availability of materials, ease of maintenance, structural requirements, fire protection considerations and economy are all factors in the selection of materials and thus in determining the construction type.

Inherently fire resistant construction or directly applied protection provide the greatest flexibility for interior design, since there are fewer restrictions on the type of ceiling materials, lights, air diffusers, column enclosures, etc. that planners can use in their office design.

Fire protection considerations involve construction materials or assemblies that are able to withstand fire for a specified time to permit occupants to evacuate, to protect firefighting personnel in the building, and to minimize property damage. This involves structural and nonstructural elements and the interior finish of the building.

Fire protection of the building structure can be attained by several methods. The structure may inherently have the required fire resistance rating, as in the case of concrete or masonry walls, floors, roofs, columns or beams. The protection can be provided by directly applied fire-resistant materials, such as sprayed on fireproofing or cast-in-place materials. The protection can also be provided by protective membranes such as gypsum board or suspended acoustical ceilings.

Building codes establish minimum types of construction based on occupancy, height and area limits, area separations, and provision of automatic sprinkler systems.

Interior finish is a principal element in determining the fire hazard of buildings. Interior finish includes the materials that form the walls, partitions, ceilings, and other finish surfaces and/or the materials, such as paint, that are applied to these surfaces. The characteristics of interior finish materials relevant to fire problems are their ability to spread fire and generate smoke when burning. Materials that have high flamespread characteristics, or produce large quantities of smoke, are obviously undesirable.

In addressing life safety, building codes limit the flamespread and smoke developed rating that an interior finish material may have (Table 5A-1 in Appendix 5A) according to the building's occupancy, suppression equipment and location of the material used. When selecting finish materials, the planning and design team must therefore be aware of the code requirements for various office areas and select materials accordingly.

Lists of tested fire-resistance rated constructions and ratings on tested materials are published by various independent laboratories, such as Factory Mutual Research, Omega Point Laboratories, Underwriters Laboratories, the model code groups, industry associations, and individual manufacturers.

DETECTION

The first step in combating a fire is to realize that it exists. Smoke detectors, heat detectors and automatic sprinkler systems increase the probability that a fire will be detected in its early stages before major harm has been done to life and property because they work automatically (often before humans are aware of the fire). In addition, manual alarms should be provided in case a fire is detected by office occupants and as a backup to the automatic devices. For detection purposes, the open-office landscape offers a distinct advantage in that all occupants in an open office are immediately aware of a local problem. Building occupants can then activate manual alarm units, and standpipe systems with waterflow indicators or other fire safety features. The effectiveness of automatic systems is enhanced if building size and configuration allow them to be "zoned" to give an accurate location of a fire within a building.

The kind of detection devices required by building codes is based on the occupancy hazard. Generally, manual fire stations are required for a business occupancy. For details, see Tables 5A-1 and 5A-2 in Appendix 5A.

Smoke Detectors

Types of smoke detectors include ionization and photoelectric. The ionization type detects invisible particles of combustion at the earliest stage of a fire while photoelectric detectors require visible products of combustion. However, the difference in response time in an office is negligible.

Smoke detectors generally are not mandated within the occupied space of an office building. However, they may be required within the air handling system as a part of the smoke control requirements. This is typically found in buildings designed with an atrium or in highrise office buildings. The spacing and coverage of the smoke detectors may vary for different manufacturers and the conditions of their testing and listing must be considered in designing the system.

Heat Detectors

Heat detection devices fall into two categories: fixed temperature and rate-of-rise. Fixed temperature detectors respond at a predetermined temperature, while rate-of-rise devices activate on an increase in heat at a greater rate than normally expected. Some detectors combine both operating principles.

Heat detectors are also located at the ceiling level and are generally visible so that they are exposed to heat generated from a fire. Spacing and area coverage of these detectors vary from different manufacturers.

AUTOMATIC SPRINKLERS

Automatic sprinkler and standpipe systems should be equipped with water-flow indicators which will activate an alarm upon flow of water. These devices are generally concealed along with the sprinkler piping or are on the main risers.

The location and layout of the sprinkler heads are affected by the performance characteristics of the specific sprinkler head being used, the hazard of the occupancy being protected, and the layout of the office space. The involvement of these devices with the ceiling system demonstrates again the importance of mutual consultation between lighting, sound, HVAC and fire specialists as part of the planning process.

Manual Alarms

Manual alarm units are generally mounted on walls located near stair entries and exit doors. Manufacturers' catalogs can be reviewed for finishes and mounting conditions.

OCCUPANT RESPONSE

Occupants can play a role in providing a safer building when an emergency action program is planned. Occupants should be instructed in exiting procedures and the use of manual alarms, portable fire extinguishers, and standpipe hose systems. Knowing the emergency egress pattern beforehand can save time, thus minimizing the hazards to personnel. Trained office personnel can provide on-the-spot firefighting capabilities for small fires and aid in crowd control during the emergency.

NOTIFICATION AND COMMUNICATION

Another necessary component of a fire safety system is a rapid means of letting occupants and firefighters know that a fire has been detected. For lowrise buildings, this component can be supplied by fire detection devices that, when activated by heat or smoke, set off a general alarm. However, highrise buildings need a more sophisticated system of voice communication for the selective evacuation of floors and for firefighting operations.

Alarm devices such as horns, bells or speakers can be concealed since they are meant to be heard rather than seen. With proper design it is possible to incorporate the alarm system into the masking system, music or intercom systems if the elements of those systems provide the necessary reliability and audibility. This option will require close consultation between acoustics and fire specialists.

EXITING

The detection/notification system must be coupled with an adequate exit system if the fire safety plan is to be considered complete. A good exit system is essential for protecting the lives of occupants and permitting firefighters access to the building. Codes require adequate exit schemes based on calculated travel distance to specified exits (Table 5-1). Giving planners greater flexibility, the systems approach bases exit design on the ability to move occupants from the fire area to an area of internal or external safety within a reasonable period of time.

An effective exit system is characterized by clear travel paths, separation of exits, and adequate exit capacity. Exit routes follow the normal travel pattern in an open office and are marked by distinctive wall graphics or creative exit signs. Space dividers must not confuse occupants or make it hard for them to find the exits. Exits and exit signs must be properly illuminated.

As with the notification system, creating an effective exit scheme for highrise buildings poses special problems for office planners. Studies show that it is impossible to evacuate a highrise building totally within a reasonable time. Therefore, in such buildings occupants of a fire area must be able to move to a place within the building that affords safety from fire and smoke. Occupants can move horizontally to a protected part of the same floor or vertically to a floor above or below the fire.

To provide for escape to a protected part of the same floor, a way of passage—or horizontal exit—must be constructed through a wall of two-hour fire-resistant material. This wall divides the floor into separate areas that function as places of refuge in the event of a fire (Figure 5-1). Double egress doors are used to provide a door swinging in the direction of exit travel from either side of the wall.

Besides its value in establishing fire refuge areas, the horizontal exit may reduce the distance to vertical exits (stairs) and the number and width of such exits. These benefits may make the horizontal option appealing to the planning team. On the other hand, planners may feel that the construction of fire-resistant walls limits the flexibility of their office design and may prefer to design separate floors of buildings as refuge areas.

Table 5-1. Building Code Requirements: Number of Persons per 22-inch Unit of Exit Width

	Doors		Stairs	
	NS[a]	AS[b]	NS[a]	AS[b]
1988 Uniform Building Code[c,d]	91.5	91.5	91.5	91.5
1988 Standard Building Code	110	110	59.5	59.5
1990 BOCA National Building Code	110	147	73	110
1985 National Code of Canada[e]	90	90	60	60
1988 NFPA Life Safety Code	110	110	73	73

[a] NS—Nonsprinklered.
[b] AS—Automatic sprinklers.
[c] The number of persons given for a 22″ width is based on 50 persons per lineal foot.
[d] Stair capacity from a floor is based on the occupancy load of that story plus 50% of the adjacent story which exits through the level under consideration.
[e] Includes revisions through January 1989.

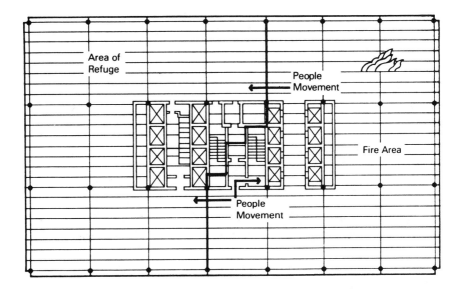

Figure 5-1. Fire separation

SMOKE CONTROL

Smoke control is important in assuring the effectiveness of the exit scheme. The objective of smoke control is to limit the spread of smoke until occupants can reach a place of safety and until the fire department can respond to the fire. Methods that can be used to accomplish this include building pressurization, mechanical exhaust, natural ventilation, and stair pressurization. Most smoke control systems are combinations of these techniques.

The pressurized-building approach involves exhausting the fire area while pressurizing the surrounding area. This will create a lower pressure in the affected zone relative to the unaffected areas. This pressure differential will reduce the migration of smoke. While other mechanical smoke control devices can be provided, this form of system is the most common and requires only a minimal amount of additional equipment. Its installation must, of course, be coordinated with the planning team's HVAC specialist.

Natural venting systems use shafts or operable windows to exhaust smoke from a building. Another means of venting is to provide a vestibule at each stair with direct access to the outside atmosphere. This would essentially be a smokeproof tower.

Stair pressurization involves forcing air into the stair shaft at the top, at the bottom, or at several different levels to prevent smoke migration into the shaft.

Building codes also deal with smoke control through a combination of stair pressurization, smokeproof towers and HVAC systems. The major difference between the building codes and the systems approach is the specification aspect of the code versus the performance criteria of the systems approach.

FIRE CONTROL/SUPPRESSION

A major component in a fire safety plan is the in-building means of controlling or suppressing the fire. The most common devices are automatic sprinklers, standpipes, and portable extinguishers.

Automatic Sprinklers

Automatic sprinklers are activated by the heat of a fire and direct water only on those areas where a fire is actually occurring. Thus, water damage is minimized while the chances of saving lives and property are improved. Performance records documented by the National Fire Protection Association show sprinklers to be effective and reliable in controlling and extinguishing fires in approximately 97 percent of those U.S. offices having sprinkler systems.[1]

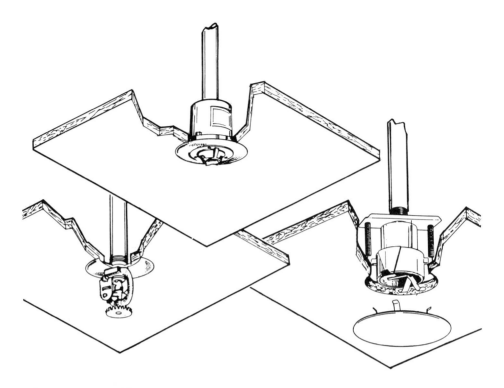

Figure 5-2. Sprinklers

Sprinklers are located at the ceiling and may be concealed, recessed, or readily visible (Figure 5-2). Manufacturers can provide an assortment of styles and finishes. Sprinkler piping concealed above the ceiling and recessed or concealed sprinklers provide a reliable source for fire fighting yet remain unobtrusive (Figures 5-3, 5-4).

When detailing or specifying sprinklers, the desired location of the sprinklers in the ceiling should be made clear. Building officials usually require automatic sprinkler installations to be designed in accordance with the National Fire Protection Association's *Standard for the Installation of Sprinkler Systems* (NFPA 13) which specifies the pipe size based on the number of sprinkler heads being supplied. It also limits the coverage per head to 200 square feet. As an alternate, it allows office areas to be designed for light hazard which will allow the pipe sizes to be hydraulically calculated and the sprinklers to be spaced up to fifteen feet on centers, and up to seven and one-half feet from walls. This allows a coverage of 225 square feet per sprinkler and possibly reduced pipe sizes.

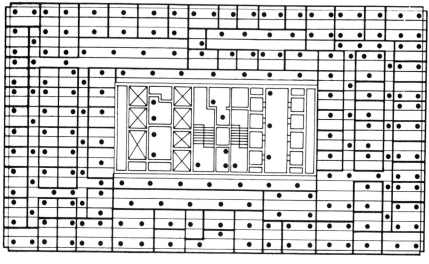

226 Sprinklers

Figure 5-3. Reflected ceiling plan showing atypical placement of sprinklers with closed-office layout

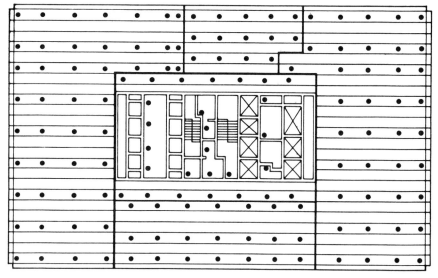

146 Sprinklers

Figure 5-4. Reflected ceiling plan showing uniform placement of sprinklers with open-office layout. Since there are no full-height partitions in office landscape, it is possible to achieve an optimum uniform pattern. Full-height partitions necessitate more sprinklers to provide required coverage of all floor areas. A cost-sensitive design and integration of sprinkler locations on a modular basis in the ceiling geometry are achieved.

194

The open office layout can result in a much more economical sprinkler installation. An added advantage is that office arrangements can be changed without affecting the sprinkler head location. In the conventional closed-office layout the movement of a partition may necessitate the relocation, removal, or installation of additional sprinkler heads.

Standpipes

Standpipes provide a local concentrated source of water for firefighting operations. They can be used by trained office personnel or firefighters. National Fire Protection Association Standard 14, *Standpipe and Hose Systems,* provides guidelines for the design and installation of standpipe systems. Standpipes are generally located in stairways and other portions of a building so that all portions of the building will be within 30 feet of a nozzle when attached to 100 feet of hose.

Extinguishers

Portable fire extinguishers also give occupants and firefighters a tool for controlling or extinguishing fires. They should be provided in accordance with the local code or with the National Fire Protection Association's *Standard for the Installation, Maintenance, and Use of Portable Fire Extinguishers* (NFPA 10). This standard recommends that extinguishers suitable for Class A fires (combustible materials) be located so that the maximum travel distance from any point to an extinguisher does not exceed 75 feet. Extinguishers for protecting Class A hazards should be water types or multipurpose dry chemical. The amount of floor space an extinguisher will protect depends on its rating. For example, an extinguisher with a 2A rating can protect 6,000 square feet while one with a 4A rating can protect 11,250 square feet of office occupancy.

FIRE DEPARTMENT RESPONSE

Alarms from detection devices should be relayed automatically to the local fire department. Additional telephone lines can provide immediate voice communication with the fire department. An annunciator panel, indicating the zone of fire alarm origin, should be located at the department response point. Elevators must be provided with an automatic recall override system to assure their safety and to enable firefighting personnel to reach the floor where the fire began.

EMERGENCY POWER

To ensure the operation of fire safety features, emergency power should be provided for detection and alarm circuits, HVAC systems, exit lighting, exit signage, communications systems, elevators and fire suppression systems.

Generally, this is provided by a permanently installed on-site power generation system which must operate within ten seconds of primary power failure for certain systems. The emergency lighting system can be operated off some types of electric batteries, but must provide power for at least one and one-half or two hours depending on the applicable code (see Table 5A-1 in Appendix 5A).

HIGHRISE BUILDINGS

In recent years, highrise buildings have become of special concern. Although fire safety is a function of the same elements as any other building, there are special considerations which pertain only to highrise buildings:

- The building is usually beyond the reach of the fire department's ground-operated aerial equipment (usually 75 feet or higher), thus requiring internal fire suppression.
- The building is of such a height as to result in an unreasonable evacuation time.
- There is a potential for a significant stack effect which can spread smoke throughout the building.

Because of these special concerns, building regulations generally contain special sections with specific provisions for highrise business or residential buildings.

To solve these problems of fire safety in the highrise, three design approaches may be considered:

- Automatic sprinklers—providing complete automatic sprinkler protection that is hydraulically calculated, fully supervised, and served by a two-source water supply.
- Vertical compartmentation—separating a building into five-story sections with each group of floors being independently contained by substantial construction and vertical shaft intervention.
- Horizontal compartmentation—dividing each floor by fire walls into segmented fire areas.

The decision on which approach to implement is made during the design phase. When working on an existing building, the approach is set and the office plan must evolve around existing conditions. Provisions of the model building codes for highrise buildings are listed in Table 5A-2 in Appendix 5A.

BUILDING CODES AND STANDARDS

Almost every structure and building system must meet the provisions of a building code. A building code or standard, when adopted through legislative action, mandates minimum requirements for the design and construction of buildings.[2] Adoption of codes tends to follow a geographic pattern; the Uniform Building Code is favored in the West; the Standard Building Code in the South; and the BOCA National Building Code in the East and Midwest. (Building code provisions are listed in Tables 5-1, 5A-1, and 5A-2.) These tables show the differences between the codes as a result of divergent writing groups and their experiences.) Because of legislative changes made to the codes during the adoption process, the planning and design team should check with building authorities at all government levels to ensure design conformity within the proper code or codes. This should be done before working drawings are begun.

Codes apply primarily to new construction but can also apply to the remodeling, alteration, or repair of an existing building, depending on the value of the alteration in relation to the building value and the time frame of alteration. Changing the occupancy or use of a building will generally require bringing the building up to the fire safety requirements of the current building code. The administrative section of individual codes specifies the applicability of its code to an existing building.

Codes establish only minimum requirements for life safety and for the confinement of fire within a building, and it is often necessary for a building owner or the planning and design team to go beyond the code guidelines to meet the particular needs of the building or users.

The systems concept for fire protection described earlier in the chapter gives office design planning teams guidance in providing a total safety system that not only meets code requirements, but ensures occupant safety, minimum fire damage, and protection of essential services within the context of a particular building. Planning teams wishing to integrate a fire safety system into their total office design must, however, understand that despite the obvious value of building codes, their very nature may impose constraints on their preferred design. The system of "equivalencies" enables the planning team to find satisfactory compromises between building code constraints and the design they wish to implement.

PROBLEM AREAS

Planning teams may find themselves frustrated by the lack of coordination between various code requirements. Codes address the necessary elements for fire safety on an item-by-item basis and may not seem to be concerned with the relationship of the parts to the whole. For example, exiting design parameters may be constant for all buildings without regard to differences in the combustibility or noncombustibility of the particular construction, the nature of the occupancy, or the smoke control system in the building. Codes also do not spell out the options or equivalencies by which planning teams might meet individual code requirements.

A second problem is that codes may not reflect the latest developments in design and materials. The basis for code requirements is the result of testing, experience, and consensus judgment of the code-making body. This development process creates a time lag which can span several years between the introduction of a new concept or product and its recognition in a code. As a result, building codes seldom keep pace with new concepts, materials, and construction.

The poor relationship of building codes to the open-office concept exemplifies the rigidity and their tendency to lag behind new concepts. The codes do not address themselves to the open-plan concept, but only to the elements of compartmentation of a building layout. Corridors, for example, are divisions of space that act as a protection device by physically separating people from hazards within a floor of a building. The "intent" of codes regarding corridors is to limit the spread of smoke, heat, and fire, thereby achieving adequate life safety for the building occupants and reducing exposure to surrounding environments. Therefore, the codes usually require corridor partitions to extend from floor to floor, and to comply with fire-resistance and interior finish flame-spread requirements. Within the open-office plan, there are no "corridors" as defined by building codes. How, then, could a planning team opting for the open-office plan meet building code requirements for corridors?

The solution to such conflicts between designs and code restrictions lies in the "equivalency" process. Planning teams concerned with providing fire safety within an office plan tailored to their particular organization must effectively state equivalencies to get approval from the appropriate agencies.

EQUIVALENCIES

Although codes do permit tradeoffs, they do not state which options will satisfy their requirements. Nor do they tell planning teams the procedure to follow to obtain approval for alternative means of meeting requirements. It is entirely up to planners to find options and justify them to approval agencies. Incomplete or improper tradeoffs may result in rejection of the design. In order to avoid such rejection, a qualified fire protection engineer might well be engaged to assist the planning and design team in designing protection equivalent to the intent of code requirements. This method would provide valuable savings in both time and money.

When the planning team's specialist finds that the proposed plan is not in compliance with the specification requirements of an applicable code or standard, and at the same time believes that it is meeting the performance levels desired, he or she should prepare an equivalency statement as soon as possible. This statement should contain three basic elements:

- The provisions of a code or standard that are not being complied with, and their intent.
- The additional or alternate methods provided to achieve the required level of performances.
- The professional judgment of the planning and design team (including the fire protection engineer) that the alternate methods, as provided, are equivalent to the provisions of the code or standards.

The equivalency statement is submitted to the appropriate official (building department, fire department, fire marshal) for approval and, when approval is granted, design or construction can proceed. All letters of equivalency and approval should be maintained by the planning and design team and the building owner in a permanent file to avoid problems with future fire inspections.

SUMMARY

We have looked at fire safety from the viewpoint of meeting code requirements without having to unduly sacrifice desired elements of an office plan. This is a negative approach to integrating fire safety into an efficient design. A more positive approach to fire safety, one that goes beyond mere adherence to codes or even the stating of equivalencies to prove that a particular design meets code standards and intent, is discussed earlier in the section on the Systems Concept. Planning teams should expect and insist that the fire safety elements of their design form a coherent system for maximum protection of life and property.

When all these features of fire safety are integrated properly by the planning and design team, the goal of a fire-safe environment can be achieved. The system will:

- Detect the presence of a fire and alert supervisory personnel, the fire department and building occupants.

- Establish a system of orderly evacuation to a safe area.
- Control the movement of smoke and other combustion products.
- Provide the fire department with access, in-building communication, fire-fighting water supply, and ventilation.

The elements previously discussed are necessary components in a fire safety program. But when making planning considerations, team members should be able to recognize any potential problem areas and the solutions for these areas, and be prepared to integrate these solutions into the overall design scheme.

Notes

1. National Fire Protection Association, Sprinkler Performance Tables, 1974.
2. Model codes are written and published by fire safety and building specialists, and serve as guidelines for building officials in state and local jurisdictions. For the sponsoring organizations who publish the model codes, refer to Appendix 5B.

APPENDIX 5A

Table 5A-1. Building Codes

General Building Code Provisions	1988 Uniform Building Code	1988 Standard Building Code	1990 BOCA National Building Code	1985 National Building Code of Canada	1988 NFPA Life Safety Code
Occupancy use group (business) designation	B2 701	B 405.1	B 303	D 3.1.2.1.(1)	Business 4-1.8
Travel distance					
Sprinklered	200'	250'	250'	45 m (148ft)	300'
Not sprinklered	150'	200'	200'	40 m (131ft)	200'
	3303 (d)	1103.1	807.5	3.4.2.4. (1)	26-2.6
Doors to swing in direction of exit travel	Hazardous areas or over 50 people	Hazardous areas or over 50 people	Hazardous areas or over 50 people	If more than 60 people.	Hazardous areas, in exit enclosures, or over 50 people
	3304 (b)	1114.1.2	813.4	3.3.1.8(1)	5-2.1.4.1

General Building Code Provisions	1988 Uniform Building Code	1988 Standard Building Code	1990 BOCA National Building Code	1985 National Building Code of Canada	1988 NFPA Life Safety Code
Minimum exit corridor width	44″ if serving 10 or more occupants 36″ if serving less than 10	44″	44″ if serving 50 or more occupants 36″ if serving less than 50	1100 mm (44″)	44″
	3305(b)	1105.3	810.3	3.4.3.1 (1)	26-2.3.2
Minimum exit corridor ceiling height	7′ 3305 (c)	7′ 2001.2.1	7′ 708.1	2100 mm (7′) 3.4.3.5 (1)	7′-6″ 5-1.5
Maximum dead-end corridor	20′	20′	20′	9 m (30′)	20′ 50′ if sprinklered
	3305 (e)	1104.2	810.2	3.3.5.2(1)(c)	26-2.5.2
Minimum of 2 exits	30 or more occupants, 10 or more people on second story, any basement, or more than 2 stories Table 33A	Accessible to each tenant space on every story	Every floor area. One exit allowed if not over two stories, 3500 sq. ft. and 75′ travel distance. 809.2	More than 60 people, or more than 200 m² per floor and not more than 2 stories in height	Every part of every floor
	3303(a)	1103.2.1	809.3	3.4.2.1(1)(2)	26-2.4
Maximum allowed capacity exiting horizontally	50% of total required exits	50% of total required exits	No Limit	50%	50%
	3308 (a)	1116.1	815	3.4.1.3(1)	5-2.4.1

Table 5A-1. Building Codes (*Continued*)

General Building Code Provisions	1988 Uniform Building Code	1988 Standard Building Code	1990 BOCA National Building Code	1985 National Building Code of Canada	1988 NFPA Life Safety Code
Capacity of floor area providing horizontal exit	3 sq. ft. per person	3 sq. ft. per person	3 sq. ft. per person	0.5 m² (5 sq.ft.) per person	3 sq. ft. per person
	3308(c)	1116.3.1	815.3	3.4.7.10(1)	5-2.4.2.4
Exit signs	Required if over 50 people	Required	Required	Required if over 2 stories, or over 150 people.	Required
	3314(a)	1118.2	823.1	3.4.6.1(1)	26-2.10
Maximum flame spread rating for interior finish	4204(a) Tables 42A, 42B	704.3 Table 704.3	922.5 Table 922.5	3.4.4.1(1) 3.1.11	26-3.3
Enclosed vertical exitways					
NS[a]	25	75	25	25	75
AS[a]	75	200	75	25	200
Other exitways					
NS	75	75	75	75(walls) 25(ceiling)	75
AS[b]	200	200	200	150	200
Rooms or areas					
NS/AS	200	200	200	150	200
Emergency lighting	Required when over 100 persons	Required when over 150 persons	Required for 1hr in all buildings required to have more than one exit	Required for ½ hr.	Required for 1½ hr. when building is 2 or more stories above level of exit dis-

Table 5A-1. (*Continued*)

General Building Code Provisions	1988 Uniform Building Code	1988 Standard Building Code	1990 BOCA National Building Code	1985 National Building Code of Canada	1988 NFPA Life Safety Code
					charge, or 100 or more occupants above or below exit discharge, or more than 1,000 total occupants.
	3313(b)	1118.2.5	823.4	3.2.7.3 (1) & (2)	26-2.9.1
Automatic sprinklers	Required in buildings not accessible from the exterior by the fire dept. and in rubbish chutes and terminal room	Required in buildings not accessible from the exterior by the fire dept.	Required in buildings over 75′, in hazardous areas and in windowless stories	Required in basements, buildings not accessible from the exterior by the fire dept. and in trash chutes	Required in buildings over 75′ and in hazardous areas
				3.2.1.5(1) 3.2.5.1(5)	
	3802(b)1	901.5	1002	3.5.3.2(6)	26-4.2.2
Dry standpipes required if	4 or more stories but less than 150′ in height	NA	Buildings more than 30′ above or below level of fire department access	NA	NA

203

Table 5A-1. Building Codes (*Continued*)

General Building Code Provisions	1988 Uniform Building Code	1988 Standard Building Code	1990 BOCA National Building Code	1985 National Building Code of Canada	1988 NFPA Life Safety Code
	3805(b) Table 38-A	902.4	1012.2.1 1012.3.1		
Wet standpipes required if	More than 150' in height or less than 4 stories in height but more than 20,000 sq. ft. per floor. Not required with automatic sprinklers	2 stories or more and over 50' in height	Buildings more than 150' in height.	Over 3 stories or exceeds areas in table 3.2.5A	NA
	3805(b) Table 38-A	902.3	1012.2.1 1012.3.1	3.2.5.4(1)	
Minimum of 3 exits where population exceeds	500 people	500 people	500 people	NA	NA
	3303(a)	1103.2.2	809.2		
Minimum of 4 exits where population exceeds	1000 people	1000 people	1000 people	NA	NA
	3303(a)	1103.2.2	809.2		
Minimum construction of wall providing horizontal exit	2 hour	2 hour	2 hour	2 hour	2 hour
	3301(b)	1116.1.1	815.2	3.1.8.8(1)	5-2.4.3.1
Minimum construction of openings in horizontal exits	1½ hr. automatic closing	1½ hr. self- or automatic closing	1½ hr. self- or automatic closing	1½ hr	1½ hr. self- or automatic closing

Table 5A-1. (*Continued*)

General Building Code Provisions	1988 Uniform Building Code	1988 Standard Building Code	1990 BOCA National Building Code	1985 National Building Code of Canada	1988 NFPA Life Safety Code
	3308(b)	1116.2.2	916.1	Table 3.1.6.A	6-2.3.2 5-2.1.8
Exits illuminated all times building is occupied	Required	Required	Required	Required	Required
	3313(a)	1118.1.1	823.1	3.2.7.1(1)	26-2.8
Minimum intensity at floor level of exit illumination	1 fc	1 fc	1 fc	10 lx (1fc)	1 fc
	3313(a)	1118.1.1	823.2	3.2.7.3(1)	5-8.1.3
Manual fire alarm	NA	Required if over 500 people total or more than 100 people above or below the street floor	Required if sprinklered and over 75′ in height, or not sprinklered and over two stories above or below level of exit discharge	Required if over 300 people, more than 3 stories, or more than 150 people above or below the first story.	Required when building is 2 or more stories above level of exit discharge, or 100 or more occupants above or below exit discharge, or more than 1,000 total occupants.
	903.1.1	1016.9		3.2.4.1(1)	26-3.4.1
Automatic fire alarm	NA	NA	NA	NA	NA

a NS = nonsprinkled
b AS = automatic sprinklers

Table 5A-2. Building Code Provisions for Highrise Buildings

General Building Code Provisions	1988 Uniform Building Code	1988 Standard Building Code	1990 BOCA National Building Code	1985 National Building Code of Canada	1988 NFPA Life Safety Code
Definition of highrise building	Floors used for human occupation located more than 75 ft above the lowest level of fire department access.	Floors used for human occupation located more than 75 ft above the lowest level of fire department access.	Floors used for human occupation located more than 75 ft above the lowest level of fire department access.	More than 36 m (118 ft) between grade and top floor level or more than 18 m (59 ft) with total occupant load above the first level exceeding 300 persons per available unit of stair exit width	A building more than 75' in height above the lowest level of fire department vehicle access to the floor of the highest occupiable story.
	1807(a)	506.1	602.1	3.2.6.1.(1)	3-2
Compartmentation	NA	In lieu of AS 506.9	NA	Optional 3.2.6.2.(5)	NA
Automatic sprinkler	Required	Required if building over 150' in height	Required	Optional. Required if floor area exceeds 1000 sq. m. (10765 sq. ft.) 3.2.6.2.(6)	Required
	1807(a)	506.10	602.3	3.2.6.6.(1)	26-4.2.2
Smoke control	Required 1807(g)	Required 506.5	Required 602.10	Required 3.2.6.2.(1)	NA
Detectors in hazardous areas	Required 1807(d)	Required 506.2	Required 602.6	Required 3.2.4.10.(1)	NA

Table 5A-2. (*Continued*)

General Building Code Provisions	1988 Uniform Building Code	1988 Standard Building Code	1990 BOCA National Building Code	1985 National Building Code of Canada	1988 NFPA Life Safety Code
Fire department communication system	Required 1807(e)3	Required 506.3.4	Required 602.8	Required 3.2.6.7.(1)	Required 26-4.2.3.3
Public voice communication system	Required 1807(e)2	Required 506.3.3	Required 602.7	Required if more than 36 m (118 ft) between grade and top floor level. 3.2.6.8	Required 26-4.2.3.2
Voice alarm	Required 1807(e)1	Required 506.3.2	Required 602.7	Required 3.2.6.7.(1)	NA
Emergency telephones	Every 5th floor in each required stairway. 1807(j)	Every 5th floor in each required stairway. 506.8.2	NA	NA	NA
Fire department standpipe	Required if over 150 ft Table 38A	Required 902.3.3	Required if over 150 ft 1012.3.1	Over 3 stories or exceeds areas in table 3.2.5A 3.2.5.4(1)	NA
Elevator for fire department access	Required 1807(h)	Required 506.6	Required 602.11	Required 3.2.6.4.(1)	Required 26-4.2.4(e)
Standby power and light	Required for 2 hours 1807(i)	Required for 2 hours 506.7	Required for 2 hours 602.12.1.1	Required for 2 hours 3.2.6.10.(1)	Required 26-4.2.4

Table 5A-2. Building Code Provisions for Highrise Buildings (*Continued*)

General Building Code Provisions	1988 Uniform Building Code	1988 Standard Building Code	1990 BOCA National Building Code	1985 National Building Code of Canada	1988 NFPA Life Safety Code
Travel distance	200'	250'	250'	AS 45 m (148 ft) NS 40 m (131 ft)	300'
	3303(d)	1103.1	807.5	3.4.2.4.(1)	26-2.6
1 1/2 inch hose line and nozzle	Not required	Not required w/AS	NA	NA	NA
	Table 38A	902.3			
Manual fire alarm	NA	Required w/com-part, not required w/AS	Required	Required	NA
			1016.9	26-3.4.1	
Automatic fire alarm	Required 1807(d)	NA	NA	NA	NA

APPENDIX 5B

Building Codes and Standards Sponsoring Organizations

UNIFORM BUILDING CODE
International Conference of
Building Officials, Inc.
5360 South Workman Mill Road
Whittier, California 90601

BOCA NATIONAL BUILDING CODE
Building Officials and Code
Administrators International, Inc.
4051 W. Flossmoor Road
Country Club Hills, Illinois 60478-5795

STANDARD BUILDING CODE
Southern Building Code Congress
International, Inc.
900 Montclair Road
Birmingham, Alabama 35212

LIFE SAFETY CODE NFPA 101
National Fire Protection Association
Battermarch Park
Quincy, Massachusetts 02269

Chapter 6

POWER AND SIGNAL DISTRIBUTION

David A. Harris

Distribution of power and signal to the work station has imposed new requirements on the office environment. Office productivity studies have demonstrated that dramatic increases or decreases in output and efficiency are the direct result of the reliability of electronic support equipment. With the sudden multiplication of video display terminals, microprocessors, personal computers, copiers, facsimile machines, and many other electronic devices, today's office productivity is integrally linked to power and signal distribution.

Buildings designed without careful consideration for both immediate and future power and signal distribution requirements are destined to be obsolete the day they open. Office vacancies are invariably tied to lack of adequate power and signal capability. The astute building owner and facilities manager must give top priority to providing an efficient, reliable, and flexible means to provide power and signal distribution. Prime examples of how quickly we make buildings obsolete can be seen by an evaluation of the thousands of buildings constructed in the 1970s with under-floor duct distribution systems. The ducts filled so quickly with power lines and telephone cables that they were literally abandoned shortly after the grand opening ceremonies. There are those who proposed to purchase the mining rights for all that abandoned copper! More recently, the switch from central computers to personal computers and networks has dramatically changed the criteria for power and signal. Clean signals and 100 percent reliability of service are required. Given the need for security as well, selecting a power and signal distribution system now requires great care in identifying present and future user needs.

Selection and analysis of the power and signal distribution for a new or remodeled office is best accomplished by a systems procurement technique (see Chapter 7 for details). The user or facilities manager must clearly identify user needs for both now and the future. Selection and design of the system(s) should be done by the systems team, with representation from all the design and construction disciplines, users, and the owner. (See Chapter 1, Figure 1-3 for the interaction matrix.)

The complexity of the power and signal dilemma is amplified by the multitude of options available to the user. The open plan office gives a choice of under-floor ducts with power poles, castles and recessed boxes, ceiling distribution with poles and/or poke-through devices, flat wire cabling, column distribution, raised floor systems, and system furniture distribution. The need for dedicated circuits and widely varying power requirements, many with backup generation and power surge controls, will vary with each upgrade or replacement of office electronic equipment.

Design for the future is vital. Many new buildings are already being equipped with fiber optic cables, microwave, and video signal distribution. With the expansion of cellular phones, we are rapidly approaching the time when most of our signal requirements will be transmitted via radio frequencies. Compact and low-cost microchips have also changed user requirements. The trend to mix closed- and open-plan offices creates an even newer challenge. To be efficient, the power and signal distribution system must now be adaptable to both the closed and the open layout without disrupting the flexibility to alter a plan from open to closed or vice versa overnight.

HOW TO ORGANIZE

This chapter is designed to assist the core group to identify, evaluate, and select the power and signal options suitable for specific circumstances. The process of selecting a system will vary widely, depending on user needs. The first step is to identify and make a detailed analysis of user needs for both the present and the future. For example, if the building is expected to be an expanding corporate headquarters with long-term ownership lease contracts, the analysis must focus on life-cycle costs and future needs. An office park that anticipates rapid turnover and changing uses over a short life span must focus on power and signal systems with maximum flexibility and minimum first costs. For this reason, in this chapter we will dwell primarily on the options available, and on their attributes and limitations.

Readers who want an in-depth understanding of power and signal technology are urged to obtain the services of a recognized expert. Responsible manufacturer representatives can provide a wealth of information and in many cases can be valuable members of the design team. The design process discussed in Chapter 1 and the systems procurement techniques of Chapter 7 must be used. To select the power and/or signal system best suited for your project, the owner/user should identify user needs at the initial core meetings. The core group that selects and establishes priority for the power and signal needs should include user representatives, designers, and industry experts. The importance of selecting a team with representation from all areas is amplified by the significant impact that the power and signal distribution have on all the other building subsystems. Key experts include the acoustician, the lighting engineer, the HVAC systems engineer, the furniture systems representative, the space planner, the power supplier, the outside system signal supplier, the architect, the general contractor, and pertinent subcontractors and code officials.

Identification of User Needs

User needs must be identified prior to analysis and selection of the power and signal distribution options. A preliminary evaluation is best accomplished by the facilities manager, the facilities consultant, or the architect. The process should build on the information generated in Chapter 1. Detailed information is required as follows.

WORK STATION POWER NEEDS. Identify each type of work station (secretarial, technical, manager, conference room, copy station, reception) and list the specific kinds and quantities of equipment each work station will require. It is recommended that this analysis be broken down into the following categories: Equipment required now, and in 2 years, 5 years, 10 years, and logical segments to the expected life span of the building. With the assistance of a power expert, this equipment list should be identified in terms of the amounts and types of power required (amps, voltage, grounding, guaranteed availability, protection, purity, number of lines, surge protection) for each work station and at each future use.

WORK STATION SIGNAL NEEDS. For each work station type, identify the type of signal required. Will it be an internal connect only? long distance? dedicated? mainframe connect? network connect? With assistance from a communications expert, identify each work station requirement in terms of the types and quantities of connects required. These criteria should also be categorized in terms of immediate or present need, 2 years from now, 5 years, 10 years, and in logical segments to the expected life span of the building.

BUILDING LIMITATIONS. In existing structures, many limits are imposed at the onset. The team must determine those that cannot change under any circumstances and those that can change within specific financial or technical limitations. For leased space, these items will be spelled out in the lease negotiations. For new buildings, these limitations will be dictated by short-term and life-cycle cost analysis. It is imperative that these limitations be identified prior to analyzing and selecting the power and signal distribution system. For a large project, which may more readily justify the effort, a power and system expert should be engaged to provide a life-cycle cost-benefit analysis. Final identification of the limits must be made with input from users, owners, and financial backers.

Some physical limitation examples to consider are these:

- Floor to ceiling heights. For example, in Washington, D.C., building height restrictions essentially eliminate use of a raised floor or suspended ceiling plenum for distribution of power and signal lines.
- Code restrictions. In Chicago, for example, union and code limitations suggest that power and signal be contained in a conduit. In the early days of systems furniture, this requirement essentially negated their flexibility. Once the wiring was installed, usually at a substantial cost increase, the movable work stations were rendered immovable.
- Aesthetic considerations. Power poles are likely to be the most cost-effective way to distribute power and signal to most open offices. However, many office designers and users have eliminated this option on aesthetic grounds.
- Interface with other building systems. The economic impact of incorporating several systems can be significant. A prime example is combining of fire management system and the background masking and paging systems. Selection of the distribution system will be dictated by the physical criteria for each system. Similar considerations for interfacing the lighting, HVAC, and sprinkler systems will dictate criteria for power and signal distribution. The economic impact of good subsystem interface was dramatically demonstrated in the United States Government Services Agency (GSA) Systems Procurement Program for Office Buildings. In one project, the systems offeror provided lights that were cooled by water lines connected with the HVAC system and the sprinkler system. The result was a substantial reduction in the power consumption of both lighting and HVAC systems. This allowed the power distribution to be downsized with considerable first use and life-cycle cost savings.

- Future innovations. As our propensity for individual computers that go with us in a briefcase, cellular phones, use of fiber optics and microwave expand, there will be power and signal requirements unique to those systems. The author also envisions the day when signals will be superimposed over power lines. If these items are in the future plans for expansion, they will dictate power and signal criteria.
- FCC deregulation policies. The Federal Communications Commission (FCC) has implemented significant changes in recent years. The most important is ruling CC docket 79-105 allowing station or telephone connections to be listed as an expense item. No longer is the installation expense included in the telephone company's rate base. In addition, the FCC has completely deregulated inside wiring and ordered the telephone companies to relinquish ownership of inside wiring. The result is that owners or users may contract for their own system and then hook into a local or long distance service of their choice. Prior to this ruling, each local phone service severely limited the equipment and distribution system. Flat wiring was, in effect, excluded from use by the Bell System. It required an expensive filtering mechanism to ensure that its lines were not "contaminated" by faulty signals. The result was a cost item so high that the savings for flat wire were negated. When deregulation went into effect, flat wire became viable. An owner or user could purchase, lease, or contract for their own system, and many options became available. While considerable savings are now possible, the complex nature of the electronics, options, and flexibility warrant retaining a communications expert to sort out the best solution for your circumstances. Likewise, the selection of equipment will dictate the most efficient distribution system.

CODES AND STANDARDS FOR POWER AND SIGNAL

Five major codes and standards documents are typically the basis for most state and local regulations for power and signal distribution. Each city, state, or county has the authority to create its own codes. While most will adopt one of the major codes, many adopt part of one standard and some of another or alter specific portions to meet their own criteria. For any major installation, it is imperative that the local code be studied carefully. Such subtle changes as a word change from "shall" to "should" could alter wiring criteria. The major codes are updated periodically and are vulnerable to political and technological change. Consequently, the reader should consult a code expert familiar with the applicable code when working on a major project. In general, the codes are well written and explicit. To avoid interpretation problems, most small communities, cities, and government agencies adopt one of the major codes. Larger cities and government entities usually make significant alterations.

The Major Code Bodies

It is indeed fortunate that there is a considerable amount of interaction between code officials and the code bodies. Consequently, widely divergent requirements tend to be minimal. Be aware, however, that the local authority has the prerogative to change the code. There are many instances where the local officials mix the national codes and enter seemingly small changes of their own. The major code bodies are six national and regional agencies:

- UBC/ICBO
- BBC/BOCA
- SBC/Southern Building Code
- NBC/American Insurance Association
- NEC/NFPA
- FCC

The *Uniform Building Code (UBC)* is produced and maintained by the *International Conference of Building Officials (ICBO)*, located at 5360 South Workman Mill Road, Whittier, California 90601. Note that the terms UBC and ICBO are used interchangeably in the industry. The UBC is widely used in the western portion of the United States.

The *Basic Building Code* is produced and administered by the *Building Officials and Code Administrators (BOCA) International, Inc.*, located at 17926 South Halsted Street, Homewood, Illinois 60430. The BOCA Basic Building Code is used primarily in the Midwest.

The *Standard Building Code (SBC)* is produced by the *Southern Building Code Congress International, Inc.*, located at 900 Montclair Road, Birmingham, Alabama 35213. SBC is commonly referred to as the Southern Building Code and is widely used in the southern states.

The *National Building Code (NBC)* is produced by the *American Insurance Association*, 85 John Street, New York, New York 10038. NBC was conceived with the hope that it would eventually replace all the other codes. Unfortunately, that has not materialized. The UBC, BOCA, and SBC are more entrenched than ever, and few communities use NBC.

The National Electric Code (NEC) is published by the *National Fire Protection Association (NFPA)*, Batterymarch Park, Quincy, Massachusetts. Called NFPA #70, this document is the world's most widely adopted electrical safety regulation. It has also been adopted by the American National Standards Institute (ANSI). It is updated periodically; the most recent addition is #70E, covering electrical safety for employee workplaces. Most code authorities have adopted the NEC for their own jurisdictions. Some have altered the document to meet their own requirements.

The following chapters of the code apply to the planning and placement of communication systems:

- Chapter 2, Wiring Design & Protection, addresses grounding and terminal identification methods.
- Chapter 3, Wiring Methods & Materials, discusses wiring systems, materials, insulations, raceways, hardware, temporary wiring, and related items.
- Chapter 5, Special Occupancies, covers wiring systems and equipment in hazardous areas and special occupancy.
- Chapter 6, Special Equipment, addresses installation of manufactured wiring and data processing systems.
- Chapter 7, Special Conditions, covers systems operating at less than 50 volts. This covers many signaling systems such as fire protection signals, and background masking systems.
- Chapter 8, Communication Systems, addresses communication circuits including radio, television, and CATV.

The *National Fire Protection Association (NFPA)* has a series of codes that apply to the fire safety of power and signal distribution systems in an office building. Given the recent concern for fire safety in offices and in particular in highrise buildings, the following standards should be used as appropriate:

National Electrical Code (NEC)	70 (A–E)
Central Station Signaling Systems	71
Local Protective Signaling Systems	72A
Auxiliary Protective Signaling Systems	72B
Remote Station Protective Signaling Systems	72C
Proprietary Protective Signaling Systems	72D
Automatic Fire Detectors	72E
Protection of Electronic Computer/Data Processing	75
Lightning Protection Code	78
Life Safety Code	101

It is impossible to cover all aspects of wiring related to fire safety, but several items deserve special attention when selecting a power and signal system for a building. For example, wiring in spaces that distribute environmental air is prohibited; it must be of special noncombustible materials, contained within special enclosures, and/or bear special approvals. A typical criteria for acceptance is a product label indicating the material or system was tested by an independent agency and inspected to ensure compliance with a specific set of manufacturing criteria. Examples are labels provided by Underwriters Laboratories (UL), Warnock Hersey (W-H), and Omega Point Laboratories.

Buildings that incorporate open ceiling plenums for either air return or supply and that have wiring located in these spaces must have wiring specially designed to avoid the rapid spread of smoke and toxic fumes from an electrical fire. Other spaces that fit this category include elevator shafts, vertical risers, and raised floor plenums. Where wires penetrate barriers and in particular those designed as fire stops, it is imperative that the penetration be sealed with approved materials. These criteria severely limit the location and type of some power and signal systems. And if not prohibited by code, the upgraded requirements will substantially affect installed costs for many systems.

Federal Communications Commission (FCC) has FCC Regulation #68, Connection of Terminal Equipment to the Telephone Network, which addresses requirements for telephone wiring and equipment connected to public telephones.

POWER AND SIGNAL DISTRIBUTION ALTERNATIVES

The office environment poses a special set of criteria for the proper distribution of power and signal. Key elements include: safety; adequate outlets with sufficient capacity; flexibility; satisfaction of code requirements; aesthetics; convenience; reliability; and compatibility with the other subsystems that make up the interior environment. The task of bringing power and signal to the office location has a whole different set of criteria specified or discussed at length in other texts. This section is intended to acquaint you with the types of systems available for use in the office environment; later sections will discuss their merits and limitations.

Power Poles

Power poles arrived with the open-plan office. With no full-height partitions to support or contain the power and telephone wiring, a simple pole was devised. This pole contained or otherwise provided protection for wires running from the floor or ceiling to office equipment. Subsequently, this pole served as a distribution mechanism for special wiring needs, including dedicated computer lines (Figure 6-1).

The main distribution source for power poles is typically installed within the ceiling plenum or in some cases in the floor system. Designed specifically for the open office, the power pole usually provides a quick connect to the main source. The name "power pole" is a misnomer today, since most units have the capability to distribute signal wiring as well. Early versions were a simple pipe or conduit fixed to the floor and ceiling, with junction boxes placed judiciously for power access. As the open plan concept grew, the power pole evolved into an ever more sophisticated, durable, and more attractive

Figure 6-1. Power poles/integrated ceiling

distribution device. Widely accepted in most code jurisdictions, the power pole has created considerable controversy from both safety and aesthetic standpoints.

Underfloor Duct Systems

In the 1970s the building trades began utilizing new flooring systems that incorporated deep flutes and eventually cellular deck systems to span great lengths between main support beams. The most widely utilized system was a formed metal deck with tubular open cells (Figure 6-2). Spanning 10 feet or more, these systems decreased construction time and formed an excellent base or form for poured concrete. Like forms that stayed in place, the cellular deck rapidly became popular and provided a natural conduit for the horizontal distribution of wiring of all types. With many cells, the decks could separate power wiring from telephone cable, thereby limiting interference. Cellular decks made of various materials evolved, and a precast concrete unit is still popular. Wiring typically is strung through the cells and penetrates the floor above, with a receptacle for access from the floor above. All manner of receptacles have been developed, from the "castle" or boxlike unit that fits over the penetration conduit on the finished side of the floor, to recessed units that have the concrete poured around them so that their top edges are flush with the floor. Fitted with a hinged lid or cover, the receptacle box contains the connector for power and amphinol for telephone connections.

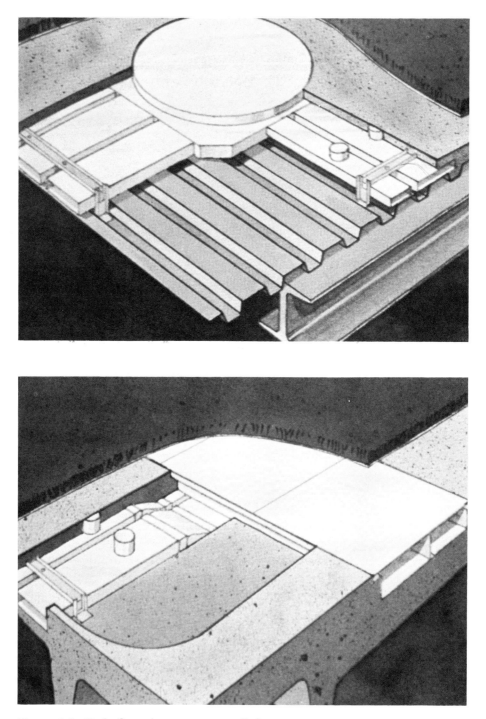

Figure 6-2. Underfloor duct systems—cell duct

Later units were totally cast into the concrete. Access is gained by drilling through the concrete deck to the box. Called *core drilling,* the process is noisy, messy, and intrusive in the office environment. Several variations place the boxes just below the concrete floor surface so access may be gained with a hammer that can break away the thin cover. Located judiciously, usually on a grid pattern of some 6 feet on center, the "castles" theoretically provided easy access from any location.

Poke-Through

Horizontal distribution of power wiring in conduit is typically installed on the underside of the floor slab or deck. Installed prior to the suspended ceiling system, junction boxes (Figure 6-3) provide power to the lighting systems installed as a part of the suspended ceiling system and HVAC fan units installed in the plenum space. Service to the floor above is achieved by drilling a hole through the floor assembly and finished flooring, allowing for the installation of a standard power and signal outlet. The poke-through method is the most widely used technique in existing highrise office buildings.

Screen or Systems Furniture Wiring

The concept of placing horizontal and vertical distribution within the partition barriers in the open office arrived slowly. At this point, nearly every systems

Figure 6-3. Poke-through system

Figure 6-4. Screen wiring system. Courtesy Rosemount Office Systems, Inc.

furniture manufacturer of note offers an integral power and signal distribution system (Figure 6-4). The means of incorporating the wiring into the part high space dividers varies widely. The distribution channel is usually contained within the base of the divider panel. In some versions, wiring can be contained within the vertical post sections. Recent offerings allow distribution at unlimited locations.

Manufacturers have developed a wide array of interconnect devices to allow adjoining panels to be plugged in as panels are installed or moved. Access to a power and signal source is typically via a column, cellular floor, poke-through or power pole.

Flat Conductor Cable (FCC)

Usually called "flat wiring," the FCC has only been available for general use since the early 1980s. The invention of FCC was initially touted as the lifesaver of the open office. Initial development efforts came from grants and assistance from the National Aeronautical and Space Administration (NASA) and a task force of private corporations. The conductors for both power and signal are contained in a flat strip approximately 3 inches wide and the thickness of several sheets of paper. Applied directly to a flat concrete or other structural floor with adhesive and covered with a metal protective sheet, FCC is installed beneath carpet tiles (Figure 6-5). Special interconnect devices allow FCC to be connected to conventional power and signal outlets at columns or other central locations. Flat conductor cable must be installed with carpet tiles or similar finished floor coverings. Outlets are contained in special boxes that are installed over the cable at any location. Relocatability and access for maintenance is the main reason why approvals require the use of carpet tiles.

The first use of FCC was marred by the effort required to gain acceptance from the National Electric Code for the power version and from the Bell System for the signal version. Safety was a prime concern in the acceptance of the flat power conductor. Many tests of the effect of penetration by nails, spike heels, rolling carts, and the like were required. The system now enjoys full

Figure 6-5. Flat conductor cable (FCC). Courtesy Thomas and Betts, Inc.

approval by Underwriters Laboratories and the National Electric Code. Early versions of the signal conductor were hampered by limitations on the number of lines and the need for a precise connection. Of even greater importance was the political issue of deregulation of the Bell System. The splitup of the national telephone system and the emergence of competitors allowed the technical advantages to be reconsidered. Flat conductor cable is now approved in most municipalities.

Ongoing facilities management and rearrangements are not as simple as they may appear. Relocating work stations typically requires moving power and signal outlets. To relocate an outlet, a substantial amount of wire must be ripped up and relaid. This requires temporary relocation of many more work stations than those involved in the change. To facilitate moves, it is recommended that power and signal layout drawings be kept current at all times. Flat wires can build up when crossing. If more than two wires cross, a noticeable lump will telegraph through the finished flooring.

Raised Floor Systems

Known initially as "computer floor systems," the raised floor has come of age as an efficient way to provide the optimum flexibility for distribution of power and signal to the office. The initial concept was developed to provide a support for mainframe computers. The plenum provides convenient access with sufficient space to distribute a wide array of services, including power wiring, cabling for signal distribution of telephones, computer terminals, fire alarms, communication lines, background masking wiring, air distribution ducts, and plumbing lines between work stations (Figure 6-6).

Composed of a plurality of base leg supports resting on a structural floor system with removable panels, raised floor systems provided easy access for maintenance and relocation of wiring and other service lines. Height may vary from 6 to 18 inches, depending on the circumstances. Removable floor panels are typically 18 to 30 inches square and may be composed of welded steel panels, reinforced concrete, wood, or a combination of materials. Some come with the finished flooring material already installed, while others need a finish carpet or tile floor covering.

When choosing a raised floor system, a wide variety of physical characteristics should be evaluated, including:

• Floor loads. These may vary from several pounds per square foot to hundreds of pounds per square foot.
• Height adaptability. Finished floor level must match or allow transition to fixed locations found at hallways and core areas of the building.

Figure 6-6. Raised floor system. Courtesy Donn® Access Floor Systems, USG Interiors, Inc.

- Ease of access. Some systems are bolted in place; others have simple lay in capability.
- Sag resistance. Permanent set or deflection under load.
- Point impact resistance. Dents from furniture and other equipment.
- Acoustical. There must be no hollow sound or flanking transmission.
- Ability to accommodate other distribution systems such as HVAC and plumbing lines.
- Ease of installation, durability, resistance to warping.

Raised floor systems have been used on an increasing scale in recent years. Several projects have over a million square feet of raised floor systems.

Combination Distribution Systems

Two or more of the systems described above can be used on the same project. A common mix is the use of systems furniture distribution for the open spaces, with an interconnect with any one of the other systems. There are many examples for each combination (Figure 6-7).

Systems for the Future

By the time this book is published, there will probably be several other viable systems on the market. Most probable is the use of fiber optic cable to distribute signals. Already in use to distribute signals over long distances, glass fiber optic cable has the capability to superimpose many more signals with less interference. Fiber optic cable allows the use of light beams as the signal carrier. With greater speed than conventional electronic frequencies, light beams are actually bent as they traverse the cable. An ideal medium for transferring a massive amount of data, fiber optic cables are most practical for trunk lines. Their use as a distribution network within the office is presently impractical due to the effort required in splicing the cable.

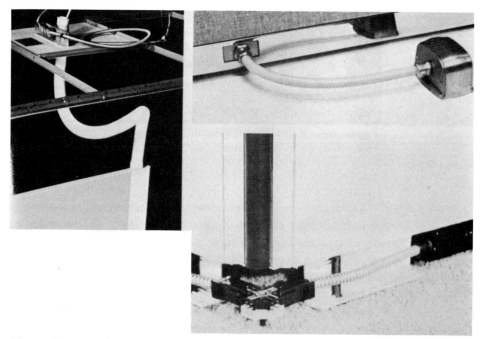

Figure 6-7. Combination of systems

The use of cellular phones and microwave already has proved to be an effective means of transferring information signals. This technology may become practical for office use in the near future. Limitations include insufficient frequencies, interference, and government regulation by the Federal Communication Commission (FCC).

AN EVALUATION OF THE ALTERNATIVES

The selection of which power and signal system best meets your user needs is a complex process. You will quickly discover that there is no right or wrong selection. The system or combination of systems that best suits the situation now will be totally wrong when a series of changes occur. The most successful systems will be designed to match potential changes. You may tire of the continuous references to "establishing user needs," but this effort is key to the selection process. If you properly define potential future changes in the organization, you will find the job of selecting a power and signal system a simple and rewarding task. If you do not, or if you are the victim of unanticipated change, you will be burdened with the result. An example of how potential changes in an organization can dramatically affect the selection of the power and signal system can be best described by reviewing the scenario at Owens Corning Fiberglas. In the early 1970s OCF contracted to move into a new corporate headquarters in Toledo, Ohio. The organization was growing at a pace that quickly outgrew its space. In anticipation, OCF management chose the open-plan concept to accommodate the rapid changes expected. The thirty-story building was designed with a cellular floor system thought to be able to accommodate power and signal changes well into the 1980s. Change and growth were much more rapid than anticipated, and within two years all the cellular floor system was filled with wire. OCF facilities management soon realized that the space was inadequate and began searching for alternatives. With office space spread all over downtown, they eventually decided to convert a defunct department store into modern office space. To accommodate potential changes, OCF chose a raised floor system for the entire complex. Fortunately, the high ceilings and other attributes of the planning process allowed a life-cycle cost analysis that eventually supported the higher cost of the raised floor system.

With further growth, OCF took over other space and attempted to implement similar design criteria for power and signal distribution. All went well until an unknown entity entered with a hostile takeover attempt that resulted in substantial downsizing. With it came many more moves and reorganizations. The early analysis of user needs paid off when the company was able to utilize the flexibility designed into the system. Even though the designs were selected on the basis of growth, the flexibility became even more valuable when negative growth occurred. The process of making the evaluations became a matter of knowing the attributes and limitations of the potential system solutions. The key to success is proper assessment of potential user needs. Once these needs are established, the evaluation will clearly indicate which system is best.

SYSTEM ALTERNATIVE ANALYSIS
Power Poles

ATTRIBUTES

Easy to move. Poles may be moved by maintenance personnel in most instances.

Distribution lines in ceiling plenum. Conventional power and signal lines are utilized to provide horizontal distribution, out of sight in the ceiling plenum (Figures 6-8, 6-9).

Figure 6-8. Power pole example 1. Courtesy Wiremold, Inc.

Figure 6-9. Power pole example 2. Courtesy Wiremold, Inc.

Low cost. The price per outlet is substantially less expensive than any other means of distributing power and signal.

Handles both power and signal.

Tax writeoff. Because they move, poles are not fixtures in the building and therefore qualify for accelerated depreciation.

Additional outlets. As more lines are required, they may be economically installed in the ceiling plenum to accommodate additional poles (Figure 6-10).

LIMITATIONS

Aesthetics. Many designers refuse to allow "power pole pollution." Many attempts have been made to make the poles more acceptable. When they are spread out over the floor, they tend to be unnoticed. However, typical needs call for at least one and possibly two poles for each work station. The result is chaotic whether disguised or amplified to look high tech (Figures 6-11, 6-12). Damaged ceiling systems add to the dilemma.

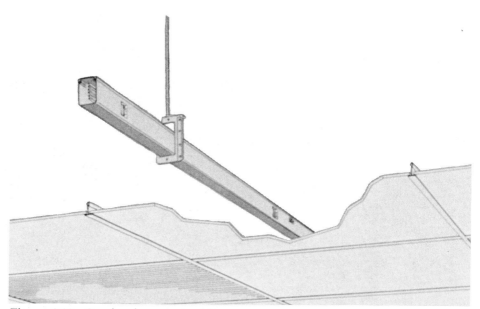

Figure 6-10. Overhead raceway grid system

Durability. Poles are subject to a lot of abuse and are vulnerable to all
   sorts of moving objects. They tend to come apart easily if not
   constructed in a very sturdy fashion. As they are moved and/or
   replaced, damage typically occurs to the ceiling materials.
Code restrictions. Some local code authorities will not allow poles unless
   they are "hard wired," rendering them immovable.
Require special ceiling systems. Poles must interconnect somewhere and
   the most typical spot is the suspended ceiling system. Unless the
   ceiling system is designed to accommodate the power pole, the pole/
   ceiling interface will limit flexibility and reduce the aesthetic
   consideration even more. The ceiling grid dictates pole location,
   thereby limiting flexibility.
Not suited to future electronics. Most poles have limited space for extra
   lines so extra or new poles are required.
Electromagnetic interference. Fluorescent and HID light fixtures located
   in close proximity to horizontal distribution lines in ceiling plenum
   will cause interference with data transmission.
Safety. Being vulnerable, poles are potential safety hazards electrically
   and physically. Manufacturers present case studies to refute the
   hazard, but many lawsuits have been filed naming power poles as a
   hazard.

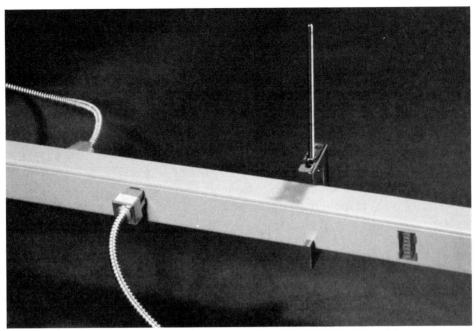

Figure 6-11. Raceway/power pole interconnect 1. Courtesy Wiremold, Inc.

Figure 6-12. Raceway/power pole interconnect 2. Courtesy Wiremold, Inc.

Underfloor Duct Systems

ATTRIBUTES

A building standard. Everyone is familiar with them (Figures 6-13, 6-14).

Low fire hazard. Containment in cells isolates fires.

Available in concrete or metal deck systems.

Satisfy all code requirements.

Good appearance. They are not seen.

Low-cost solution for new construction.

Handle both power and signal and special cables.

LIMITATIONS

Flexibility. Once a grid is set in concrete, you are locked into that location for the life of the building. Alternate methods to effect changes are prohibitively expensive.

Poor wire management. Box location is fixed requiring long chords or furniture to be moved to accommodate.

Overloaded cells. Abandoned wires quickly fill cells causing overloaded system.

Cannot be used in remodeling unless building has system.

Not suited to future expansion or future electronics.

Figure 6-13. Underfloor duct system

Figure 6-14. Underfloor duct system example

Poke-Through

ATTRIBUTES

Initial costs are low. Major costs are delayed until occupants move in.
Design freedom. Initial services may be installed nearly anywhere desired
(some limits due to structural members).

LIMITATIONS

Capacity limited. Codes typically restrict poke through to one per 65
square feet and no closer than 2 feet on center.
Structural damage. Caused by hole drilling, the structure may be
compromised as will the fire- and sound-resistant ratings of the floor/
ceiling system.
Disruptive to occupants. The process of drilling holes for access is noisy,
dirty, and generally distasteful and disruptive if conducted during
normal working hours to occupants above and below. Off-hour
installation requires overtime pay.
High relocation costs. Relocation costs in excess of $100 per outlet are
the norm. On a life-cycle cost basis these systems have a poor chance
of being competitive.
Limited security. Cables may be accessed from below.

Screen or Systems Furniture Wiring

ATTRIBUTES

Flexibility. Outlets may be located in the most convenient place for the
specific need.
Excellent wire management. Equipment chords may be kept to minimal
length or confined in special compartments (Figures 6-15, 6-16).
Good aesthetics. Wires are contained within system cavities.
Power and signal. Conductors of all types may be accommodated by
most furniture systems (Figure 6-17).
Accommodates future electronics. Additional outlets of all types are
offered by most system manufacturers.
Low installation and move costs. Plug-in features at panel junctures are
easy to maintain and relocate.
Tax writeoff. The IRS has ruled that these systems are furniture and are
therefore eligible for early depreciation.

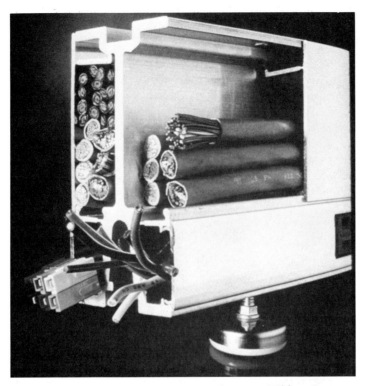

Figure 6-15. Screen wiring system. Courtesy Tibbet, Inc.

LIMITATIONS

Must interconnect. Panels must plug into another wiring system at column, wall, underfloor, or power pole. Interfacing hardware is not always readily available. Installation may require electrical expert.

May hinder movement. Depending on the manufacturer and the design, the wiring may significantly hinder the flexibility and ease of installing or moving the screen or furniture system. If local code requires "hard wiring" (i.e., wires in a metallic conduit) the ability to move the system may be completely negated. This actually happened on some early installations in Chicago (Figures 6-16, 6-17).

Trade required is variable. In most instances the power and signal distribution systems may be installed by maintenance personnel or systems furniture contractor. However, there have been trade disputes that resulted in a requirement that licensed electricians be required to hook up the panels on installation or revision.

Figure 6-16. Panels pre-wired

Figure 6-17. Screen wiring example

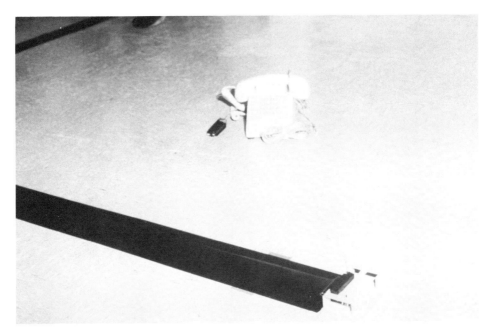

Figure 6-18. Flat wiring system. Courtesy Thomas and Betts, Inc.

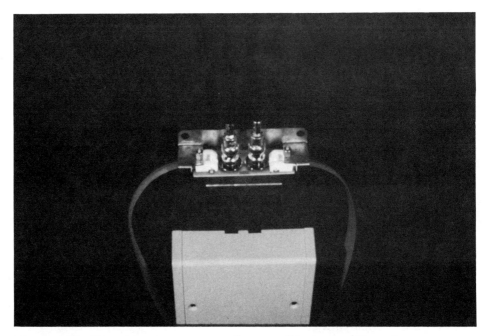

Figure 6-19. Flat wiring interconnect. Courtesy Thomas and Betts, Inc.

Flat Conductor Cable (FCC)

ATTRIBUTES

Ideal for remodeling (Figures 6-18, 6-19). Many older existing buildings have poured concrete floor systems that make it nearly impossible to install any form of conventional horizontal wiring. Poking holes from a suspended ceiling plenum is nearly impossible or at least very expensive. FCC may be the only reasonable solution for most remodeling situations.

Flexible. FCC may be installed at any location desired and may be relocated at minimal expense and disruption.

Accommodates power and signal. Present systems have been updated to accommodate most common office needs for power and signal requirements.

Tax writeoff. The IRS has ruled that FCC is not a fixture in the building and therefore qualifies for accelerated depreciation and investment tax credit.

Aesthetically acceptable. Located under the carpet tiles, FCC is out of sight. Wire management at the work station may be optimized.

Acceptable for most future electronics.

Floor integrity preserved. Because FCC is surface-mounted, the structural, acoustical, and fire resistance characteristics of the floor/ceiling system are preserved and/or optimized.

Installation on move in. FCC is installed as a part of the finish floor installation, one of the last items to be installed before the furniture. This allows for last-minute adjustments to the layout, an inevitable event in a dynamic organization. For some, the cost of installation becomes a part of relocation expense, making it a leader item for rental properties.

LIMITATIONS

Carpet tile is required. Approvals of FCC by code authorities and from a practical standpoint require the use of carpet tile. The aesthetic characteristics may be detrimental to some, and there is an economic impact, since carpet tiles command a premium price compared to other floor-covering materials. Note that carpet tiles fare well when analyzed on a life-cycle cost basis over the building life. Most of the wear happens in high traffic areas, allowing for only partial replacement.

Wire management imperative. FCC layouts require care in locating distribution lines to avoid crossovers and turns. Each time either event occurs, there is a real possibility that the cable will telegraph through the carpet tile, causing extra wear and tripping hazards. When relocations occur, the old lines must be removed. Layout drawings are vital to the efficiency of relocations. They must be kept up to date and accurate. There is a tendency to let this aspect slide, causing unnecessary work at time of relocation or maintenance.

Installation is special. While the technique for installation appears simple and assignable to maintenance workers, it requires a degree of skill that is not part of most construction trades. It is imperative that the floor be smooth, clean, and free of particles. Particles such as sand can damage the cable when walked on or rolled over with a heavy cart. In addition, the adhesive systems and tape will not provide adequate bonding. Cable joints and interconnects with other wiring systems require special tools and connection devices. Outlet boxes or "castles" must be installed with special tools.

Safety. While FCC has been tested and retested under all kinds of potential hazardous conditions with good results, it is a simple fact that the cables are located in a very vulnerable location with little protection against vandals, accidents, and the like. The jury is still out on this issue. FCC is clearly only usable in a low-traffic office environment. Safeguards against short circuits, water intrusion, and the like appear adequate but have not been extensively field-tested.

Signal interference. Placing power and signal cables parallel and close to each other raises the potential for communication interference. Proper wire management should minimize this issue.

Limited security. Because FCC is so flexible and easy to access it also can be easily accessed by others. For high security data transmission, FCC is a poor choice.

Durability is in doubt. Although FCC has been installed in a number of installations for several years, there is no long-term data on system durability or expected life span.

Limited electronic capability. At this time only 120 volt power and 20 communication circuits are generally available. Special cables for other demands are available on a limited basis.

Labor/code acceptance. Acceptance will vary depending on the municipality or authority. Some major city codes have not yet approved FCC, even though it has National Electric Code approval and carries a U-L label. Some unions have objected and held up installations. It is not clear what trade has responsibility.

Raised or Access Floor Systems

ATTRIBUTES

Optimum flexibility. The entire floor is accessible for installation ease
and relocation convenience, with plenty of room for expansion of all
types of distribution lines (Figures 6-20, 6-21, 6-22).

Relocation labor and costs minimal. With such easy access and use of
conventional wiring techniques, relocation costs will be very
reasonable.

Life-cycle costs are low. May vary by manufacturer.

Tax credit. Because of the flexibility and relocatability, raised floor
systems may qualify for investment tax credits and fast depreciation.

Accommodates all future electronics. There seems to be no limit to
adding new lines of any type including dedicated circuits.

Communication interference is minimal. By grounding the metallic
panels, this system should be simple to maintain low interference with
signals on communication lines.

Figure 6-20. Raised floor installation

Figure 6-21. Raised floor schematic. Courtesy Donn® Access Floor Systems, USG Interiors, Inc.

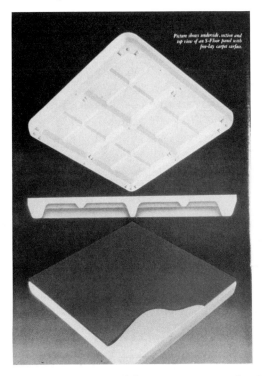

Figure 6-22. Raised floor concrete panels. Courtesy Innocent Systems, Inc.

Accommodates other equipment and distribution lines. Raised floor systems may also serve as a distribution space for other services such as plumbing, air handling, gas, and special services.

No cleanup or damage. On removal, there are no holes, patches, or related damage to deal with. This is probably the best feature of these systems.

LIMITATIONS

Extra floor to floor height required. By raising the floor system above the face of the structural floor system, the floor/ceiling height will be compromised. This means that for existing buildings, there may not be sufficient height to accommodate the raised floor and allow acceptable floor/ceiling heights for the occupied space. Since large open spaces tend to lower the apparent height, the raised floor will compound the problem. For buildings in cities like Washington, D.C., with overall building height limits, there will likely be no available space for a raised floor in either new or existing structures. The raised floor requires special consideration for transition to conventional areas of the building without raised floors. Ramps or offsets will be required. This is not a large problem for new construction, but is significant in existing space.

High initial cost. While initial installed costs have been reduced substantially in recent years, the raised floor is inherently the most expensive first-cost way to provide power and signal distribution. Life-cycle costing (the first cost plus the cost of relocating work stations and maintenance over the life span of the building) is required to demonstrate an economically viable program. Initial costs may be double to triple other wiring options (Figures 6-23, 6-24).

Limited security. Ease in opening panels for access also allows others to gain easy access.

Limited acoustical performance. Many raised floor systems have a hollow sound that is unnatural and annoying to many. For closed offices or conference rooms, the raised floor serves as a potential sound flanking path. More expensive and heavy systems are available to correct these limitations.

Limited floor loads. Raised floor systems generally have substantial limits on how much floor load they will carry. While systems may be designed to handle most conditions, they are more expensive and must be specified at time of purchase.

Durability is limited. Except for the heavy-duty systems, raised floors tend to warp and bow over the years. Warping causes panels to rattle

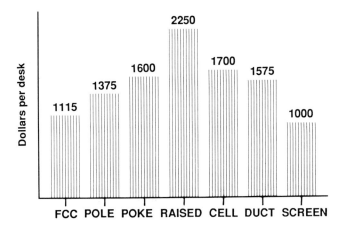

Figure 6-23. Distribution system cost comparison: ten-year accumulated cost comparison.

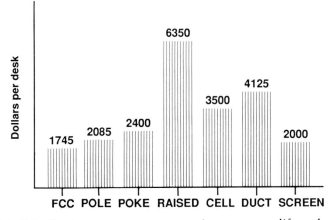

Figure 6-24. Distribution system cost comparison: ten-year life-cycle costs and time value of money.

when stepped on. After many changes, the fit between panels and support becomes worn or damaged, causing potential durability questions.

Limited finish floor options. Carpet tiles or integral floor covering on the individual units is required. The monolithic floor covering preferred by many designers may not be used by code. Even if it were approved, you must forego the other attributes of a raised floor—flexibility and accessibility.

Installation must be level. Special care must be taken to assure systems are level. Laser beams are now standard equipment by the installing contractor. Even so, some panels rock on their supports.

Security is moderate. While wires are contained in service cells, they are relatively accessible to everyone.

Surface Raceways (Exposed)

Mounting power and signal distribution lines on the surface of walls and ceilings is likely the oldest known technique. In today's modern office building this technique is relegated to the factory environment or those design situations where it is prohibitive to provide a more aesthetically pleasing installation. However, there is a preponderance of equipment manufactured for this method of power and signal distribution to warrant consideration. The hardware is usually a surface-mounted conduit and is available as standard EMT conduit attached to the structural elements of a building with clips attached with nails, screws, or the like. More sophisticated versions of the conduit utilize snap-off covers and quick-inset outlets.

ATTRIBUTES

Low initial cost. Probably the least expensive technique.

Flexibility is optimum. All wiring is easily accessible and therefore inexpensive to relocate.

Cable lengths are kept to a minimum. Wire management is optimum. Multiple outlets may be placed close to equipment location, requiring short power and signal chords.

Future electronics easily accommodated. Extra lines may be added.

LIMITATIONS

Aesthetics are poor.
Security is poor.
Safety is poor.

COMMUNICATION CABLING NETWORKS

The prime need in today's office building is for cabling to handle voice networks. Most of the signals we use today are transmitted via a phone line. Switching is commonly handled by a digital Private Branch Exchange (PBX). Consisting of common equipment, a PBX may include a switchboard or switching equipment shared by all stations, a telephone or key telephone system, and the wiring connecting the terminals to the station equipment. Smaller cable sizes are the norm in new installations. In the past, cable sizes up to 400 pair were common; 25-pair unshielded cable was common to most telephones. With increased competition, technological advances, and deregulation, digital electronics have substantially reduced interior cable to 3- and 4-pair with four-conductor station wire.

Shared communication services are becoming commonplace, particularly in large office parks or complexes. Shared services can provide voice and data signal distribution, for local and long distance, with services such as message centers, voice mail, switching, and Local Area Networking (LAN) and teleconferencing at attractive rates. Called "intelligent buildings" or "tenant shared telecommunications" by some marketers, building services may also include access to central computer systems, HVAC control, lighting controls, fire management systems, paging or central music, and background masking sound distribution. Multitenant occupants find these systems particularly attractive, since they may have access to state-of-the-art communication systems heretofore limited to large single owner/occupants.

Wiring for today's office building is usually from 3- to 25-pair unshielded inside wiring cables. Composed of 24 AWG copper conductors insulated with flame-resistant, semirigid polyvinyl chloride (PVC), wires may be color coded. To reduce cross-talk between circuits, a staggered-pair lay system is utilized. Wires are given extra strength by wrapping them together with a nonhygroscopic yarn or propylene binder tape and covered with a PVC outer jacket. To allow for future expansion and rearrangements, closed raceways usually have a wiring fill capacity of 50 percent for the cross-sectional area. Depending on the wire used, various size conduits will be required to accommodate the number of cables required. The actual wire and conduit size should be calculated by a wiring professional. Note that he or she will require detailed information on present and future user needs, information that must be supplied by the owner/user representative.

Wiring fire safety concerns have been amplified by some recent dramatic highrise fires. The spread of toxic fumes, smoke, and flames via plenum chambers that handle environmental air are of particular concern. It is traditional and convenient to utilize the ceiling plenum and vertical air shafts to contain the wiring. Code requirements have become more stringent in recent years and will likely become even more so in the years to come regarding the fire resistance and toxicity of the wire covering. Both the raised floor and suspended ceiling are being marketed as a space to contain the distribution and return of both heated and cooled air. Rightly so, any wiring in these spaces must be placed in a conduit or encased in materials that have demonstrated acceptability in the ASTM E-84, *Standard Test Method for Surface Burning Characteristics of Building Materials,* modified for wire and cable. Metallic conduit and fluoropolymer covering materials are generally required to meet the flamespread and smoke criteria. These criteria are generally required by most codes for all forms of cabling including power, and signal distribution including voice, data, fire and burglar alarm, and masking sound systems. The National Electric Code and some local codes have made an exception for low-voltage wiring if it is classified as "having adequate fire resistance and low smoke producing characteristics."

Shielded Cables

The demand for signal integrity has given rise to a plethora of products. Many are proprietary. Local Area Networks (LANS) are in effect a distribution system designed to ensure that outside electromechanical (EMI) and radio frequency (RFI) interference is minimized. The most common technique is to utilize shielded cable. A single shield will suffice for many applications. Where protection of signal integrity is critical, multiple-shield configurations designed to block both EMI and RFI signals may be utilized. The selection of cable shields is therefore directly related to the kind of signal being transmitted. For this reason, the owner/user must clearly identify the type of equipment antici-pated for both the near term and long term and convey that information to the power and signal designer/contractor, who will then specify the proper shields. A life-cycle cost analysis will assist all members of the design team to choose the system best suited for the circumstances.

Optical Fiber Systems

Optical fibers are ideally suited to transmit many signals over long distances while requiring a comparatively small cable. They are being utilized extensively by long distance phone vendors. Their use in office buildings has been limited to vertical-riser and communication and data cable placements. Normal office data cables do not require the high bandwidth capability that fiber optic cables provide. Consequently, there is no significant advantage to offset the added cost for the cable and the "pulse code modulation" system required at each end. In addition, sharp corners and splices require unique precision to assure proper alignment. Signal sources are usually light emitting diodes (LEDs). Fiber optic cable designs and sheaths primarily vary the fiber count. Higher fiber counts (more than 12) and heavy flame-retardant sheaths are used as riser cables. Jumper cables generally have a low fiber count (less than 4). One positive aspect of fiber optic cables is their inherent resistance to flamespread and smoke. To be cost-effective within the office, fiber optic cables require additional develop-ment that is presently under way.

Cellular Phones/Microwave Relays

While not yet practical for inner office communication, the day is coming when the office designer must prepare for the needs of the cellular phone and microwave relay. Using only radio waves, these systems have the potential to make obsolete all the present signal distribution systems. Recent Federal Communications Commission (FCC) regulations have made it practical for many who must be on the road a lot to have instant phone communication with their offices. Via internal system hookups on the conventional phone system, the user of a cellular phone has all the advantages of a standard phone system without the wiring. For more complex signals, the microwave relay is becoming an amenity, along with video conferencing. While it is beyond the scope of this book to explain the systems, they must be considered in any future planning. Specific performance parameters may significantly affect the location, frequency, and normal power/signal requirements for facilities that accommodate these technologies.

SUMMARY

Reliability and ease of access to power and signal in an office will directly affect office productivity. The challenge is to identify present and future user needs early in the planning process. Selecting the distribution system that best meets future needs will eventually be the most successful.

Planning and selecting the power and signal distribution option is a key role of the core group and must be based on user needs, code criteria, and building limitations. This chapter is organized primarily to assist the planning team and user group to evaluate the options of the many and varied type of distribution systems. The major systems such as power poles, underfloor ducts, poke-through, furniture wiring, flat conductor cable, raised floor, combination of systems and systems for the future are discussed. Individual system attributes and limitations are presented in a fashion that will aid the planning team to assess and then select the system best suited for the project.

The only sure thing about power and signal distribution systems is that technology is constantly changing. Together with vastly different office equipment, power and signal distribution system selection is a major challenge. Only by focusing on future user needs and implementation of the planning process described in Chapter 1 will the planning team achieve success.

Chapter 7

SYSTEMS PROCUREMENT

David A. Harris

The emphasis of this book has been on utilizing a structured planning process and a systems approach to office design. The planning and technical complexities involved with this approach are numerous, yet it offers comprehensive and innovative solutions to today's most challenging and fluid situations.

The necessary design tools, as well as the identification of issues that may arise and who should be responsible for their resolution, were provided in Chapter 1. Chapters 2, 3, 4, 5, and 6 then discussed the hardware needed to provide an acceptable physical environment. Integrating these elements and assuring their compatibility is the key to success. The process involves establishment of minimum performance criteria and a single-source responsibility capable of coordinating the interior system design with equal thought to each element and criteria.

One final element must also be rated: cost. Specifically, the ultimate goal is to meet *all* the criteria and user requirements at the lowest user cost. Of the many ways to handle this complex process, a technique with proven success is systems procurement. The largest and most successful party to utilize the system procurement process has been the U.S. General Services Administration. The GSA's book, *Performance Specification for Office Buildings,* was the primary document for the structure, HVAC, lighting, finished floor, finished ceiling, and space divider subsystems for over three million square feet of office space in the Social Security Administration Payment Centers and Headquarters project. Similar documents covering the Integrated Ceiling System were used on over twelve million square feet of other government office buildings during the late 1970s.

Several private sector projects also utilized the same process. In all projects, the systems procurement process was instrumental in providing the environment required to meet user needs. Best of all, these projects all were completed on schedule and within budget allowances—a major accomplishment for any construction project. While there are other processes that could produce a successful "built environment," it benefits the prudent owner/user to consider systems procurement for a large project.

HOW DOES THE PROCESS WORK?

After initiating the systems approach in a design project, the core group would naturally want to guarantee the success of the project, in as much as possible, by ensuring that the established requirements are met. This is accomplished by preparing performance specifications[1] that transmit a clear statement of purpose as well as the previously established short- and long-term needs of the organization. The specifications are then sent to bidders, generally called "offerors," who can, in turn, respond to these needs. These specifications usually include specific ground rules on testing procedures, where the tests are to be conducted (i.e., usually in the lab for bid qualification, prototype for construction approval, and in the field for building acceptance), and bidding procedures. With today's escalating energy and maintenance labor costs, the lowest or winning bid is usually based on life-cycle cost. Details of the process for determining the life-cycle cost bid must accompany the performance specifications.

The offeror is given an abundant opportunity to meet the organization's needs and to be truly innovative because he or she is limited only by the requirement that certain *performance* criteria be met. In other words, an important selection of building products can be made based on performance and not on preselected product lines. The key to the success of the interior system is that each subsystem and its components are selected and designed to complement, interact and be compatible with other building components.

Considerable verbiage on systems, systematized building, and performance criteria in recent years has produced conflicting ideas concerning the systems concept and environmental performance, probably to the point of exasperation in some cases. However, the concept has many specific benefits, both obvious and not so obvious. Thus, a detailed discussion of the benefits—as they apply to the interior system—is in order. An effectively planned system will do the following:

OPTIMIZE COSTS WITH ASSURED PERFORMANCE. By specifying a minimum level of performance for each environmental or design attribute, the offeror can make the necessary tradeoffs to lower costs. If, for example, it is known that a flat ceiling containing a uniform lighting level of 70 ESI foot-candles and a speech privacy of NIC' $\geq$ 20 is required, the least expensive ceiling system that meets this combined criteria can then be selected. If only the lighting criteria were required, the fixture chosen might be considerably cheaper, and possibly inefficient. However, by combining the lighting, acoustical and aesthetic criteria, the ceiling subsystem bidder is encouraged to select material and equipment that when combined meets all end user needs. In essence, the user will be assured of an effective work environment.

ASSURE COMPATABILITY. Minimum performance must be provided for fit tolerances between components and subsystems. Therefore, it is necessary for the offeror to become totally familiar with the project at its inception or prior to bidding. The best way to lose valuable time and money in construction is to have to redesign or rebuild an entire subsystem because it is not compatible with other subsystems. These issues are clarified early in the project since the ground rules are clear. Arguments over who caused the problem are efficiently eliminated.

ENCOURAGE INNOVATION. When an offeror understands the minimum performance requirements and that a contract can be won by finding a better or less expensive way to meet the requirements, he or she is motivated to be innovative. The offeror probably knows the competition better than anyone. If, for example, the specifications call for a 1' × 4' light fixture model no. X from the manufacturer Y, *or its equivalent,* the only opportunity to beat the competition is to buy or install the fixture less expensively.

A minimum performance criteria allows the producer to utilize a multitude of lighting techniques, some of which may be incorporated with another subsystem, possibly with improved performance and at an overall lower cost. In this sense, innovation and creativity are encouraged with usually interesting and successful results.

IDENTIFY OPTIONS AND TRADEOFFS. The process of selecting the optimum solution yields an interesting by-product—options. There are always several ways to satisfy criteria, many times with no real change in cost. By identifying these items early, it may be possible to select a solution that enhances another physical, aesthetic, or economic attribute.

ENCOURAGE VALUE ANALYSIS. By specifying price based on a life-cycle cost (first costs plus the costs of owning and operating the building), the offeror will be encouraged to determine true life expectancy for the product or system and its maintenance requirements. With today's inflationary economy, it is entirely feasible that an item costing two times another could be the least expensive solution because it lasts twice as long or requires less maintenance or energy to keep it operating. As with innovation, the offeror knows the product and competitors better than anyone else and is therefore in the best position to make a realistic value analysis. This type of specification encourages the offeror to make product changes or improvements.

PROMOTE COMPETITIVE BIDS AND SINGLE-SOURCE RESPON-SIBILITY. The idea of competitive bidding and single-source responsibility is highly desirable. By packaging the performance requirements in system or subsystem parts, the offeror does the shopping for the lowest-cost individual components that are compatible with the system proposal. By prequalifying the system performance, an efficient bidding process then yields a winning bid from a single-source responsibility. In return, the core group receives a guarantee of installed performance. In essence, the core group is shifting a great deal of the selection process and quality control to an offeror who is, in most cases, better qualified to make these decisions.

COORDINATE SUBSYSTEMS AND TRADES. When an offeror knows he must provide a coordinated subsystem within the specified tolerances and with other building elements or systems, he has an incentive to assure compliance or make direct contact with the interfacing system offeror. In this fashion, interface problems are usually resolved without owner participation.

SUMMARY

The core group must provide a carefully devised list of standards and short- and long-term goals which respond directly to the planned-for organization's needs. This list, when prepared properly, becomes the parameters for performance specifications that encourage an innovative and cost-conscious guide for bidders.

By providing these parameters, the planning team and, hence, the organization, can effectively control the success of their project. Each interior system has been considered as both a separate entity and as it interrelates with other systems. From these considerations, the subsystem and its components can be selected and designed to complement other subsystems. This procedure ensures that the performance of the system as a whole is maintained.

In essence, the system procurement process of planning, designing, fabricating, constructing, maintaining and operating a group of interrelated and interdependent activities is an effective tool for ensuring a successful, enduring project.

Note

1. Several existing documents contain excellent examples of performance specifications. Most notable is the *PBS Building Systems Program and Performance Specification for Office Buildings*, third edition, U.S. Government Services Administration (GSA) Public Building Services (PBS), November 1975. The Construction Research Council (CRC), a private- and public-sector funded organization, is in the process of preparing similar specifications. American Institute of Architects (AIA) also has baseline performance recommendations.

Glossary

Accommodation. The process by which the eye changes focus from one distance to another.

Acoustical baffles. Sound-absorbing materials mounted in a position to absorb reflected sounds such as ceiling baffles or window wall baffles.

Acoustically transparent (material). A material that will not attenuate or block sound.

Acoustical material. Any material considered in terms of its acoustical properties. Commonly a material designed to absorb sound. (ref. ASTM C-634)

Acoustical system. The elements that affect or define the hearing environment. An acoustical system is generally an amalgam of materials and products having sound-absorption, transmission loss, or masking properties such as ceilings, walls, floors, and background masking systems.

Acoustician/acoustical engineer/consultant. An individual having credentials to be called an expert in acoustical technology, particularly architectural acoustics. A specialist in open-office acoustics is recommended to provide speech privacy.

Acoustics/acoustical environment. The elements that establish and/or control how sound is perceived by the occupant of a space.

Adaptation. The process by which the eye becomes accustomed to more or less light than it was exposed to during an immediately preceding period.

Air conditioning. In enclosed spaces, the combined treatment of the air to control temperature, relative humidity, velocity of motion, and radiant energy level, with consideration of the need for removal of airborne particles and contaminant gases.

Ambient air. The surrounding air, usually outdoor air or the air in an enclosure under study.

Ambient lighting (re acoustics). Light sources mounted to reflect a light from a surface before reaching the occupant, such as an uplight. These fixtures are ideal for achieving optimum speech privacy.

Ambient lighting (re lighting). Lighting (generally uniform) throughout an area that provides general illumination to the area.

American Society for Testing and Materials (ASTM). An independent organization of users, producers, testers, and specifiers that promulgates industry standards, specifications, and test procedures for materials, systems, and products.

Articulation Class (AC). A single-number rating that identifies the amount of transmitted speech intelligence between office spaces as determined by ASTM Classification E-1110.

Articulation Index (AI). A numerical value (0 to 1) of speech intelligibility derived from an analysis of background sound, expected speech effort, and the acoustical qualities of the area and its components. An AI of 0.1 is low, indicating that little, if any, of a conversation will be intelligible to listeners on the other side of a screen. An AI of 0.6, on the other hand, will make for poor speech privacy or good speech intelligibility.

Background masking sound. The collective ambient sounds in an occupied space. In an office, masking sound is usually composed of noise from HVAC equipment, business machines, speech, and sometimes an electronic background masking sound system.

Bacteriostatic. The property of any substance that inhibits the growth of bacteria.

Ballast. A device used with an electric-discharge lamp (fluorescent or HID) to obtain the necessary circuit conditions of voltage, current, and wave form for starting and operating.

Brightness. The strength of sensation that results from viewing surfaces or spaces from which light comes to the eye. May refer to luminance, although its use for luminance is discouraged.

Building code. A document that specifies minimum performance criteria and/or materials and systems acceptable for a specific building type. Each community may be different. Most subscribe to the nationally recognized building codes such as the Uniform Building Code (UBC), Southern Building Code

(SBC), or the National Building Code. Specific codes may be referenced, such as the National Electric Code (NEC) and the like.

Building envelope. An outer shell which encloses conditioned space through which thermal energy may be transferred to or from outdoors.

Built environment. The space within a building. The term is used extensively by those utilizing the systems procurement process to define the office building interior or similar space within the building envelope, in terms of acoustical, thermal, lighting, safety, and aesthetic performance.

Bullpen. A derogatory term for open-plan offices, usually reserved for a square layout with low (4-foot or lower) space dividers between work stations.

Bureaulandschaft (office landscape). A synonym for creative innovation through systematic cooperation of many disciplines to create an office design/ environment.

Candela. The SI unit of luminous intensity. One candela is defined as one lumen per steradian.

Candlepower. Luminous intensity expressed in candelas.

Carpet tile. Carpet squares laid like tile. Individual sections can be removed for access to flat wires, raised floors, etc.

Castles. Floor-mounted boxes that contain connection points for power and signal connections. The newer version is recessed in the floor to prevent a trip hazard.

Ceiling plenum. The open space between a suspended ceiling and the structural floor or roof above.

Cellular phones. Speech communication system that utilizes radio frequencies to transmit signals.

Change of state. Change from one of the three phases—solid, liquid, or gas—to another phase.

Chlorofluorocarbons (CFC). Refrigerants, typically Refrigerant 11, 22, and 113.

Circulation pattern. The routes office users take to perform their daily tasks.

Clear sky. A sky that has less than 30 percent cloud cover.

Closed-plan office. An office layout composed of primarily full-height walls (walls that extend from floor to ceiling). The walls may be fixed or demountable partitions and may contain doors, windows, and other elements to support normal office user needs such as wiring, furniture, and so on.

Cloudy sky. A sky that has more than 70 percent cloud cover.

Code. A collection of laws, regulations, ordinances, or statutory requirements adopted by governmental (legislative) authority.

Coefficient of utilization (CU). The ratio of the luminous flux in lumens from a luminaire calculated as received on the work plane to the luminous flux emitted by the luminaire's lamps alone.

Co-generation. The generation of electric power that is electrically compatible with the electric supply from the serving utility.

Communications analysis (tally or matrix). A detailed listing and comparison of the communications in an office, such as voice, telephone, electronic, and paper over a given time frame.

Condensation. The change of state of a vapor into a liquid by extracting heat from the vapor.

Conduction. The process of heat transfer through a solid due to molecular activity.

Consultants. Individuals or firms hired by the user or design team with specific expertise to aid in the design or preparation of specifications, such as an acoustician, architect, space planner, engineer.

Convection. Transfer of heat by movement of a fluid.

Cooling load. The amount of cooling per unit of time required by the conditioned space; the heat a cooling system must remove from a system over time.

Core group. Key members of the user group and planning team, usually composed of top management of the user, the architect, and the space planner.

Correlation diagram. A graphic representation of the ideal spatial relationship between work groups.

Damper. A device used to vary the volume of air passing through an outlet, inlet, or duct.

dB$_A$. Decibels, measured on the A scale of a sound level meter. The A scale is preferred for speech privacy measurements because it corresponds closely to the sensitivity of the ear. Like the ear, it virtually ignores low-frequency sound, but responds accurately to the frequencies of normal speech.

Decibel (dB). The basic unit of sound level. In acoustics, "the term used to identify ten times the common logarithm of the ratio of two like quantities; it has no dimensions." It is, however, common practice to treat decibel as a unit as, for example, in the sentence, "The average sound pressure level in the room is 45 decibels." (Reference; ASTM C-634) In the frequency range of normal speech, the ear can perceive sound differences of 1 or 2 dB. Normal male speech is 65 dB on the A scale of a sound level meter within 3 to 5 feet.

Decision committee. Management personnel from the highest possible level in the user organization.

Dehumidification. The process of removal of water vapor from air.

Demountable/movable wall systems (partitions). Full-height space dividers designed to be disassembled and reassembled in a new location to accommodate a new office layout with a minimum of aesthetic impact on the interfacing elements such as existing walls, floors, and ceilings.

Design condition. The conditions (temperature, humidity, purity, etc.) required to be produced and maintained by an air conditioning system.

Desiccant. An absorbent or adsorbent, liquid or solid, that removes water or water vapor from a material.

Diffuser. An air distribution outlet, generally located in the ceiling and comprised of deflecting members in various directions.

Disability glare. Glare resulting in reduced visibility and that may cause discomfort.

Discomfort glare. Glare resulting in discomfort; does not necessarily cause reduction in visibility.

Document (paper) flow study. A map showing where a document goes in an organization or facility.

Electromagnetic interference. Electrical signals that interfere with a user's signal.

Electronic background masking sound. Electronically produced sound used to obscure intrusive speech sounds. In an office, the masking sound should not exceed the NC_{40} rating, a single-number rating of the speech-masking performance of a background masking sound system.

Emergency lighting. Lighting designed to supply illumination upon loss of normal supply for life and property safety.

Emergency power. Self-contained device that will provide electricity for safety devices in the event of a power failure.

Environmental conditions. Natural or controlled conditions of air and radiation prevailing around a person, an object, or a substance.

Environmental criteria. A physical measurement and established minimum values for those elements required for a specific user task, such as acoustical control, speech privacy, visual comfort, and thermal comfort.

Environmental system. All the elements within the office interior envelope that establish the acoustical, thermal, lighting, and human comfort levels.

Equivalent sphere illumination (ESI). The level of illumination in a sphere which would produce visibility of the task equivalent to that produced by a specific lighting system.

Executive core plan. An office layout where senior-level employees are collected in a central part of the building, with support staff located on the periphery.

Exfiltration. Air leaking outward (see infiltration).

Exhaust air. Air intentionally discharged from any conditioned space to outside the space.

Exit system. Procedures designed to aid occupants to exit a building in an emergency.

Fan-coil unit. A fan and heat exchanger for heating and/or cooling assembled within a common casing.

Federal Communications Commission (FCC). The United States government agency that regulates all communication systems, such as telephone, radio, television, cellular telephone.

Fenestration. Any opening in the building envelope for the admission of light.

Fiber optics. A signal distribution system that superimposes data transmission on light that is transmitted over optical fibers.

Filing system analysis. An identification of how files are managed, utilized to establish an efficient filing system for a particular user group or organization.

Fire control/suppression. A major component of a fire safety plan to contain or reduce a fire, such as a sprinkler system.

Fire management system. A computerized central control that monitors fire and smoke sensors and automatically activates fire prevention systems such as sprinklers, fire alarms, smoke control, and communication/annunciator systems.

Fireproofing. Materials or systems that are applied to or encapsulate structural members such as a steel beam or column to protect it from weakening and collapsing under the high temperature of a fire. Some materials are spray applied, others are gypsumboard enclosures. A common material from the 1950s to the 1970s was asbestos, now considered a health hazard. Current materials are mineral fibers, gypsum, and cement.

Fire protection (material/system). A material or system that provides improved resistance to flames, suppression of flames, a barrier to fire, heat, and smoke, and warning devices.

Fire protection engineer. An acknowledged expert in design and application of fire protection materials, systems, and codes.

Fire-safe environment. A place protected from heat, flames, and toxic fumes.

Flamespread. The movement of a flame front. Flamespread is usually evaluated in an ASTM E-84 test where 0 flamespread is assigned to cement board and 100 flamespread is assigned to red oak.

Flanking path. The route sound takes in circumventing a sound barrier. Typical flanking paths are apertures or openings such as a ceiling plenum, air duct, open window, and unsealed cracks at interfaces such as a wall-ceiling juncture.

Flat wire or flat conductor cable (FCC). Thin power and signal wiring designed to be installed on the floor beneath the carpet so that it will not be noticed.

Floor-ceiling sandwich. *See* Interstitial space.

Fluorescence. The emission of light as a result of the absorption of the radiation of other wavelengths.

Fluorescent lamp. A low-pressure mercury electric discharge lamp in which a coating of phosphor transforms some of the ultraviolet energy generated by the discharge into light.

Follow-up planning. That portion of the planning process which reviews actual occupied space to ensure satisfaction of the initial plan and correct identified problems; sometimes called "ongoing facilities management."

Foot-candle (fc). The unit of illuminance in the English system. The illuminance on a surface for which all points are located one foot from a directionally uniform point source of 1 candela.

Foot-lambert (fL). The uniform luminance of a perfectly diffusing surface emitting or reflecting light at the rate of one lumen per square foot. The average luminance of a reflecting surface is the product of the illumination in foot-candles by the reflectance of the surface.

Freestanding furniture. Desks, work surfaces, and so on that do not require any other element to support them.

General lighting. Lighting designed to provide an essentially uniform level of illumination throughout an area.

Glare. The sensation produced by luminance within the field of view of the eye that is sufficiently greater than the luminance to which the eyes are adapted.

Graphics. Those elements of a user space that inform, identify, or direct people in the office: may be signs, colors, arrows, lighting, art.

Grid. Metallic members, usually a T shape, used to support ceiling system components.

Hard wiring. Power and/or signal wires contained in a metallic conduit, usually for safety reasons.

Heat detectors. A device to warn occupants of the presence of fire by reacting to elevated temperatures.

Heat-of-light system. A system that uses heat from high lighting intensity for heating spaces in a building.

Heating. The process of adding heat to a space to offset the heat losses from the space.

Heating load. The heating rate required to replace heat loss from the space being controlled.

Hertz (Hz). The unit of frequency. One Hertz equals one cycle per second. The frequency of the human voice can range from 100 to 10,000 Hz, though the frequencies of intelligible speech lie between 400 and 2000 Hz.

High-intensity discharge lamp (HID). A group of lamps commonly known as mercury, metal halide, or high-pressure sodium.

High-tech look. An architectural design for interiors that became popular in the 1980s, typified by the exposure of basic structural elements in the finished space.

HVAC. Heating, ventilating, and air conditioning system; *see* Chapter 4.

Illuminance. The density of the luminous flux incident upon a surface.

Illumination. The act of illuminating or state of being illuminated.

Incandescent lamp. A lamp in which visible light is produced by a heated filament powered by an electric current.

Indirect lighting. Lighting by luminaries that distribute 90 to 100 percent of the light upward.

Induction unit. A device that injects treated air to entrain recirculated air through a heat exchanger enclosed within a cabinet or enclosure; nozzles or fans may be used for the jet action device.

Infiltration. The uncontrolled inward air leakage through cracks and interstices in any building element and around the windows and doors of a building caused by the pressure effects of wind or the effect of differences in indoor and outdoor air density.

Intelligent buildings. A building containing the latest in electronic communication and control devices, usually a shared computer system with access by different users.

Interdisciplinary planning team. Several design specialists working together toward a common goal, such as designing an office.

Interface. The point or plane where two or more disciplines or architectural surfaces meet (architect and acoustician, wall and ceiling).

Interior designer. A professional individual or group trained in the discipline of translating user needs into work relationships, space layout, and work station design criteria.

Interior zone. Controlled zones that do not interact with the building envelope; *see also* Perimeter zone.

Interstitial space. That space between the floor above and the ceiling below in buildings which is commonly used and available for mechanical, electrical, structural, acoustical, and fire protection devices.

Interzone attenuation. The difference in decibels, at a given frequency, between the sound level on one side of a screen and the level on the other side. The distance between the source and the point measured is referred to as the interzone distance.

Landscape office. A synonym for creative innovation through systematic cooperation of many disciplines to create an office design or environment.

Latent cooling load. The cooling load to remove latent heat.

Life-cycle cost (LCC). An evaluation method to measure the economic performance of a building, or building system, over a specified time period (the defined life). LCC totals, in either present-value or annual-value terms, all relevant costs associated with a building or building system over the defined life of the project.

Life cycle (costs). The useful life of a building, space, or equipment; costs for the element and all maintenance over the useful life of the building or facility.

Life safety (system). Elements utilized to protect humans from the hazards of fire.

Light. Radiant energy that can be seen; that portion of the spectrum from 380 to 770 nm wavelength.

Lighting system. The elements that provide sufficient light to perform a human task; *see* Chapter 3.

Local area networks (LANS). A telecommunication distribution system protected from intrusive signals.

Lumen. SI unit of luminous flux.

Luminaire. A general term for a lighting unit consisting of lamps and other parts designed to distribute the light, to hold the lamp in position, to protect the lamps, and to provide a means for connecting the lamp to the power supply.

Luminance. The luminous intensity per unit of projected area of a given surface viewed from a given area. (*See* IES handbook for complete technical definition.)

Luminaries. Light fixtures, usually mounted in the ceiling. Conventional flat lens fluorescent luminaries act like acoustical mirrors.

Lux (lx). The SI unit of illuminance. One lux is defined as one lumen per square meter.

Microwaves. Signal distribution via microwave radio frequencies. This system is used extensively in long-distance transmission and for satellites.

Movable walls. Full-height space dividers affixed to a track at floor and/or ceiling that allows the divider to be closed and opened on a daily basis to accommodate changes in space needs. A typical application is to subdivide a conference room.

National Electric Code (NEC). An independent organization that promulgates electrical product and system performance, test procedures, and specifications.

National Fire Protection Association (NFPA). An organization dedicated to preparing fire standards and specifications.

Natural air circulation. Air circulation induced by differences of density caused by differences of temperature.

Noise. Unwanted sound.

Noise path. The route unwanted sounds take to reach a receiver.

Noise receiver. Person or group that hears unwanted sounds.

Noise reduction coefficient (NRC). A single-number rating derived from measured values of sound absorption coefficients in accordance with ASTM test method C-423. It denotes the sound-absorptive property of an acoustical material. Ratings range from 0 to approximately 1.2.

Noise source. Object or system that creates unwanted sounds.

Noncombustible. Materials or systems that will not support fire. Building code authorities have varying definitions. A common use is a material or system that has a flamespread under 25 when tested in accordance with ASTM E-84. Typical materials are concrete, most metals, masonry, gypsum wallboard, plaster.

Occupancy. A designation by code authorities of the degree of fire protection required for a particular building type or use.

Office environment. Space defined by the interior envelope of a building or facility, typically composed of the acoustical, lighting, thermal, air, aesthetic and other elements required for humans to function efficiently in a workplace.

Office landscape. A synonym for creative innovation through systematic cooperation of many disciplines to create an office design or environment.

Office planning. The process of planning an office facility.

Ongoing facilities management. The process of implementing the planning team objectives over the life span of the office facility.

Open-plan office. Any office layout devoid of full-height walls.

Open-plan office acoustics. The technology of achieving speech privacy in an open layout.

Organization chart. A representation of who works for whom in a user organization.

Orientation. The directional relationship of a building with respect to points on the compass.

Outdoor air. Air outside a building or air taken in from outdoors.

Ozone. Triatomic oxygen, O_3, sometimes used in air conditioning as an odor eliminator; can be toxic in certain concentrations. Present in the atmosphere; absorbs harmful radiation from the solar system. Believed to be destroyed by CFCs.

Paper flow. The route that office documents follow from creation to final storage.

Parabolic (light) fixtures. Light fixtures having a parabola-shaped light reflector to distribute the light source. Parabolic fixtures with large size cells (4 × 4 inch or larger) will generally equal the speech privacy properties of top-quality sound-absorbing ceiling tiles.

Performance specification. Specific criteria established for a product or system by referencing a test procedure without mention of the product name or manufacturer.

Perimeter zone. The controlled zone that is exposed on at least one surface to exterior surfaces of the building. Usually considered to be the area enclosed by a line 15 feet parallel to the walls or the areas directly under the roof; *see also* interior zone.

Phasing effect. In masking sound, sound produced by two or more speakers may cause a subjective response of increased or decreased perception of loudness or tone change if the sounds are in or out of phase. The effect is usually annoying to the user.

Planning team. Group of individuals assigned the task of defining user needs, and establishing environmental criteria and space requirements for specified tasks.

Plenum chamber (ceiling plenum). A space where air travels at a pressure slightly different from the space on the other side of the enclosure. The floor-ceiling sandwich is often used as a return-air plenum in some office systems.

Power. In an office, the electricity required to provide lights, and operate office machines and electronic devices. Typically the power in an office is 120 or 240 volt.

Power pole. A device used to move power and signal distribution wires from a floor or ceiling source location vertically to a desk, table, or the like.

Power and signal distribution system. The wires or devices that carry, connect, and switch power and signal from source to user locations; *see* Chapter 6.

Primary air supply. Treated air introduced at a diffuser or terminal unit, where it mixes with recirculated air.

Primary flanking position. Surfaces located in a position to reflect sound from a source to a receiver. A screen located perpendicular to a barrier or the wall opposite an open door are in the primary flanking position and should be highly sound-absorbent.

Psychoacoustic response. The subjective response to sound, which may not correlate to physically measured values.

Quality of lighting. The level of favorable visual performance, ease of seeing, safety, and aesthetics for specific visual functions.

Radiation. The transmission of energy by electromagnetic waves emitted due to temperature.

Raised floor system. A subfloor system that provides a plenum space between the finish floor and structural floor for easy distribution and relocation of power and signal wires; originally used for computer floors to accommodate extensive dedicated wiring.

Reflectance (of a surface). The ratio of the reflected flux to the incident flux. *Note:* Reflectance values vary depending upon the viewing angle and the incidence angle.

Refrigerant. A fluid used for heat transfer in a refrigerating system; the refrigerant absorbs heat at a low temperature and low pressure and transfers heat at a higher temperature and a higher pressure, usually with changes of state.

Retrofit. The act of installing or changing elements within the office envelope after initial construction.

Return air. Air extracted from the conditioned space and totally or partly returned to the air conditioner.

Screen. Self-standing, individual space dividers used to delineate or separate individual work stations; may be curved or straight and are usually 5 feet by 5 feet in size, easily moved, and provide a degree of visual and/or acoustical privacy.

Screen system. A power and signal distribution incorporated in a space divider, systems furniture, or the like.

Secondary air. Air recirculated or mixed with primary air in a terminal unit or at the outlet of a diffuser.

Seismic restraint. Elements of a building system designed specifically to restrain movement or failure in an earthquake.

Sensible heat load. The cooling load to remove the sensible heat.

Sentence intelligibility. A subjective measure of speech privacy; the percentage of words a listener can hear and understand.

Shading coefficient. The ratio of absorbed and transmitted solar heat relative to fenestration fitted with shading devices to that occurring with unshaded single-strength glass.

Signal. Electric current that carries telephone, computer, or voice data; usually a low voltage such as 24 or 70 volt.

Signal to noise ratio. A comparison of the loudness of a sound source with the ambient or background sound. A zero ratio yields speech privacy; a positive ratio will yield increasing degrees of speech intelligibility.

Smoke. The product of combustion.

Smoke control. Devices, design, or system that limits the spread of smoke in a building.

Smoke detector. A device designed to warn occupants of the presence of fire by reacting to the presence of smoke.

Sound absorption. The process by which sound is absorbed by a medium, material, or system. Materials such as concrete and glass which are highly sound reflective have little or no absorbing properties. Soft, porous materials generally absorb sound. The open sky is considered a perfect absorber, since no sound is reflected.

Sound transmission class (STC). A single-number rating derived from measured values of sound transmission loss in accordance with ASTM Classification E-413. An STC of 0 means there is no attenuation of the sound source. An STC of 60 is equivalent to a 12-inch-thick solid concrete barrier.

Sound transmission loss (TL). The reduction of sound as it passes through a barrier. TL is approximately the sound source level minus a sound receiver level adjusted for the sound-absorbent conditions; *see* STC.

Space divider. Any element in an office that provide a degree of visual and acoustical separation between work stations or user groups; may be screens, systems furniture, filing cabinets, demountable partitions, or fixed walls.

Spatial uniformity. Uniform sound within a space.

Specification. A precise statement of a set of requirements, satisfied by a material, product, system, or service.

Speech privacy. A measure of the degree to which a user can understand the sense of a conversation from an adjoining work station or common area. See Chapter 2 for explanation of levels for minimum, normal, and confidential speech privacy.

Speech privacy noise isolation class, NIC'. A single-number rating of the acoustical performance of any screen or space divider and ceiling combination. NIC′ is a gauge of the degree of speech privacy provided by the components of an acoustical system. The higher the rating, the higher their attenuation, and the better the possibility of achieving speech privacy.

Speech privacy potential, SPP. A single-number rating that measures whether or not an office will achieve speech privacy. SPP may be measured objectively or subjectively. Objectively, SPP is the sum of the NIC′ and the NC_{40} level of the background masking sound. To achieve speech privacy, the SPP should be greater than 60 in the open-plan office and 70 in the closed plan.

Standard. A document that defines properties, processes, dimensions, materials, relationships, concepts, nomenclature, test methods, or rating methods. Usually prepared by professional or trade associations and reviewed by the consensus process. May be national or international in scope.

Standpipe. A local, concentrated source of water.

Status symbol analysis. Identification of individuals or work functions that deserve a particular level of recognition in a user organization and what elements will identify that level in the office environment, such as a closed office for manager and above, an oriental rug for the CEO, bars or stripes for grade level.

Subjective space. A user space identified for a specific work group; is usually identified by color, sign, space dividers, or similar means.

Supply air. Air supplied through ducts to a space.

Surface raceways. Exposed conduits for power and signal wires.

Surge controls. Devices that protect against excess power supply that could damage on-line equipment.

Systems approach. A design principle that focuses on building systems and performance rather than products.

Systems concept for fire protection. The integration of all services, materials, building systems, and warning devices to provide an efficient, safe, and economical office environment.

Systems furniture. An integrated and interdependent design that provides visual and acoustical separation between work stations plus work surfaces, power and signal distribution, bookshelves, and the like. A typical system has interlocking panels that support hang-on desks and cabinets.

Systems performance concept. The process of defining the components of the built environment in terms of specific criteria related to real-world tests that can be conducted in the actual building and correlated with equivalent laboratory analysis.

Systems procurement. The process of selecting, specifying, purchasing, and installing construction systems by performance. The system is a collection of products and materials that, when assembled, form a building component such as a wall, ceiling, lighting, or acoustical system.

Task-ambient lighting. A combination of task lighting and ambient lighting.

Task lighting. Lighting directed to a specific surface or area that provides illumination for visual tasks.

Tax writeoff. Nontaxable item; usually not a building fixture.

Temporal uniformity. Uniform sound over time.

TL backing. A material applied to the back of a sound-absorbing product to improve its sound attenuation or transmission loss characteristics, such as foil or gypsum board.

Translucent. A property of a material that transmits light.

Underfloor ducts. Spaces in a floor system designed to carry power and signal wires or devices.

User. Person or group of individuals who occupy and utilize an office facility.

User group. Users who represent members of the planned-for organization.

User interaction. A representation of how office users communicate or otherwise contact associates to achieve group goals.

User needs. User tasks defined in environmental criteria terms, such as acoustical, lighting, thermal needs.

User tasks. Any of a variety of things people do in an office, such as reading, creating documents, and operating equipment.

Value analysis. An investigation of costs versus return on investment; synonymous with life-cycle cost.

Veiling reflection. Regular reflections superimposed upon diffuse reflections from an object that tend to conceal the details by reducing the contrast.

Ventilating. The process of supplying or removing air by natural or mechanical means to or from any space. The air may or may not have been conditioned.

Vertical surface treatment. A sound-absorbing material applied to walls, columns, and the like.

Visibility. The state of being seen by the eye.

Visual comfort probability (VCP). The rating of a lighting system expressed as a percentage of people who will be expected to find it acceptable in terms of discomfort glare.

Visual display terminal (VDT). A display such as the monitor screen of a personal computer, a computer terminal, a word processor, or some other electronically activated visual display.

Visual task. The details of an object that must be seen for the performance of an activity, including the foreground and background of the object.

Voice mail. Computerized electronic voice message system.

White (or pink) noise. In acoustics, white noise has equal sound intensity at all frequencies; pink is slightly shaped. The terms *white* and *pink* noise have been widely misused to describe masking sound. Masking sound is not unwanted and therefore is not noise. Furthermore, masking sound should have a shaped frequency spectrum, or it will be ineffective and annoying.

Wire management. The process of containing or controlling power and signal chords/wires.

Work flow (analysis). The route a specific office task follows from inception to fulfillment (similar to paper or document flow).

Workplace. A location where office activities occur.

Work station. A specific space allocated for an *individual* to perform office-related functions.

Work time distribution matrix. A chart that indicates the kinds of functions the user performs at the workplace. These data are valuable in establishing performance criteria for lighting, acoustics, and so on.

Zone. A space or group of spaces within a building with heating or cooling requirements sufficiently similar that comfort conditions may be maintained by a single controlling device.

Zoning. The division of a building into separately controlled spaces (zones), where different conditions can be maintained simultaneously.

Index